PARTY PRIMARIES IN COMPARATIVE PERSPECTIVE

Party Primaries in Comparative Perspective

Edited by

GIULIA SANDRI
Catholic University of Lille, France

ANTONELLA SEDDONE
University of Turin, Italy

FULVIO VENTURINO
University of Cagliari, Italy

ASHGATE

© Giulia Sandri, Antonella Seddone and Fulvio Venturino 2015

All rights reserved. No part of this publication may be reproduced, stored in a retrieval system or transmitted in any form or by any means, electronic, mechanical, photocopying, recording or otherwise without the prior permission of the publisher.

Giulia Sandri, Antonella Seddone and Fulvio Venturino have asserted their right under the Copyright, Designs and Patents Act, 1988, to be identified as the editors of this work.

Published by
Ashgate Publishing Limited
Wey Court East
Union Road
Farnham
Surrey, GU9 7PT
England

Ashgate Publishing Company
110 Cherry Street
Suite 3-1
Burlington, VT 05401-3818
USA

www.ashgate.com

British Library Cataloguing in Publication Data
A catalogue record for this book is available from the British Library

The Library of Congress has cataloged the printed edition as follows:
Sandri, Giulia.
  Party primaries in comparative perspective / by Giulia Sandri, Antonella Seddone and Fulvio Venturino.
    pages cm
  Includes bibliographical references and index.
  ISBN 978-1-4724-5038-8 (hardback) – ISBN 978-1-4724-5039-5 (ebook) – ISBN 978-1-4724-5040-1 (epub) 1. Primaries. 2. Comparative government. I. Title.
  JF2085.S36 2015
  324.5'4–dc23
                                                                        2014048313

ISBN: 9781472450388 (hbk)
ISBN: 9781472450395 (ebk – PDF)
ISBN: 9781472450401 (ebk – ePUB)

Printed in the United Kingdom by Henry Ling Limited,
at the Dorset Press, Dorchester, DT1 1HD

Contents

List of Figures and Tables		*vii*
Notes on Contributors		*ix*
Acknowledgements		*xiii*
List of Abbreviations		*xv*
1	Introduction: Primary Elections across the World *Giulia Sandri and Antonella Seddone*	1
2	Leadership Selection versus Candidate Selection: Similarities and Differences *Ofer Kenig, Gideon Rahat and Reuven Y. Hazan*	21
3	The American Experience of Primary Elections in Comparative Perspective *Alan Ware*	41
4	Democratising Party Leadership Selection in Spain and Portugal *Oscar Barberà, Marco Lisi and Juan Rodríguez Teruel*	59
5	Democratising Party Leadership Selection in Belgium and Israel *Bram Wauters, Gideon Rahat and Ofer Kenig*	85
6	Democratising Party Leadership Selection in Japan and Taiwan *Yohei Narita, Ryo Nakai and Keiichi Kubo*	105
7	Democratising Candidate Selection in Italy and France *Marino De Luca and Fulvio Venturino*	129
8	Democratising Candidate Selection in Romania and Slovakia *Sergiu Gherghina and Peter Spáč*	145
9	Democratising Candidate Selection in Iceland *Indridi H. Indriðason and Gunnar Helgi Kristinsson*	161

10   Conclusion   181
     Giulia Sandri, Antonella Seddone and Fulvio Venturino

Bibliography   *199*
Index   *215*

List of Figures and Tables

List of Figures

2.1	Candidate selectorate continuum	25
2.2	Leadership selectorate continuum	26

Tables

1.1	Overview of main cases of primary elections across the world (up to 2014)	10
2.1	The use of primary selections to various political positions around the world	23
2.2	Dimensions of leadership and candidate selection methods	28
2.3	Leadership selectorates in 71 parties	30
2.4	Eligible voters and turnout in 57 leadership contests	35
2.5	Women prime ministers and their selectorates (as of 2012)	37
4.1	Main features of primary election processes in Spain and Portugal	68
4.2	Main features of primary elections in Spain and Portugal	72
4.3	Effects of primary elections on political parties in Spain and Portugal	78
5.1	Main features of primary election processes in Belgium and Israel	92
5.2	Main features of primary election competitions in Belgium and Israel	95
6.1	Main features of primary election processes in Japan and Taiwan	112
6.2	Main features of primary election competitions in Japan and Taiwan	116
6.3	Effects of primary elections on political parties in Japan and Taiwan	120

6.4a	The level of party support before and after the leader selection in Japan: LDP	124
6.4b	The level of party support before and after the leader selection in Japan: SDPJ	125
6.4c	The level of party support before and after the leader selection in Japan: DJP	126
6.4d	The level of party support before and after the leader selection in Japan: NFP	127
7.1	Main features of primary election processes in Italy and France	135
7.2	Main features of primary election competitions in Italy and France	139
7.3	Effects of primary elections on political parties in Italy and France	141
8.1	Main features of primary elections processes in Romania and Slovakia	151
8.2	Main features of primary election competitions in Romania and Slovakia	154
8.3	Effects of primary elections on political parties in Romania and Slovakia	158
9.1	Features of primary election processes in Iceland, 2012–2013	166
9.2	Example of rank ordered plurality voting	169
9.3a	Party leaders: features of primary election competitions in Iceland	171
9.3b	Candidates: features of primary election competitions in Iceland	171
9.4	Women on party lists by nomination method	174
9.5	Effects of primary elections on political parties in Iceland, 2013	175
9.6	Votes, participation in primaries and membership density in Iceland, 2013	176
9.7	Effects of campaign spending on primary success in Iceland	179
10.1	Dimensions of analysis of the effects of primary elections	194

Notes on Contributors

Oscar Barberà is a lecturer in the Constitutional Law and Political Science Department of the University of Valencia. His research concerns political parties, party members and activists, party funding, political elites, devolution, Spanish politics and comparative politics. He has recently published articles in *Regional and Federal Studies* and *Pôle Sud*, and other works include 'Challenges for the political representation of moderate Catalan nationalism: the case of CiU (1974–2006)', in A. Elias and F. Tronconi (eds), *Minority Nationalist Parties and the Challenges of Representation* (2011, with A. Barrio).

Marino De Luca received his PhD from the Department of Sociology and Political Science of the University of Calabria, Italy. He is now a research fellow at the University of Cagliari, also in Italy, and in 2011 was Visiting Fellow at the University of Paris VII. He is a member of the Standing Group of the Italian Political Science Association on Candidate and Leader Selection. His areas of research concern intra-party democracy, party primaries, political communication and e-democracy. His work has been published in the *International Journal of E-Politics* and *French Politics, Culture and Society*.

Sergiu Gherghina is a lecturer in the Department of Political Science, Goethe University, Frankfurt. He holds a PhD in Political Science from Leiden University, with a comparative thesis on party organisations and electoral volatility. His research interests lie in party politics, legislative and voting behaviour, democratisation and direct democracy in Central and Eastern Europe.

Reuven Hazan is a professor in and chair of the Department of Political Science at the Hebrew University of Jerusalem, Israel. His areas of research include parties and party systems, legislative studies and inter- and intra-party (s)elections. He is the author of several books, most recently *Democracy within Parties: Candidate Selection Methods and Their Political Consequences* (2010, with Gideon Rahat), and dozens of articles in journals such as *Comparative Political Studies*, *Electoral Studies*, *Journal of Legislative Studies*, *Party Politics* and *West European Politics*.

Gunnar Helgi Kristinsson is Professor of Political Science at the University of Iceland. His main areas of research include the politics of the executive, clientelism, political parties and local politics. His work has appeared in journals such as the *European Journal of Political Research*, *Party Politics*, *West European*

Politics and *Scandinavian Political Studies* as well as in several edited volumes by international publishers.

Indridi H. Indriðason is Associate Professor of Political Science at the University of California, Riverside, and Adjunct Professor of Political Science at the University of Iceland. His current research focuses on coalition politics, cabinets, campaign strategies and elections. His work has appeared in, among others, *American Journal of Political Science*, *Journal of Politics*, *British Journal of Political Science*, *European Journal of Political Research* and *Legislative Studies Quarterly*.

Ofer Kenig is Senior Lecturer at Ashkelon Academic College, Israel, and head of the political parties' research group in the Israel Democracy Institute's Political Reform Project. His research fields are comparative politics and Israeli politics, and particular interests include leadership and ministerial selection, party members and constitutional change.

Keiichi Kubo is Associate Professor at the Faculty of Political Science and Economics, Waseda University, Japan. He holds a PhD from the London School of Economics and Political Science, where he specialised in comparative politics. His research interests include democratisation, political parties and party systems, quality of democracy, civil war and post-conflict peace building, and ethnic identity, with a regional focus on post-socialist countries.

Marco Lisi is a lecturer at the Universidade Nova de Lisboa, Portugal. His research focuses on political parties, electoral behaviour, democratic theory and political communication. His main interest concerns the transformation of political parties, especially in Southern Europe. He is author of several works, including *Os partidos políticos em Portugal: continuidade e transformação* (2011); 'The importance of winning office: the PS and the struggle for power', in Anna Bosco and Leonardo Morlino (eds), *Party Change in Southern Europe* (2007); and 'The democratisation of party leadership selection: the Portuguese experience', *Portuguese Journal of Social Science* (2010).

Ryo Nakai is an assistant professor at the College of Law and Politics of Rikkyo University, Japan. His research interests include party systems, elections and ethnopolitics in newly democratised countries. Among his most recent articles is 'The influence of party competition on minority politics: a comparison of Latvia and Estonia', published in the *Journal on Ethnopolitics and Minority Issues in Europe* (2014).

Yohei Narita received his MA in Political Science from Waseda University, Japan. His research interests include experimental political science and political processes. He has collaborated on several presentations at international conferences, such as the European Consortium for Political Research.

Gideon Rahat is an associate professor in the Department of Political Science at the Hebrew University of Jerusalem and a senior fellow at the Israel Democracy Institute. His areas of research and teaching are comparative politics (especially democratic institutions) and Israeli politics. He has authored and co-authored numerous articles and chapters on the politics of reform, candidate and leadership selection, the personalisation of politics, legislative behaviour and electoral reform. The latest of his three books, *Democracy within Parties* (with Reuven Hazan), was published in 2010.

Giulia Sandri is Assistant Professor at the European School of Political and Social Sciences of the Catholic University of Lille, France. She was previously a research fellow at Christ Church and at the Department of Politics and International Relations of the University of Oxford. Her main research interests are party politics, intra-party democracy and political behaviour. She has recently published in *Politics and Policy*, *Acta Politica*, *Comparative European Politics*, *Religion, State and Society*, *Ethnopolitics* and *Regional and Federal Studies*.

Antonella Seddone is currently a research fellow at the University of Cagliari, and lecturer on opinion polls and public opinion in the Department of Culture, Politics and Society at the University of Turin, from where she holds a PhD in Political Science. Her main research interests are intra-party democracy. From 2010 to 2012 she was a research fellow in the Department of International Politics and History, University of Cagliari, where she collaborated on a project on primary elections and their consequences on parties, leaders and voters, collecting survey data on local primary elections in Italy. At the University of Turin (2012–14) she worked on a project on the communication of public policies, and has also collaborated on a project on Italian election campaigns. She is coordinator of the work package on the direct election of party leaders of the Standing Group of the Italian Political Science Association on Candidate and Leader Selection. She has also published several books and articles in peer-reviewed journals.

Peter Spáč is an assistant professor in the Department of Political Science, Masaryk University, Brno, Czech Republic, and a research fellow at the International Institute of Political Science. His fields include elections, electoral systems and their reforms, candidate selection processes and Slovak politics. He is author of several books, chapters and articles, and his current work focuses on several topics, including the factors of preferential voting, the development of populist parties and support of the radical right.

Juan Rodríguez Teruel is a senior lecturer at the University of Valencia, and his research focuses on ministers, political elites, party politics and decentralisation. He is also a member of various international research networks, such as the Selection and Deselection of Political Elites (SEDEPE), and the International Political Science Association (IPSA) Research Committee on Political Elites and the IPSA Research Committee on Political Sociology. Recently he has published 'A new political elite in Western Europe? The political careers of regional prime ministers in newly decentralised countries', *French Politics* (2010, with Joan Botella, Oscar Barberà and Astrid Barrio).

Fulvio Venturino is currently Associate Professor at the University of Cagliari, and was previously a research fellow at the University of Genoa. Between 2005 and 2010 he was a member of the scientific board of the Italian Society for Electoral Research. In 2011 he launched the Candidate and Leader Selection Standing Group of the Italian Political Science Association, and is currently coordinating a three-year project, 'Primary Elections and their Consequences on Parties, Participation, and Competition' funded by the Sardinia region. He has published several books and articles on the issue of intra-party democracy.

Alan Ware is an Emeritus Fellow of Worcester College, University of Oxford, and a Senior Research Associate at University College London. Much of his earlier research focused on American politics and political parties; however, he is currently writing a book on the political economy of British education in the twentieth century.

Bram Wauters is Professor of Political Science in the Department of Political Science at Ghent University, Belgium. His research deals with political parties, political participation and substantive representation. He has written several works on these topics, with special focus on participation within parties; for instance 'Explaining participation in intra-party elections: evidence from Belgian political parties', *Party Politics* (2010). He has also recently published in several international journals, including *Local Government Studies*, *Political Studies* and *Res Publica*.

Acknowledgements

This volume originates from discussions between the editors and the contributors at Workshop n. 19, 'Party Primaries in Europe. Consequences and Challenges', held at the European Consortium for Political Research (ECPR) Joint Session of Workshops in Antwerp in April 2012. The discussions continued at the ECPR General Conference in Bordeaux, in September 2013, where two workshops on primary elections were held: 'Causes and Consequences of Primaries as Instruments for Candidate Selection' and 'Democratising Party Leader Selection Primaries: Challenges and Opportunities Beyond Intra-Party Democracy'.

After the first meeting, all the researchers involved in the project agreed on the need for a comprehensive comparative examination of both the concept and practice of primaries around the world. The tricky part was to find a way to assemble a group of scholars who could contribute theoretical or case-study expertise. At the same time, we needed to elaborate a common framework of analysis and a standard set of empirical indicators that could be used in all the case studies. We are confident of having achieved our first goal, given the significant earlier contributions to the study of party politics and primary elections of each of the contributors and the quality of their current work. We are really proud of the team of leading party scholars, and deeply grateful for all their work and contributions to this project. This has truly been a collective effort, and each contributor has brought a collegial approach to the project by participating in discussions on the scope and structure of the study, on the preliminary drafts of chapters and on the measurements and indicators to be used.

Concerning the second goal, we would like to point out that the cross-national analytical framework and set of indicators proposed in this volume represent the first phase of an ongoing research project. It took more than two years to complete this first phase, but we are putting in as much effort as possible to expand the current research design to new comparative cases and further indicators.

The project was initially funded by the Wiener-Anspach Foundation, Belgium, and we thank the foundation's board for its generosity. We would like also to thank Professor Ken Carty for his useful comments. It has been a pleasure to work with the team at Ashgate Publishing; we are really thankful to Rob Sorsby and Brenda Sharp, and look forward to publishing with them again.

Finally, we thank our spouses and partners – Cristina, Dario and Thomas – for tolerating our dedication to this project over the past two years. We know we are in their debt far beyond our capacity for repayment.

List of Abbreviations

Short name of party	Full name	Translation	Country
AP	Alianza Popular	People's Alliance	Spain
BE	Bloco de Esquerda	Left Bloc	Portugal
BF	Björt framtíð	Bright Future	Iceland
CD	Centro Democratico	Democratic Centre	Italy
CDA	Christen-Democratisch Appèl	Christian Democratic Appeal	Netherlands
CD&V	Christen-Democratisch en Vlaams	Christian Democratic and Flemish	Belgium
CDH	Centre démocrate humaniste	Humanist Democratic Centre	Belgium
CDS-PP	Centro Democrático e Social Partido Popular	Democratic Social Centre – People's Party	Portugal
CiU	Convergencia i Unió	Convergence and Union	Spain
DL – La Margherita	Democrazia è Libertà – La Margherita	Democracy is Freedom – The Daisy	Italy
DPJ	民主党 Minshutō	Democratic Party of Japan	Japan
DPP	Simplified Chinese: 民主进步党; traditional Chinese: 民主進步黨	Democratic Progressive Party	Taiwan
DS	Democratici di Sinistra	Democrats of the Left	Italy
Ecolo	Écologistes Confédérés pour l'organisation de luttes originales	French-Speaking Greens	Belgium
EELV	Europe Écologie – Les Verts	Greens	France
FCN	Parti Communiste Française	French Communist Party	France
ERC	Esquerra Republicana de Catalunya	Republican Left of Catalonia	Spain
FDF	Fédéralistes Démocrates Francophones	Francophone Democratic Federalists	Belgium

FDI	Fratelli d'Italia	Brothers of Italy	Italy
FDNS	Frontul Democrat al Salvării Naționale	Democratic National Salvation Front	Romania
FI	Forza Italia	Forward Italy	Italy
FN	Front National	The National Front	France
FSN	Frontul Salvării Naționale	National Salvation Front	Romania
Groen	Groen	Flemish Greens	Belgium
ICV	Iniciativa per Catalunya Verds	Initiative for Catalonia Verds	Spain
IDV	Italia dei Valori	Italy of Values	Italy
IP	Sjálfstæðisflokkur	Independence Party	Iceland
IU	Izquierda Unida	United Left	Spain
Kadima	קדימה Qādīmāh	Forward	Israel
KMT	Kuomintang	Nationalist Party	Taiwan
Labour Party	יִתְלָאְרְשִׂיַה הָדֹבְנֲעָה תֶגֶלְפִמ Mifleget HaAvoda HaYisraelit	Israeli Labour Party	Israel
LDP	自由民主党 Jiyū-Minshutō	Liberal Democratic Party	Japan
LGM	Vinstrihreyfingin – grænt framboð	Left-Green Movement	Iceland
LIKUD	דוּיכִּלָה HaLikud	The Consolidation	Israel
LN	Lega Nord	Northern League	Italy
M5S	Movimento 5 Stelle	Five Star Movement	Italy
MCC	Mouvement des Citoyens pour le Changement	Citizens' Movement for Change	Belgium
Meretz	צֶרֶמ	Energy	Israel
MR	Mouvement Réformateur	Reformist Movement	Belgium
NFP	新進党 Shinshintō	New Frontier Party	Japan
NRP	Mafdal	National Religious Party	Israel
N-VA	Nieuw-Vlaamse Alliantie	New Flemish Alliance	Belgium
Open Vld	Open Vlaamse Liberalen en Democraten	Open Flemish Liberals and Democrat	Belgium
PA	Alþýðubandalagið	People's Alliance	Iceland

PC	Partidul Conservator	Conservative Party	Romania
PCE	Partido Comunista de España	Communist Party of Spain	Spain
PCF	Parti Communiste Français	French Communist Party	France
PCP	Partido Comunista Português	Portuguese Communist Party	Portugal
PD	Partito Democratico	Italian Democratic Party	Italy
PDL	Popolo della Libertà	People of Freedom	Italy
PDL	Partidul Democrat-Liberal	Democratic Liberal Party	Romania
Pirate Party	Píratar	Pirate Party	Iceland
PNL	Partidul Național Liberal	National Liberal Party	Romania
PNV	Partido Nacionalista Vasco	Basque National Party	Spain
PP	Partido Popular	People's Party	Spain
PP	Framsóknarflokkurinn	Progressive Party	Iceland
PRD	Partido Renovador Democrático	Party of Democratic Renewal	Portugal
PRG	Parti Radical de Gauche	Radical Party of the Left	France
PS	Partido Socialista	Socialist Party	Portugal
PS	Parti Socialiste	Socialist Party	Belgium
PS	Parti Socialiste	Socialist Party	France
PSC	Partit dels Socialistes de Catalunya	Socialists' Party of Catalonia	Spain
PSD	Partido Social Democrata	Social Democratic Party	Portugal
PSD	Partidul Social Democrat	Romanian Social Democratic Party	Romania
PSOE	Partido Socialista Obrero Español	Spanish Socialist Workers' Party	Spain
PvdA	Partij van de Arbeid	Labour Party	Netherlands
RC	Partito della Rifondazione Comunista	Communist Refoundation Party	Italy
RPR	Rassemblement pour la République	Rally for the Republic	France

SDA	Samfylkingin-Jafnaðarmannaflokkur Íslands	Social Democratic Alliance	Iceland
SDK	Slovenská demokratická koalícia	Slovak Democratic Coalition	Slovakia
SDKÚ-DS	Slovenská demokratická a kresťanská únia – Demokratická strana	Slovak Democratic and Christian Union-Democratic Party	Slovakia
SDPJ	日本社会党 Nihon Shakaitō	Social Democratic Party of Japan	Japan
SEL	Sinistra Ecologia e Libertà	Left Ecology Freedom	Italy
SP	Socialistische Partij	Socialist Party	Netherlands
sp.a	Socialistische Partij Anders	Socialist Party – Differently	Belgium
SPD	Alþýðuflokkurinn	Social Democrats	Iceland
The Jewish Home	יְדהוֶיָה תיָבַה HaBayit HaYehudi	The Jewish Home	Israel
UCD	Unión de Centro Democrático	Union of the Democratic Centre	Spain
UDF	Union pour la Démocratie Française	Union for French Democracy	France
UDEUR	Unione Democratici per l'Europa	Union of Democrats for Europe	Italy
UDMR	Uniunea Democrată Maghiară din România Romániai Magyar Demokrata Szövetség	Democratic Alliance of Hungarians in Romania	Romania
UMP	Union pour un mouvement populaire	Union for a Popular Movement	France
UPyD	Unión Progreso y Democracia	Union, Progress and Democracy	Spain
VB	Vlaams Belang	Flemish Interest	Belgium
VVD	Volkspartij voor Vrijheid en Democratie	People's Party for Freedom and Democracy	Netherlands

Chapter 1
Introduction:
Primary Elections across the World

Giulia Sandri and Antonella Seddone

The Spreading of Intra-Party Democracy Instruments

A recent article by Sasha Issenberg argued that several parties in different countries are nowadays inspired by one 'unique creation of the American 20th century' and are introducing party primaries for choosing their leaders or candidates for office, strengthening the quality of party internal democracy. Issenberg notes that several parties 'in France, Italy, Argentina and Canada are now led by figures chosen under new systems designed to spur intramural competition by widening the circle of people empowered to choose party leaders', and the same goes for candidates nominated to be on party lists. The article is an example of the increasing visibility gained by the topic in recent years, and not only within academia.[1]

The number of parties that have undergone significant organisational and legal reforms to promote intra-party democracy is constantly growing. During the last two decades, several parties in advanced and new democracies have introduced primary elections, allowing their members, and sometimes voters or sympathisers, to democratically select their candidates running for elected office or as leaders.

For instance, the UK Labour has recently changed the method for selecting its leader, during the March 2014 Special Conference in London. The reform process, launched by Ed Miliband, entails the use of full OMOV system (= 'one member one vote') for the next leadership elections, with a selectorate composed by full members, affiliated members, and registered supporters.

The scientific interest in these processes of intra-party democratisation has grown since the turn of the millennium.[2] However, primaries as a tool of intra-party democracy are essentially studied within the American context (for a literature review, see Ware, 2002; Cohen et al., 2008). Analysis of the implementation of primary elections outside the United States is not equally developed despite recent trends towards more party primaries (Kenig, 2009; Pasquino and Venturino, 2010).

---

1 Sasha Issenberg, 'America exports democracy, just not the way you think', *New York Times*, 14 March 2014. <http://www.nytimes.com/2014/03/15/opinion/sunday/a-safer-way-to-export-democracy.html?_r=0>.

2 For instance, in 2001 *Party Politics* published a special issue on the topic.

This book explores the introduction of party primaries. There are very few comparative studies on the adoption, functioning and consequences of primary elections in advanced and new democracies (and, more specifically, outside the US) that go beyond analysis of a country or party case study and that are developed on the basis of electoral or individual level data. Nonetheless, the use of primary elections is spreading so quickly that a significant amount of data is being collected, even concerning non-US cases. Data availability has now reached a point that seems to allow rigorous cross-time and cross-country comparative analysis.

The Rationale for a Comparative Study of Primaries

The rationale for this book arises from two observations. First, as underlined above, primary elections for choosing party leaders and candidates are becoming usual events for European, African, Asian and American (both North and South) parties. Second, so far most studies on primaries in advanced and new democracies – or more generally outside the US – have just underlined the differences between European (or non-US) and American cases (Pasquino and Venturino, 2009), without reflecting further on how to conceptualise this democratisation instrument disregarding the varying political contexts.

Here we consider that context plays a crucial role insofar that primaries are particular kinds of political decision-making instruments ('rules of the game') that are applied within a given context. We also need to take into account factors such as electoral rules, political system features or meso-level features (for example party organisational models and internal distribution of power and resources). This is because primaries are rules that interact with other rules (either at party or systemic level) and that operate within a specific structure of party politics. For instance, party organisational structures – and particularly the role and nature of party membership – differ significantly in the American context and, broadly speaking, in the European one.

Moreover, the main comparative studies on candidate and leadership selection methods have either focused on large datasets analysing very different typologies of selection methods across a large number of countries (Cross and Blais, 2012; Pilet and Cross, 2014) or on case studies or small-N comparisons (Gallagher and Marsh, 1988; LeDuc, 2001). Although the theoretical and methodological reflection on primaries is quite extensive – especially concerning the development of this instrument within the US political system (Ware, 2002) – the analysis of the implementation of primary elections outside the US, and in particular within the European context, is not equally developed. A cross-country study which focuses specifically and solely on primary elections as a method for selecting candidates and leaders and which identifies the trend towards this particular type of intra-party democratisation beyond the US is still missing.

More recently, cross-national or case studies on the adoption and consequences of primaries outside the US have been published, but they mostly focus either on new democracies or on geographically limited areas such as Africa (Öhman, 2004; Ichino and Nathan, 2012) or Latin America (De Luca et al., 2002; Carey and Polga-Hecimovich, 2006).

However, we consider that there is still need for a volume which is specifically dedicated to the study of the processes of primary elections and of their consequences; which analyses at the same time candidate and leadership selection procedures; and also which is structured comparatively, expanding research on primaries away from the US and exploring parties in Europe and the Middle East (more specifically Israel) as well as in Asia.

Four scholarly works just have been published on topics dealing with highly inclusive methods for selecting leaders and candidates. The first is the comparative volume by William Cross and André Blais (2012). They provide an overview of the formal influence that rank-and-file members have on the selection of party leaders in the five English-speaking Westminster democracies: Australia, Canada, Ireland, New Zealand and the United Kingdom. The second comprises two studies published by Gilles Serra (2007b, 2011) on the origins of primary elections in Latin America, and in comparative perspective. Serra explores the rationales that lead political parties to hold competitive primary elections in the United States, Europe and Latin America.

The third study is the seminal volume by Reuven Hazan and Gideon Rahat (2010), in which they develop a comparative analytical framework for studying the political consequences of all the different methods for selecting candidates for office, and this in comparative perspective. The fourth work, edited by Jean-Benoit Pilet and William Cross (2013), analyses the various procedures for selecting party leaders in comparative perspective. It covers 12 European Union (EU) members, plus Australia, Canada and Israel.

Other seminal studies have also been published, in the form of edited volumes or monographs on party primaries, but they focused on the origins of American party primaries (Ware, 2002; Reynolds, 2006) rather than on the empirical or theoretical exploration of the phenomenon outside the US or on the dimension of organisational or electoral consequences.

In terms of empirical operationalisation and findings, besides the comparative datasets analysing separately leadership or candidate selection procedures mentioned above, a specific data collection focused on primaries in comparative perspective but integrating both candidate and leadership selection procedures is still lacking. This volume aims to complement and advance the two books already published on candidate selection (Hazan and Rahat, 2010) and leadership selection (Pilet and Cross, 2013) by developing further the analysis on party organisational democratisation. These works constitute the basis for bridging the two approaches – the latter focusing on leadership selection, the former on candidate selection – within a more comprehensive approach specifically targeted at exploring the functioning and consequences of primary elections.

In sum, the literature on the political consequences of leadership and candidate selection processes is now quite varied.[3] However, this stream of research seldom focuses specifically on primaries. In addition, primaries as a tool for enhancing intra-party democracy are basically studied within the US context (Ranney, 1972; Cohen et al., 2008). Studies addressing the political consequences of primaries in comparative perspective and on the basis of a common, standardised methodological and analytical framework are still lacking. But then the scholarly relevance of primaries (and more generally of internal democratisation and leader and candidate selection processes) is currently increasing.

This book aims to fill the abovementioned gaps in the literature on primary elections and addresses growing public and scholarly interest in intra-party democracy processes.

What Do We Know About Primary Elections?

The first angle from which primary elections have been studied concerns the rationales for adopting such internal democratisation instruments. This strand of research has focused more recently on the observation of empirical cases beyond the US, but of course originated in America. The first primaries were organised in Crawford County, Pennsylvania in 1842, and the rationales for adopting this democratisation instrument have been widely studied in the US literature (Key, 1949; Meinke et al., 2006). In the US the use of primaries for selecting candidates has mostly been imposed exogenously by state laws,[4] but the growing use of primary elections since the 1960s shows that parties have also played a role in choosing their methods of candidate selection (Serra, 2011). For instance, the US Democratic Party decided to adopt primary elections following internal discussions by the McGovern-Fraser Commission in the 1970s (Aldrich, 1980; Geer, 1989).

The key issue addressed by these studies is why parties should voluntarily adopt such inclusive methods for selecting candidates (and, outside the US, party leaders). Why hand out the nomination procedure to members or even non-members when party leaders can choose their candidates in closed-door negotiations ('smoke-filled room', as the Americanists say), and therefore fully control the outcome? Ware (2002), in his seminal history of primary elections in the United States, underlined that the origins of primaries are to be found in a cost-benefit evaluation by party leadership: state legislatures could not have adopted primaries if the leadership of the Democratic and Republican parties had not supported the decision. Several studies show that this decision is more tactical than ideological, and mainly linked to the will of party elites to find ways to interact with supporters outside the election season (Scarrow, 2005; Serra, 2011).

---

3 See for instance Ranney, 1972; Scarrow, 2005; Barnea and Rahat, 2007; Maravall, 2008; Cross and Pilet, 2014.

4 The first state regulation of primaries in the US was adopted only in 1912.

In countries where, unlike the US, party internal nomination processes are not (entirely) regulated by law, the significance of identifying the causes of adopting primaries appears to be even greater. An emerging literature has recently addressed the question, especially in Latin America; but the issue remains quite understudied both at empirical and theoretical level (Alcántara and Freidenberg, 2001).

An analytical model has been developed by Barnea and Rahat (2007) to explain the democratisation of candidate selection procedures, but it does not address specifically the adoption of primary elections. According to them, the motivations that explain the process of internal democratisation relating to candidate selection are found at three levels: political system level, party system level and intra-party level. At the political system level, the key explanatory factors are identified in the processes of personalisation of politics, decline of party membership and overall democratisation of contemporary societies, which force the parties to adapt to the changes in their social and political environment. At the party system level, parties are considered to be more likely to internally democratise after an electoral defeat (Cross and Blais, 2012). Also, the contagion effect between parties is argued to play a role. Finally, at intra-party level, the main arguments for explaining the democratisation of candidate and leadership selection deal with the internal distribution of power within parties (see below).

The second set of existing studies focuses on the consequences of party primaries. The potential effects of primary elections have been explored mostly with regard to internal organisation and party competition. Primary elections are a recurrent theme in the debate about parties and their organisational changes, even outside the US (Katz and Mair, 1995; Scarrow et al., 2000; Bolleyer, 2012). The debate on the consequences of intra-party democracy, more generally, arose within the early classical works on party politics (Ostrogorski, 1902; Michels, 2009 [1911]; APSA, 1950) and has resurfaced in the last two decades as a spinoff from the literature on party politics (Cross and Katz, 2013; Hazan and Rahat, 2010).

The arguments and theories developed so far for explaining the consequences of intra-party democratisation are different, but the empirical evidence is overall mixed (Scarrow, 2005). The American literature generally emphasises the idea that primaries inevitably lead parties to a decline because they are thought to entail a weakening of establishment control on the recruitment procedures (Miller et al., 1988; Hopkin, 2001). Conversely, in Europe the literature stresses a strategic use of this instrument by the party leadership, which tries to combine formal inclusiveness of internal selection processes with centralisation of other decision-making processes, increased veto power or leadership autonomy (Sandri and Pauwels, 2011; Wauters, 2009). The adoption of this inclusive method for selecting leaders and candidates can be explained by the creation of a new power equilibrium that combines both the increased legitimacy of direct democracy and the strategic value to serve the party leaders by weakening the middle level elites (Mair, 1994; Russell, 2005). Other recent studies show that the use of primaries in the European context does not seem to affect party organisational cohesion as negatively as expected (Indriðason and Kristinsson, 2013).

The third angle through which primaries have been discussed in the literature focuses on their effects on internal mobilisation and the role of members. Party primaries represent a new pattern in the relationship between parties and their supporters. Internal direct elections can be considered as a tool used by parties in order to compensate for the loss of legitimacy towards the electorate, and to attract new supporters less inclined to traditional party activism by giving ordinary members or voters a say (Aylott et al., 2012; Seddone and Venturino, 2013). Thus, parties are thought to provide more decision-making power to their supporters as an incentive to their own membership to mobilise internally, to present a public image of being open and to promote democratic innovation (Seyd, 1999; Scarrow, 1999). Scholarly attention on the consequences of primaries (or more generally of inclusive methods of selection) has focused also on their influence on overall levels of participation in internal ballots (Rahat and Sher-Hadar, 1999; Wauters, 2015).

The degree to which the use of open or closed primaries entails real empowerment of party members has been widely debated in the literature, and requires a clear distinction between the functioning and effects of closed and open primaries (Abramowitz et al., 1986; Mair, 1994; Sandri and Pauwels, 2011). Some authors have argued that primaries would weaken the mobilisation potential of rank-and-file members by diminishing their power over the party leadership (Katz and Mair, 1995). Others have stressed that they would enhance participation of new supporters who are not traditionally interested in intra-party participation (Heidar and Saglie, 2003). Studies show that (open) primaries could negatively affect candidate loyalty to the party because the nomination is legitimated outside the party, directly by primary voters (Ansolabehere et al., 2006; Hopkin, 2001).

Studies also show that primaries are often adopted by the party leadership for strategic reasons, and do not always respond to their rhetorical goals of democratisation (Ramiro, 2013). The empowerment of ordinary individual members is sometimes used by the leadership in order to secure greater organisational autonomy by reducing the power of activists and middle-level elites and by limiting their influence (Sandri, 2011; Corbetta and Vignati, 2013). However, these hypotheses have been assessed empirically only to a limited extent (van Holsteyn and Koole, 2009). This debate shows that the consequences of introducing primaries for political parties and democracies are uncertain and deserve to be explored empirically.

A fourth angle through which this instrument is examined concerns its impact on interparty competition. The effects of the adoption of primary elections on parties' electoral dynamics are highly contested in the US literature and empirical findings are quite mixed. The key issue concerns the electoral gain in promoting primaries. The hypotheses differ between those scholars who argue that primaries will have a negative impact and those who argue that they will produce an 'electoral bonus'.

On the one hand, several empirical studies have found that primary voters have extreme ideological views (Key, 1956; Polsby, 1983) and therefore that primaries select mainly ideologically extreme, less competitive candidates who are less likely to be supported by the general electorate (Norrander, 1986; Burden, 2004; Kaufmann et al., 2003). The argument, based on May's law of curvilinear disparity (1973), is that giving decision-making powers, especially for selecting candidates, to lower party strata or even voters would produce different candidate profiles, and therefore would affect their electability (Norris and Lovenduski, 1995). Also, the fact that the usually high turnout in primary elections could strengthen the electoral consensus for a party in general elections could be difficult to be evaluated by the general electorate (Adams and Merrill, 2008). However, the hypothesis of the negative impact of primaries in electoral terms is still debated in the US literature.

On the other hand, other empirical studies have found opposite results: they have shown that primary voters do not have extremist ideological views and that they do not select less electable, extremist candidates (Ranney, 1968; Gerber and Morton, 1998; Kaufmann et al., 2003). The empirical literature on the effects of American direct primaries is thus mixed. Studies analysing empirical cases beyond the US also show that primaries can have a positive impact on parties' electoral performance because they produce candidates more similar to party voters (Mikulska and Scarrow, 2010; Bruhn, 2011). Adams and Merrill (2008) and Serra (2011) also argue that, at least in Latin America, primary elections produce candidates who electorally benefit from having higher valence and broader appeal within the general electorate.

A fifth and last angle through which primary elections have been studied focuses on the potential contentious nature of primary election campaigns. The mutual delegitimation between primary candidates in highly competitive races could exacerbate internal conflicts and negatively affect the electoral results. Candidate and leadership selection processes are areas where party internal factions would compete and potentially clash (Ranney, 1981; Gallagher and Marsh, 1988). Some studies show that primaries emphasise intra-party conflict and attract greater media attention (Hazan and Rahat, 2010). Other studies argue that supporters, following a 'negative' primary campaign, could opt for defection in elections (Haines and Rhine, 1998; Peterson and Djupe, 2005). Primaries could also produce an 'electoral penalty' if a significant percentage of selectors are alienated because their favoured aspirant did not win the nomination (Stone, 1986). Finally, other studies refer to the concept of divisiveness, which refers to the potential intra-party conflict triggered by a highly contested and competitive primary election (Ware, 1979b; Wichowsky and Niebler, 2010). Divisiveness in primary elections is thought to demotivate party members and supporters, impacting negatively both on turnout and electoral performance.

The Importance of Primary Elections

This comparative volume focuses thus on open and closed party primaries to select candidates and party leaders. We consider that there is some scope for theory development in the treatment of these selection procedures in a cross-country perspective and in its attending guidance of empirical analysis. The study of internal selection procedures serves as a pretext to analyse whether some formal scope for intra-party democracy has an effect on actual intra-party democracy, on a party's organisational strength, cohesion and electoral success, and thus on the party as a whole. This is crucial for understanding how parties evolve both organisationally and electorally.

The book seeks to produce a theoretical and comparative empirical account of the emergence of party primaries in advanced and new democracies. In doing so it provides an account of these internal electoral processes – both concerning their origins and their mechanics – as well as an assessment of their impacts. It bridges sub-areas that are not in conversation with each other: that is, the literature on leadership and candidate selection, on party organisation and on electoral studies.

There are at least four different sets of literature that the study of primary elections beyond the US can contribute to and from which it can derive a research agenda. First, the study of primary elections integrates the debate on party organisational change and party internal regulations. The study of primaries relates to the scholarly debate on the transformation of party organisational models at the turn of the millennium (Carty, 2004; Carty and Cross, 2006). It also integrates current debate on the nature and consequences of party decline (Cain et al., 2003; Dalton et al., 2011). This matters for parties' ability to mobilise and for their claims to democratic legitimacy, especially with regard to the spreading of anti-party and anti-politics attitudes within European societies (Dalton, 2002). The public and scientific debates on the linkage function of parties and on direct citizens' participation issues underline the importance of better understanding primaries.

Second, the study of primary elections is linked to the research on the evolution of intra-party democracy. Besides the above-mentioned argument by Katz and Mair (1995; Mair, 1994) on the trade-off between internal participation and control of elites over party organisation, other studies frame primaries as an indicator of party internal democratisation processes (Cross and Katz, 2013). The way in which primary elections for selecting the leader and candidates are used not only describes how power is distributed internally but also how parties conceive democracy within their organisation, and consequently to what extent they are internally democratic.

Third, the comparative study of primaries could provide a better understanding of the evolutions of party membership and political participation. The open and inclusive nature of this instrument encourages new types of political participation (Kittilson and Scarrow, 2003). On the one hand, the adoption of primaries stimulates the internal mobilisation of members. On the other hand, primaries (especially open ones) are considered a stimulus to mass participation in politics (Ware, 1979a). Not only are primaries a way to increase membership: they are also a way for parties to mobilise electoral support; to interact with supporters outside of election season; to stabilise the involvement of casual backers; and to recruit volunteers. Primaries provide new opportunities for participation to those citizens less inclined to intra-party, traditional activism (Young, 2013).

Fourth, the study of primary elections relates to the research on candidate selection processes and, by extension, electoral studies. The literature review in the previous section has shown the scholarly debate on the relevance of primaries in electoral studies. Moreover, the comparative study of primary elections appears to be increasingly relevant with regard to its empirical scope. In the last decade the academic literature has included an increasing number of studies on primaries, and more generally on the direct participation of party members, party sympathisers and voters in general, in the selection of leaders and candidates for office.

This growing academic interest seems to follow an increase in the actual use of primaries across countries. Unlike in the US, where the specific nomination processes are regulated by law, political parties in Europe, Latin America, Asia and Africa can freely choose their selection processes. Outside the US, primaries are organised by parties themselves. Governments are not involved in the process, but parties may need their cooperation. For instance, when holding an open primary, parties might need to obtain electoral lists or to cover the territory with a sufficient number of polling stations. This may affect the capacity of individual parties to organise primaries, but nonetheless an increasing number of political organisations are voluntarily adopting primaries.

Recently, the adoption of open or closed primary elections has spread among parties in Israel, Iceland, France, Italy, Spain, Belgium, Denmark, Germany, the United Kingdom, Ireland, the Netherlands, Finland, Romania, Portugal, Slovakia, Greece, Japan, Argentina, Colombia, Chile, Mexico, Nicaragua, the Dominican Republic, Venezuela, Taiwan, South Korea, Ghana, Australia and Canada. For instance, in Latin America nowadays 'almost 40 per cent of the presidential elections in the region involved the participation of at least one candidate selected through a primary election' (Kemahlioglu et al., 2009, p. 339). If we look at the contemporary use of party primaries across the world, we can observe a clear trend of contagion between countries and among parties within national party systems. The trend of contagion also concerns different government levels (Venturino, 2013; Ramiro, 2014): in some countries, parties first adopt primaries at lower territorial levels (for instance, for selecting local elections candidates); their use then spreads to upper government levels (for instance, for selecting candidates for national election or chief executive office). Table 1.1 provides an overview of the actual use of open and closed primaries elections across the world in 2014.

Whereas closed primaries are rather common within many European countries, few political parties in Europe have already opted for open primaries. Parties generally organise primaries to nominate the party leader, less often to nominate the chief executive candidate or the candidates to put in their electoral lists. The underlying reason is that most European countries are parliamentary democracies. National governments are derived from the majority in parliament, which means that the head of the government is generally the leader of the winning party. France, of course, is one exception to this rule. Therefore, when studying primary elections it is important to distinguish their causes and consequences on the basis of the type

Table 1.1   Overview of main cases of primary elections across the world (up to 2014)

Type of Selection	Closed Primaries	Open Primaries
Party leader (national level)	Australia: Democrats Belgium: all parties Canada: Bloc Québécois, Conservatives, NDP Denmark: Socialdemokraterne, SF France: PS, UMP, EELV Ireland: Labour, Greens Israel: Likud, Kadima, Labour Italy: DS, LN Japan: LDP, SDPJ Netherlands: PvdA, VVD, D66 New Zealand: Labour Party Portugal: CDS[a], PS, PSD Spain: PSOE Sweden: MP, Liberals, SDP UK: Labour, LibDem	Canada: Liberal[b] Greece: Pasok Italy: PD
Chief executive (national or regional level)		Argentina: FPV, PRO Chile: all parties Colombia: PL, PCC, PV, PDA Costarica: PLN Dominican Republic: PLD El Salvador: FMLN Finland: all parties France: PS, PCF, EELV Honduras: LP, NP, Libre Italy: PD, SEL Mexico: PAN, PRD Nicaragua: FSLN, ALN, PLC Panama: PRD, CD, PP Spain: PSOE, UPyD Taiwan: KMT Uruguay: all parties US: Democrats, Republicans
Legislative candidates (national level)	Belgium: most parties (local level) Denmark: most parties Finland: all parties Germany: Greens, Die Linke (local level) Iceland: all parties Israel: Labour, Likud Romania: UDMR, PSD Slovakia: SDKÚ-DS	Ghana: NPP, NDC Iceland: all parties Italy: PD, SEL, M5S UK: Conservatives US: Democrats, Republicans

Notes: PvdA – Partij van de Arbeid (Labour); SF –Socialist People's Party; SPD – Social Democratic Party of Germany; NDP – New Democratic Party; D66 - Democrats 1966; MP- Environment party/the greens; SDP – Social democratic workers' party of Sweden; PL – Colombian Liberal party, PCC – Colombia Communist party; , PV – Colombian Green party; PDA – Alternative Democratic Pole; PLN – National Liberation party; FMLN – Farabundo Marti National Liberation Front; PRD – Revolutionary Democratic party; CD Democratic Change; PP – Panamanian party; FPV – Front for Victory; PRO – Republican Proposal; DLP – Dominican Liberation party; LP – Liberal party; NP – National party; PAN – National Action party; PRD – Party of the Democratic Revolution; FSLN – Sandinista National Liberation Front; ALN – Nicaraguan Liberal Alliance; PLC – Constitutionalist Liberal party; NPP – New Patriotic party; NDC – National Democratic Congress.

[a] Closed primaries have been used by the CDS between 2005 and 2011.   [b] Since 2012

of political regime they take place in, namely parliamentary or presidential, and on the basis of the electoral system of their respective countries.

Closed primaries happen in many European countries, while open primaries have so far mostly occurred in (mainly socialist) parties in Greece, France, Spain, Finland, Italy and the UK (but only in few local electoral colleges), to select the party leader, candidates for elections or the chief executive candidate at different levels (local, regional, national). One of the more recent developments in primary politics is the attempt at organising primaries at the European level. European parties that organised closed primaries – i.e. those open only to their registered party members – for the 2014 European elections were the European Green Party (EGP) and the Party of European Socialists (PES).

Primaries: Definitions and Typologies

Before presenting an overview of the scale of analysis of primary election processes and of the potential consequences of primary elections on parties, we will provide a brief general definition of the concept. Party leader and candidate selection through direct election is often labelled as open or closed primary election. Nevertheless, the adoption of the term 'primaries' or 'primary elections' for designing those specific internal elections, either open to all members or the wider electorate, is somewhat controversial in the non-US literature (Lefebvre, 2011; Cross and Blais, 2012). In fact, Hazan and Rahat (2010) define as non-party or open primaries all the selection methods that are open to all voters, even to sympathisers and non-members. Conversely, they define as party or closed primaries (or membership ballots, 'one member one vote' (OMOV) systems or direct selection methods) all the selection methods that are open only to party members (Pilet and Cross, 2013).

The term 'primary' in the American context relates to an election in which candidates for a subsequent election are chosen (Ware, 2002). In the non-US context (e.g. European, Asian) this label relates more generally to internal direct elections which are characterised by a high degree of inclusiveness (Kenig, 2009; Cross and Blais, 2012). Thus the term 'party primary' in the European (and, more broadly, non-American) context defines a selection method that is 'organised by the party, in which at least all party members are included in the selectorate and can cast their vote without having to travel beyond the region in which they live' (Koole, 2012, p. 2). We define as party primaries the internal elections for selecting political leaders or candidates for office (either for parliamentary elections or for chief executive mandates, at all levels) that entail full membership votes (FMV, closed primaries) or votes by members, sympathisers and registered voters (open primaries).

Previous studies have shown that open and closed party primaries are closer at the conceptual level than closed party primaries and votes by party delegates in congress (Pilet and Cross, 2013). The selectorate is not clearly bounded in both open and closed primaries (as for the latter we may see big ups and downs in party membership according to the electoral cycle), whereas other forms of selection, particularly by party delegates in congress, have a clearly stated selectorate defined by size in party standing orders. Also, in terms of implications for intra-party democracy, the marginal increase in the degree of inclusiveness of the selectorate when a party adopts closed primaries instead of votes by delegates in congress is higher than when a party adopts open primaries instead of closed ones (Cross and Katz, 2013).

There are three main points of variation between the American direct primaries and the direct selection of leaders and candidates within non-American (mostly European and Latin American) parties:

1. The instrument has been elaborated mainly in the framework of the nominating procedures for electoral mandates rather than for party internal mandates.
2. The primary election is thought to be regulated by (state) law and organised by external bodies and not directly by the party.
3. There is a direct and essential link between the nominating procedure and the subsequent (general) election. This is reflected in the requirement of an overall correspondence between the primary selectorate and the general electorate.

Using the same concept for identifying two objectively different phenomena – such as primary election in the US and internal elections for selecting the party leader or candidates for office within non-American parties – might represent a case of 'concept misformation' (Sartori, 1970, p. 1038). Nevertheless, this choice is justified by the lack of specific research tools for studying such new organisational features of parties and also by the undeniable similarity of several organisational dimensions and various symbolic aspects between the internal direct elections in Europe, Asia and Latin America and direct primary elections for selecting presidential and gubernatorial candidates in the US (Rahat and Kenig, 2011).

Although European primaries for selecting the leader and/or the candidates for office are mainly organised and financed by the parties themselves, in many cases the regulation of such instruments is provided by state law, as for instance in Germany and Finland (Ranney, 1981, p. 81). The same goes for Latin America, with the exception of Uruguay. In many other cases also the selection body is open to the entire general electorate and not only to party members.

Moreover, the main argument in favour of using the concept of primaries within the European or non-American context, in particular for studying elections for selecting party leaders, is that the linkage with subsequent elections might be latent but is generally present. Although the party leader is not automatically a candidate for general or presidential elections at the time of the selection procedure, in most parties the leader is designed as candidate for prime minister (or the equivalent) in subsequent elections (Kenig, 2009; Pilet and Cross, 2014).

Straying from the original model of US primaries, where direct primaries have been used for more than two centuries (Palmer, 1997; Cohen et al., 2008), parties outside the US have adapted primaries to their needs. This is mainly due to the different role played by parties within national party systems and processes of representative democracy in European, South American or Asian contexts. The very concept of party membership, crucial in the study of primary elections, has a completely different meaning in the US and other world political contexts (Stone et al., 2004; Heidar, 2006).

Also, analysis of the potential effects of such instruments of democracy outside the US needs to take into account the types of political regimes and electoral systems. The theories and studies formulated for American primaries can be generalised only to a certain extent, given that the US has a two-party system and a presidential system. Parties in parliamentary systems, which are based on the fusion rather than the separation of powers, perform a role that is significantly more important than parties in presidential systems (Indriðason and Kristinsson, 2013). The potential generalisation of theories and findings on American primaries to European and Asian primaries is discussed at length in Chapter 3 of this book.

Aims of the Study, Research Questions and Methodology

The two previous sections have shown that there is still much work to be done on party primaries. This volume tries to fill the gaps in the existing literature on primary elections in Europe and across the world. Its aim goes beyond existing work in at least two respects. First, there is a need for more comparative and empirical analysis on primary elections beyond the American case. Second, there is a need for a research agenda focused specifically on primary elections. Accordingly, the book provides a first descriptive account of the main rules governing primary election processes in various countries from a comparative perspective. It first discusses the formal rules and then it indicates how they function in practice. The study also attempts to assess the effect of the adoption and use of primaries on the electoral performance of political parties and their membership. The study develops innovative research in a field that is still embryonic in European political science, where the existing literature is highly fragmented and where cross-national and comparative studies are virtually nonexistent. This volume involves a comparative research design. Moreover, it takes into account primaries for selecting both candidates and party leaders.

The case selection has been developed on the basis of two criteria. First, a comparative, cross-country research design for studying party primaries is strictly limited by the fact that, unlike general elections, primaries are present only in some political systems across the world – and only within some parties in those countries. This entails a significant lack of data and the general need for intensive case studies. Second, on the basis of those limits, we decided to collect small-N empirical studies in which the cases are broadly comparable, culturally homogenous and mutually illuminating. In particular, the cases are integrated in the comparison on the basis of the similarity and general comparability of their political system features (electoral system, party system, form of government, concentration of executive powers vs power sharing and so on) in order to develop the analysis *ceteris paribus* and to control for cultural variables.

Case selection represents a critical phase in every work of comparative politics. On the one hand, it is necessary to avoid a selection of cases shaped only by opportunity reasons. On the other hand, the most appropriate rationales and processes for selecting cases to be explored empirically, which are identified on the basis of the research design requirements, are often problematic to implement in practical terms, because of mundane factors such as lack of funds for data collection or lack of linguistic competence. Case selection, thus, is often based on a trade-off between the research goals identified by the theoretical framework and the limitations imposed by the practical contexts of the research agenda.

As a consequence, several comparative books present a similar and comparable structure. In recent comparative researches on European political systems some chapters are dedicated to the most 'relevant' countries, usually the biggest in terms of size. If the comparison is limited to Western Europe, usually the analysis focuses separately on advanced European democracies such as France, Germany and the United Kingdom. Smaller countries are often explored together in specific chapters dealing with culturally and politically homogenous cases. For instance, this happens often with the five Scandinavian countries (Sweden, Norway, Finland, Denmark and Iceland), which are usually taken together in the analysis as the group of 'Nordic democracies'. The same goes for Spain and Portugal, usually analysed in the chapter dedicated to 'southern democracies', or for Belgium and the Netherlands, usually studied together in the chapter on the 'Low Countries'.

A research design following this well-established pattern is not feasible in the case of the analysis of primary elections. First, the traditional instruments for political representation – electoral systems, elections and parliaments – are necessarily present in all democratic political systems, while primary elections are an optional instrument of participatory democracy. Therefore, primaries are adopted and used by parties present in some countries but not in others. Second, the adoption of primaries, which are rarely regulated by state laws – except in the US and in few other countries such as Uruguay or Finland – varies significantly across time and can be abandoned after a period of intensive use.

The unequal, asymmetric use of primaries – which varies across time, is limited in geographical terms and can be totally absent in some political systems – significantly constrains the possibilities of selecting cases in the framework of comparative research designs. It compels one to limit the scope of analysis to the empirically available cases of political systems where at least one party has adopted such peculiar instruments of democracy. This situation also alters the classification criteria usually adopted for evaluating contemporary political systems. In the study of primaries, few small countries, such as Israel or Iceland, are characterised by the use of such instruments which are both intensive (in terms of the number of parties using them) and extensive (in terms of cross-time analysis), and this makes them the most relevant cases in the framework of comparative analyses.

In this study the selected cases are designed as sets of paired empirical comparisons (except for the last one which deals with Iceland alone), each exploring two countries. The cases were selected so that the comparison will develop between countries where (at least some) parties use primary elections either for selecting leaders or candidates for parliamentary elections or chief executive mandates. The countries are selected on the basis of the degree of comparability of the features at political system level and the features of the primary election processes. The chosen countries cover different geopolitical areas (Western Europe, Eastern Europe and Asia) and types of democracy (advanced and new) as well as different political regimes, dealing with both parliamentary and (semi) presidential systems. Concerning leadership selection, for instance, party leaders often also serve as prime ministerial candidates. If this fits perfectly with what happens in most Westminster-style democracies or parliamentary systems, it is not always the case in France, Taiwan or Italy, for instance. In these cases, primaries are used for selecting highly specific types of candidate, namely prime ministerial or presidential candidates. Moreover, two of these countries (France and Taiwan) have semi-presidential systems.

Therefore, in order to take into account this trend of 'contagion', or spreading of the use of primaries, the empirical focus of this book is not limited to 'old party systems' and established western democracies. The empirical chapters deal with Western European established democracies (for example France and Italy) and more recent democracies (Spain and Portugal); Eastern European post-communist new democracies (Romania and Slovakia); classical consensual democracies (for example Belgium); established and emerging Far East democracies (Japan and Taiwan); and Middle East democracies (Israel) as well as with parliamentary and semi-presidential systems. The only exception to these paired comparisons is represented by the last chapter on Iceland which, given its peculiarity, is analysed separately. Iceland is in fact one of the first countries outside the US to have adopted open primaries. Since the 1970s, all the major Icelandic parties have selected candidates through primary elections. Moreover, the method of selection has generally been decided at constituency level, which means that the same party has often used different methods of candidate selection for the same election.

Here we provide an integrated and comparative analytical framework for empirically assessing: how the primary election processes function, and the consequences of using primaries on internal party organisation and on inter-party competition. Chapters 2 and 3 give the basis of analysis for collecting empirical data, namely primaries, a much-needed conceptualisation with regard to non-US contexts and provide the framework for the analyses developed in the subsequent empirical chapters. We identify here the research questions that guide the empirical analysis and the associated possible variables and indicators, and define the dimensions along which primaries vary. This framework is elaborated on the basis of the analytical tools developed for studying the American experience, which will be adapted to the European and Asian typologies of primary elections.

The study takes as its main unit of analysis primary elections within individual parties and their organisational features. Although we assess empirically the model by Hazan and Rahat (2010), we do not identify here specific hypotheses; rather, we clarify our main research questions which provide guidance for empirical analysis. The study's three research questions (RQs), stemming from the main open debates in the North American literature, are:

RQ1: What are the main factors that lead parties to use inclusive procedures to select their leaders and candidates?

RQ2: What are the main features of the primary election processes, particularly in terms of formal rules, degree of participation in internal elections and competitiveness?

RQ3: What effect, if any, do primaries have on parties in terms of electoral performance and membership appeal?

Concerning RQ1, this study applies the model by Barnea and Rahat (2007); concerning RQ2, it analyses the formal rules for electing the party leader by looking at empirical indicators identified by previous analytical models (Scarrow, 2005; Cross and Blais, 2012), such as: who is eligible to vote in internal ballots (inclusiveness of the selectorate); the degree of territorial and functional decentralisation of the selectorate body;[5] who is eligible as a candidate (candidacy rules); the voting system; rules concerning timing; and the deselection rules (in the case of leadership selection).

According to Hazan and Rahat's model, it is crucial to look at the actual functioning of the selection processes. In particular, the most relevant dimensions for studying primary election processes are competition and participation. Here we explore the competitiveness of each selected primary election and the degree of involvement of the potential selectors (members or even non-members, sympathisers and general voters). The chapters explore in great detail the individual processes of primary elections before assessing their impact on parties.

Concerning RQ3, the empirical analysis of the effects of primary elections on the selected parties is developed on the basis of the four dimensions identified by Hazan and Rahat's model: competition, representation, participation and responsiveness. In this study we emphasise the differences between internal and external effects of the adoption of primary elections. We also focus on the dimensions of participation and competition when studying the consequences of primaries (and not only the processes). Participation is often seen as an important indicator for measuring the democratic degree of elections, both within and

---

5   For instance, all registered members at local level constitute the selectorate for choosing candidates through closed primaries when primaries are organised at the level of each local section of the party.

between parties (Franklin, 2002). Not only is this dimension the most relevant for evaluating the political consequences of intra-party democracy, but it is also the most empirically appropriate for developing a common codebook for collecting comparative data.

While the dimensions of representation and competition will be analysed as contextual ones for framing this empirical study, participation constitutes the main analytical dimension, theoretically driven and empirically informed, that is explored comparatively across the cases. Therefore, RQ3 can be specified further by dividing it into two sub-research questions:

> RQ3.1: What effect, if any, do primaries have on party organisation and cohesion?
> RQ3.2: What effect, if any, do primaries have on electoral parties?

With regard to the internal consequences (RQ3.1), the existing literature has compared current and previous situations (Heidar and Saglie, 2003; Wauters, 2014) or evaluations of the influence that the party on the ground can exert through these processes (Scarrow, 1999). As underlined, some authors argued that primaries would weaken the mobilisation potential of rank-and-file members by diminishing their power of control over the party leadership (Katz and Mair, 1995). Others stressed that it would enhance participation of new supporters who are not traditionally interested in intra-party participation. We explore the impact of primaries on intra-party mobilisation and party membership.

Concerning the external consequences of primaries (RQ3.2), the analysis focuses on the electoral gain for parties through promoting primaries (Ramiro, 2014). We have seen that the American literature is mixed on this point and that the main theoretical models are conflicting on the trade-off between electability and inclusiveness of the selection process (Kaufmann et al., 2003). We explore thus the potential link between parties' use of primaries and electoral performance.

All the empirical chapters will follow this structure: in the introduction they address the political context of the countries included in the analysis, summarising the explanatory factors at political and party system level for the adoption of primary elections by parties. In particular, authors will provide a brief account of the following explanatory dimensions identified by Gallagher and Marsh (1988): the political culture; the main features of the political system; the electoral system; the format of the party system. The empirical chapters then explore the contexts and rationales for adopting primary elections at intra-party level, thus describing each unit of analysis, with special focus on party main organisational features (degree of decision-making centralisation, role of the leader and of the dominant coalitions). An overview of the main strategic incentives for each party to resort to, inclusive processes of candidate or leader selections, is also presented.

Then, a detailed analysis of the processes of primary elections in the selected parties is provided. This explores the process as a whole, taking into account both the rules governing internal elections and the actual functioning of the latter. The descriptive analysis of the independent variables will feature a synthesis of:

- the party's formal rules. The main indicators are the degree of inclusiveness of the selectorate; the decentralisation of the selectorate; candidacy rules; voting system; timing rules and deselection rules.
- the degree of participation in internal elections, reporting overall turnout shares;
- the degree of competitiveness of primary elections. The main indicators are the number of candidates and, in the case of primaries for selecting candidates for parliamentary elections, the competitiveness index (Kenig, 2009).

Concerning the study of the consequences of primaries, we adapt Hazan and Rahat's model and focus not only on the internal processes but also on the organisational and electoral effects of primary elections. We focus therefore on two main variables: the evolution of overall membership figures of parties; and their electoral performance in general elections before and after internal ballots are held.

Especially in the case of open primaries, the exogenous legitimation of the selected candidates or leader and the participation of voters and supporters could provide an opportunity for minority factions and for individual ambitions to defy the party leadership and its dominant coalition. Thus, we focus on the evolution of the organisational relationship between members and party by looking at the effect of recruitment campaigns launched during primary elections on membership size. If the overall turnout in primaries over time might represent a pertinent and straightforward indicator of the impact of this instrument on a party's mobilising appeal, in the long term the consequences on membership internal mobilisation and roles within party structures appear to be more complex to assess. We explore thus to what extent primaries enhance participation by attracting new members. We assess to what extent the adoption of primaries attracts new members and whether these new cohorts of affiliates remain within the party or leave as 'instant members' (Rahat and Hazan, 2007). Concerning the external consequences on parties, we argue that the degree of participation in primary elections has a potential impact on party results in general elections.

In terms of indicators, the absolute size of membership in the year before and after each primary election are analysed in the empirical chapters. The absolute and percentage election results (at national, general elections for the UK's lower house) before each primary election are analysed; and the difference between each selected party's share of votes before and after each primary is also examined.

In this volume, discussion on the consequences of primaries is limited to a descriptive account of the relationship between internal ballots and membership size as well as electoral performance. It is, foremost, an explorative study, and not enough comparative data are available for developing an inferential approach (at least at this stage) on the effects of primaries on electoral performance. We do not define specific hypotheses on this point. There are too many variables intervening in explaining electoral performance, and we cannot identify explanatory factors for electoral success/defeat solely linked to previous primary election competitiveness and turnout. In the empirical chapters, we try to assess mainly whether primaries created massive registration campaigns for the parties and whether the members who joined on the eve of primaries stayed or left the party after they were over. Also, we intuitively explore whether primaries helped or maybe hindered the parties' electoral performance. In fact, especially leadership selection in most parliamentary democracies does not fit with the electoral cycle, and it is crucial to account for the political and institutional context in each selected country.

The core research in this volume is contained in the first three chapters, which provide the basis for a comparative analytical framework for studying primary elections beyond the American experience. The remaining chapters then provide empirical assessments of the proposed framework in a large set of comparative cases. Chapters 1–3 present the theoretical and methodological framework that is implemented empirically in Chapters 4–9, which focus on primaries for both leadership and candidate selection. Ultimately, the book comes down to the empirical chapters, each of which analyses two countries selected by the degree of comparability of their features at political system level and of their primary election processes (with Iceland treated separately, as mentioned earlier).

In conclusion, the 'younger' literature on primaries outside the US might not have yet reached a consensus on some fundamental definitions and methodological aspects – what a primary election is; the main dimensions to be explored when investigating the consequences of primaries on political parties – given the peculiarity of each case, both at party and national level. This volume will thus attempt to systematise (at least partially) the main elements from previous studies and supply a (very) general overview of the subject. Hence, we identify a few key variables and indicators for analysing with a unified research design both open and closed primaries and procedures for selecting leaders and candidates. Some indicators remain relevant or useful only for some specific types of primary, but the great majority of analytical dimensions suggested refer to a general, comprehensive framework for studying party primaries across the world.

Chapter 2
Leadership Selection versus Candidate Selection: Similarities and Differences

Ofer Kenig, Gideon Rahat and Reuven Y. Hazan

Introduction

The pioneering cross-national work on leadership selection (Marsh, 1993; Punnett, 1992) and on candidate selection (Gallagher and Marsh, 1988; Ranney, 1981) is only a generation old, and the research of these two topics is now more or less at similar stages of development. That is, in both cases sufficient tools have been developed for comparative analysis – classification and measurement – and both have begun to provide, albeit only a few, systematic cross-national comparisons (for example Hazan and Rahat, 2010; Cross and Blais, 2012; Pilet and Cross, 2014). Yet, problems with the availability of data still block researchers from getting closer to their mature relative, the comparative study of elections and electoral systems. Research is at the stage at which electoral studies were almost 50 years ago when Rae (1967) published his seminal work, and we hope that a Rae-like breakthrough is on the horizon.

In this chapter we delineate the differences and similarities between leadership selection and candidate selection methods. We start with a short explanation of the importance of distinguishing between the two. We then map the similarities and differences between these two related but distinct methods of selection in terms of various dimensions: candidacy, selectorate, decentralisation, appointment/voting and deselection. Then, an overview of the evidence and motivations for the democratisation of both leadership and candidate selection is presented. This is followed by an analysis of the consequences of the democratisation of each selection method, and their interaction when they occur simultaneously.

Why is it Important to Distinguish between Leadership and Candidate Selection?

Although it is tempting to treat leadership selection as an offshoot of candidate selection, the research literature that focuses on parliamentary democracies treats the two separately. There are several reasons for this.

First, the party leader is not just 'number one' on the list of party candidates for public office. A new prime minister may be selected by the ruling party, or parties, without a general election taking place. That is, the decision concerning the highest office in the country may not be in the hands of the electorate. Only five of the last 11 British prime ministers (as of 2014) initially assumed office following a general election. The others (Eden, Macmillan, Douglas-Home, Callaghan, Major and Brown) became prime ministers following an intra-party procedure between one general election and the next. This pattern is common in other countries as well. In Japan, for example, only one of the 10 prime ministers that served between 1996 and 2012 initially assumed office following a general election. The other nine became prime ministers following an intra-party procedure between one general election and the next. The selection of a party leader must, therefore, be seen as more than just an intra-party matter, and possibly as a procedure that determines who will serve as the leader of a country.

But not all parties select leaders who will compete for the prime ministership. In most instances, the party leaders are selected with the expectation – or the hope – that they will hold the senior post that the party will gain, either in the legislative or in the executive branch. The party leader, if it is the main opposition party, will be the leader of the opposition; if it is one of the other parties in opposition, the leader may be a committee chair, or fill another important legislative position. If the party is in government as part of a coalition, the leader will likely be a cabinet minister; and if it is the main party, or the only party, in government the leader will be the prime minister. In short, at least several parties in each country, when they select their leader, will perceive him or her as the party's candidate for prime minister, while other parties will select their leaders in the hope that they will be in a senior executive position. Even perennial opposition parties give their leaders more stature in party matters and in other areas such as media access.

Alternatively, some parties hold different selection processes for the position of party leader and for their candidate for chief executive (president, prime minister, chancellor). In France, for example, the Socialists held a primary contest for selecting the party chairperson in 2008. Three years later, they held another primary for selecting their presidential candidate. While such a separation mainly occurs in presidential or semi-presidential systems, it may happen in parliamentary systems as well (Table 2.1). For example, in Italy the Democrats have selected their leaders through a primary contest since 2007, while in 2012 their candidate for prime minister was selected in a separate primary contest within the framework of the wider left coalition.

Second, parties grant their leaders authority they do not grant anyone else in the party. In some parties, the leader *is* the party, as he or she makes all the important decisions, including those concerning candidate selection and policy making. But even in less autocratic parties, leaders have special formal authority – for example selecting ministers; deciding whether to join or to leave a governing coalition; supporting or vetoing the nomination of party candidates for various intra- and inter-party positions – and also many informal ones (for example dictating the agenda and schedule for the party conference).

Table 2.1 The use of primary selections to various political positions around the world

Type of Regime	Party Leader	Chief Executive	Legislative Candidates
Presidential system	–	USA	USA
Semi-presidential system	France, Taiwan	France, Taiwan	Romania
Parliamentary system	Belgium, Israel, Italy, Japan, Portugal, Spain	Italy	Slovakia, Iceland

Note: All examples are case studies that appear in this book, except for the USA.

Third, while in presidential democracies candidates for both legislative and executive posts need the support of the selectorate and the electorate, in parliamentary democracies things are different. In such systems, the party leadership position has significantly different sources of both legitimacy and survival than other party candidates. That is, after candidates are selected by the party, voters then elect the successful ones among them to parliament. This is true regardless of whether the candidates compete individually in single-member districts or as part of a team in multi-member districts. After being selected by the party, in order to be elected they must possess a wide popular base of legitimacy. Both the party selectorate and the general electorate can only oust them either on the eve of the next election (when candidate selection largely takes place) or in the general election. Leaders, on the other hand, are selected only by the party selectorate; they are not subject to the verdict of the voters in order to assume the party leadership, and in principle they can be ousted by the party at any time.

Party leaders are, therefore, judged differently according to the expectations the public, their own party members and their fellow elected representatives have both for and of them. This is so even though candidate selection is about selecting candidates for public posts while leadership selection is sometimes (in parliamentary democracies) 'only' about selecting a candidate for a party post. The political weight of a party leader is significantly greater than that of a party candidate selected to run in a district or appear on the party's list of candidates.

Similarities and Differences between Leadership and Candidate Selection

This section delineates and compares the similarities and differences between leadership and candidate selection methods, which we argue are two related yet distinct mechanisms.

Candidacy

Candidacy answers the question: Who can be selected as the party leader, its candidate for the chief executive and/or its legislative candidates? Leadership selection and candidate selection can both be assessed in terms of candidacy requirements according to a continuum from exclusiveness to inclusiveness. At the inclusive pole, any voter can present him/herself as the party candidate, with no preconditions. At the exclusive pole, a candidate must be a veteran member of the party and is required to fulfil additional preconditions linked to his/her everyday party activities. In between there are various cases in which, for example, a minimum period of party membership is required.

A common candidacy requirement, particularly for leadership races but also found in candidate selection, is the presentation of a minimum number of supporters' signatures. This measure is undertaken to make it harder for fringe candidates to run. Without this precondition, a fringe candidate might drag the party through an expensive, problematic campaign that would waste both energy and resources needed to compete in the interparty arena and could harm the party's image. Signatures can be those of parliamentarians, delegates of a selected party agency or party members. For example, the British Labour Party requires a candidate to command the support of at least 12.5 per cent of the party's members of parliament (MPs) in cases of leadership vacancy, and 20 per cent of its MPs in cases of leadership challenge. The Social Democrats in Portugal require a leadership candidate to present the signatures of 1,500 party members. Contest fees are also a common mechanism to deter candidates and limit the number of contenders. In Canada the entry fee for the 2004 Conservative leadership race was $100,000, while the Liberals set the entry fee for their 2013 leadership race at $75,000. Similar preconditions can be found in candidate selection, with the same aim of preventing fringe candidacies, though their scale is usually significantly lower, necessitating fewer signatures and less money: the Canadian Conservatives, for example, required only a $1,000 deposit in 2009.

An important difference concerning the 'additional requirements' of leadership versus candidate selection is a precondition that a leadership candidate must be an incumbent MP. This is the requirement, for example, in the major British and Irish parties. In the case of candidate selection, such a precondition would be absurd.

Selectorate

The selectorate concerns the question: Who selects the party leader, its candidate for the chief executive and/or the legislative candidates? It is arguably the most important dimension in both leadership and candidate selection. Leadership and candidate selection share most types of selectorate (see Figures 2.1 and 2.2). In addition to the extreme cases of the highly exclusive selectorate of a single leader and the highly inclusive selectorate of all eligible voters, parties use three other commonly found selectorates for choosing their legislative candidates. Moving from the exclusive pole of party leader, these selectorates are then composed of the rather exclusive group of the party elite, followed by the moderately inclusive group of delegates, then the more inclusive mass group of party members.[1]

Most exclusive *Most inclusive*

Leader	Party elite	Party delegates	Party members	Voters
Israel: Yesh Atid	Japan: LDP	Ireland: Fianna Fail Germany: several parties	Canada: several parties Finland: several parties Ireland: Fine Gael, Labour Israel: Labour	Iceland: several parties US: Democrats, Republicans

Figure 2.1 Candidate selectorate continuum
Note: Parties along the continuum are based on the most recent data available.
Sources: Indriðason and Kristinsson, 2013; Inoguchi, 2010; Hazan and Rahat, 2010; Reidy, 2011.

There is, nevertheless, one selectorate that is unique to leadership selection – the parliamentary party group (PPG). It is quite obvious why the PPG cannot serve as a selectorate in candidate selection – it would be the selectors selecting themselves. The PPG was widely used in the past, and is still in use today by some parties for leadership selection. It is less inclusive than selectorates composed of party delegates but more inclusive than the most exclusive kinds of selectorate (a single leader or members of the elite), and it still represents an element of indirect democracy – that is, the party voters elect the MPs who form the PPG. Moreover, it replicates the parliamentary logic at the intra-party level: the parliamentarians select the prime minister and the PPG selects the party leader. To summarise, we can count five types of selectorate in candidate selection (party leader, party elite, party delegates, party members and all voters); and in leadership selection we must add a sixth (the PPG).

---

[1] Recently several parties have experienced an additional category of 'supporters' (other terms for the category include 'sympathisers' and 'friends'). In terms of inclusiveness, this category should be located between party members and voters. For the sake of simplicity we combine the categories of voters and supporters. These categories can be used when analysing a simple, one-stage and uniform candidate selection method. Empirically, however, we often see complex selection methods which deserve special attention (see Hazan and Rahat, 2010).

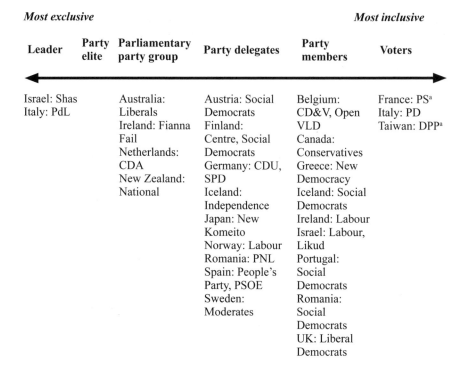

Figure 2.2   Leadership selectorate continuum

Note: Parties along the continuum are based on their position in 2012;
CDU: Christian Democratic Union of Germany; SPD: Social Democratic Party of Germany
[a] presidential candidates.

Decentralisation

Decentralisation is about asking the question: Where is the candidate selected? The answer can be territorial – the candidate is selected at local, regional or national level, or in any combination of these, with varying levels of influence. The answer may also be sociological – members of a specific social group (for example women, minorities, union members and so on) select the candidate. In most parties, in most established democracies, candidate selection is in the hands of regional or local selectorates and the national level has only a secondary role, if any. Not so when it comes to leadership selection. This is, by definition, a national event – yet attempts may be made to decentralise leadership selection by granting specific territorial regions more than their proportional share in the selectorate. For example, parties in Canada use a 'points system' for calculating votes. According to this method, each party member participates, but the votes are calculated in such a way that each electoral riding (constituency) gets the same weight as the others, regardless of how many members actually cast a vote. In general, however, and as a result of the nature of selection – national leader versus local/regional representatives – candidate selection is much more decentralised than leadership selection.

Appointment vs Voting

This dimension asks the questions: How is the leader selected? How are the candidates selected? Appointments look similar in both leadership and candidate selection. That is, a single leader, a relatively small party elite or a selection committee announces the party candidate(s). When it comes to voting, the differences are based on the number of positions that have to be filled and not the nature of the selected position (leader or candidate). When a single candidate is selected – whether for the party leadership, for chief executive or as the party candidate in a single-member district (and even if the party list is filled position by position) – the voting methods are similar. In all these cases, various kinds of majoritarian systems are implemented: plurality, two-round majoritarian, alternative vote or elimination vote. But, if more than one candidate is selected in a voting event – which can involve only candidate selection and not leadership selection – other voting methods may be employed, such as limited vote or single transferable vote. To summarise, while appointment is similar for both leadership and candidate selection, it is the number of candidacies that have to be filled in a single voting event that influences the nature of the voting method adopted, not the distinction between leadership and candidate selection.

Deselection

Candidate selection is held before a general election (except for by-elections) to choose the contenders who will compete under the label of each party. Once candidates are elected to parliament they are secure in their position until the next general election. This is also true for candidates selected for (and then elected to) directly elected executive posts (chief executive, mayor, governor). In other words, the party cannot remove them, except in rare cases.[2] Leadership selection in parliamentary democracies is different in this aspect: party leaders are not necessarily secure in their position during their entire term in parliament or in government. They may be challenged, and the rules governing these challenges vary across parties (Bynander and 't Hart, 2007; Quinn, 2012). The timing of leadership contests is thus not necessarily related to the life cycle of the legislature (unlike candidate selection) or to the timing of elections in general, like directly elected executive posts.

The fact that parties can oust their leader during a term of office is highly significant since, as we argued at the outset, leadership selection should be seen as more than just an intra-party matter, especially if such a replacement brings

---

2 In India, for instance, an MP's defection from their party results in expiry of their membership (Janda, 2009).

about a change of prime minister. The famous ousting of Margaret Thatcher by her fellow Conservative MPs (1990) and the more recent removal of Australian Prime Minister Kevin Rudd (2010) provide examples of successful leadership challenges that changed not only the leader of the party but also the leader of the country.

The difference between leadership and candidate selection in this dimension is crucial since it concerns the varying perceptions of these two posts in parliamentary democracies. The leader is selected only by the party and not subsequently elected directly by the people. Members of parliament are selected by their party, but then they are elected by the voters. MPs may, therefore, be challenged on the eve of the next elections, just before they have to face the voters, but party leaders may be ousted at any time. The party leader may thus have more incentive to act as a delegate vis-à-vis their selectorate than an MP who can act as a trustee. But this is not always the case, and many parties secure their leaders' position – at least as long as they succeed in the interparty arena, bring the party to government and, particularly, if they occupy the prime ministership.

In presidential democracies, however, the selection of candidates for both the executive and the legislative branch shares the property of pre-selection, one that must later be ratified in general elections. It is thus no wonder that, once elected, a president (unlike a prime minister) cannot be deselected by his party.

Table 2.2   Dimensions of leadership and candidate selection methods

Leadership selection	Candidate selection	Difference
Candidacy	Candidacy	Small
Selectorate	Selectorate	Small
–	Decentralisation	Irrelevant for most cases of leadership selection
Appointment/voting	Appointment/voting	Small
Deselection	–	Substantial (for parliamentary democracies)

Table 2.2 summarises the comparison between dimensions in the classification of leadership selection and candidate selection methods.[3] There are apparently more similarities than differences between leadership and candidate selection. The relatively minor differences in the case of candidacy, selectorate, decentralisation and appointment/voting system are:

- the higher threshold for candidacy and incumbency sometimes used as a requirement for leadership selection;

---

3   The classification of candidate selection essentially follows Rahat and Hazan (2001), while the classification of leadership selection follows Kenig (2009b).

- the possibility of using the PPG as a selectorate in case of leadership selection;
- the built-in centralisation of the leadership selection method; and
- the necessary use of majoritarian selection methods in case of leadership selection.

Leadership and candidate selection are, however, substantially different when it comes to deselection, but this large difference is confined to the case of parliamentary democracy.

The Scope and Causes of Intra-Party Democracy

Reacting and adapting to social changes, political parties have transformed their internal distribution of power by granting their members a significant role in various aspects of party life (Scarrow et al., 2000; Bille, 2001; Hazan, 2002). Two of the processes in which party members have received a role are in the selection of party leaders and/or candidates for chief executive and for the legislature. In other words, a process of internal democratisation has taken place within political parties in modern democracies, leading to an increase in the role of rank-and-file party members and sometimes even of a larger crowd of 'supporters'. This redistribution of power manifests itself in both similar and different ways if we compare the level of leadership selection to that of candidate selection.

The Empirical Evidence

Theoretically, when scholars write about democratisation in leadership or in candidate selection, they refer to the opening of the selectorate to broader audiences – that is, the replacement of an existing selectorate with a more inclusive one; or, in the case of complex selection methods, the addition of a more inclusive selectorate to the existing selection process. Empirically, recent decades have witnessed exactly such a process of internal democratisation by political parties in established democracies. Political parties have changed their internal distribution of power by granting their ordinary members a greater role in leadership and in candidate selection (Bille, 2001; Kittilson and Scarrow, 2003; Hazan and Voerman, 2006; Cross and Katz, 2013).

With regard to leadership selection, there are several studies that confirm such a process of democratisation. A study of 30 parties in 11 established democracies compared leadership selectorates in 2007 to those in 1975. It founded that 40 per cent of the parties opened their leadership selection methods within this period (Kenig, 2009a). Another study of 26 parties in Australia, Canada, Ireland, New Zealand and the United Kingdom compared the leadership selectorates in 2010 to those in the mid-1970s. Prior to 1976 only the three Canadian parties granted any formal role to party members. By 2010, 11 parties gave members full authority over selection, while seven parties shared authority between the PPG and the party members (Cross and Blais, 2012).

Table 2.3 outlines the leadership selectorates of 71 parties from 23 democracies. We can see that, as of 2012, almost half of the parties used inclusive selectorates (members, supporters, mixed or voters). In addition, we can compare the selectorates used in 2012 to those in use in 1975. The number of parties compared here declines to 47 because 24 parties did not exist, or existed under non-democratic regimes, back in 1975.[4] In about half of the cases (24 out of 47) we can detect an opening of the selectorate. The rest of the parties retained their selectorate, while not a single one moved in the opposite direction (adopting a more exclusive selectorate).

Table 2.3 Leadership selectorates in 71 parties

State	Party	Leadership selectorate 1975	Leadership selectorate 2012	Opening?
Australia	Labour	PPG	PPG	No
	Liberals	PPG	PPG	No
Austria	Freedom Party	Party delegates	Party delegates	No
	Greens	n.a.	Party delegates	n.a.
	People's Party	Party delegates	Party delegates	No
	Social Democrats	Party delegates	Party delegates	No
Belgium	CD&V	Party delegates	Party members	Yes
	MR	Party delegates	Party members	Yes
	N-VA	n.a.	Party members	n.a.
	Open VLD	Party delegates	Party members	Yes
	Socialists (Flemish)	Party delegates	Party members	Yes
	Socialists (French)	Party delegates	Party members	Yes
Canada	Conservatives	Party delegates	Party members	Yes
	Liberals	Party delegates	Supporters	Yes
	NDP	Party delegates	Party members	Yes
Denmark	People's Party	n.a.	Party delegates	n.a.
	Liberals	Party delegates	Party delegates	No

---

4 The CD&V, MR and Open VLD (Belgium) were compared to the CVP, PRL and PVV in 1975, respectively; the Conservatives (Canada) were compared to the Progressive Conservatives in 1975; the Social Democratic Alliance (Iceland) was compared to the Social Democratic Party in 1975; Likud (Israel) was compared to Herut in 1975; the Liberal Democrats (UK) were compared to the Liberals in 1975.

Leadership Selection versus Candidate Selection

	Social Democrats	Party delegates	Mixed	Yes
	Soc. People's Party	Party delegates	Party members	Yes
Finland	Centre	Party delegates	Party delegates	No
	Left Alliance	n.a.	Party delegates	n.a.
	KOK	Party delegates	Party delegates	No
	Social Democrats	Party delegates	Party delegates	No
France	Socialists	Party delegates	Party members	Yes
	UMP	n.a.	Party members	n.a.
Germany	CDU	Party delegates	Party delegates	No
	FDP	Party delegates	Party delegates	No
	Greens	n.a.	Party delegates	n.a.
	SPD	Party delegates	Party delegates	No
Greece	New Democracy	n.a.	Party members	n.a.
	PASOK	n.a.	Supporters	n.a.
Iceland	Independence	Party delegates	Party delegates	No
	Left-Green Alliance	n.a.	Party delegates	n.a.
	Progressive	Party delegates	Party delegates	No
	Social Democrats	Party delegates	Party members	Yes
Ireland	Fianna Fáil	PPG	PPG	No
	Fine Gael	PPG	Mixed	Yes
	Labour	PPG	Party members	Yes
Israel	Kadima	n.a.	Party members	n.a.
	Labour	Party delegates	Party members	Yes
	Likud	Party delegates	Party members	Yes
	Shas	n.a.	Leader	n.a.
	Yisrael Beitenu	n.a.	Party delegates	n.a.
Italy	Democrats	n.a.	Voters	n.a.
	PDL	n.a.	Leader	n.a.
Japan	Democrats	n.a.	Mixed	n.a.
	LDP	Party delegates	Mixed	Yes
	New Komeito	n.a.	Party delegates	n.a.
Netherlands	CDA	PPG	PPG	No
	PvdA	Party delegates	Party members	Yes
	SP	Party delegates	Party delegates	No
	VVD	Party delegates	Party members	Yes
New Zealand	Labour	PPG	PPG	No
	National	PPG	PPG	No

Norway	Conservatives	Party delegates	Party delegates	No
	Labour	Party delegates	Party delegates	No
	Progress	Party delegates	Party delegates	No
Portugal	Social Democrats	Party delegates	Party members	Yes
	Socialists	Party delegates	Party members	Yes
Romania	PDL	n.a.	Party delegates	n.a.
	PNL	n.a.	Party delegates	n.a.
	Social Democrats	n.a.	Party members	n.a.
Spain	People's Party	n.a.	Party delegates	n.a.
	PSOE	n.a.	Party delegates	n.a.
Sweden	Moderates	Party delegates	Party delegates	No
	Social Democrats	Party delegates	Party delegates	No
Taiwan	DPP	n.a.	Party members	n.a.
	Kuomintang	n.a.	Party members	n.a.
UK	Conservatives	PPG	Mixed	Yes
	Labour	PPG	Mixed	Yes
	Liberal Democrats	PPG	Party members	Yes

Notes: The table includes parties that received at least 8 per cent of votes or seats in the preceding two legislative elections, as of March 2012.
NDP: New Democratic Party; KOK: National Coalition Party; CDU: Christian Democratic Union of Germany; FDP: Free Democratic Party: SPD: Social Democratic Party of Germany
Sources: Pilet and Cross, 2014; authors' data.

This ongoing process of democratisation is exacerbated by the very recent phenomenon of selecting leaders or candidates for the chief executive position through open or semi-open primaries. This type of selectorate, rare for parties in non-presidential democracies (Carty and Blake, 1999), has been on the rise of late: the Socialists in Greece has used it twice since 2007; the British Labour Party recently considered widening the vote to some sort of open primary (Wintour, 2011); and in its 2013 leadership selection the Liberal Party of Canada opened the procedure to supporters of the party. There are also recent cases where primaries were held for the selection of presidential as well as prime ministerial candidates. In France, two parties on the left conducted semi-open primaries in 2011 to select their joint nominee for the 2012 presidential election. The centre-left coalition in Italy, a pre-electoral coalition, has twice in the last decade conducted open primaries to select a prime ministerial candidate.

There is considerable evidence that democratisation in candidate selection has also occurred in the same time period. Both Bille (2001) and Scarrow et al. (2000) identified a modest trend towards increasing members' involvement in candidate selection from the 1960s to the 1990s. Kittilson and Scarrow (2003) compared parties in 2000 to the 1960s and found evidence that the trend continues. Two large datasets that coded candidate selection methods in democracies in the last two decades

(Atmor, 2011; Shomer, 2014) confirm the impression that there is indeed a trend of democratisation. It is safe to claim that democratisation in candidate selection did occur in established parliamentary democracies despite the fact that at times there was a temporary reversal of these trends either within specific parties or as a national trend.

The democratisation of both leadership and candidate selection methods is clearly linked. They occur at about the same period and advance the same thing. They are both about widening the circle of participants through the adoption of more inclusive selectorates, and about allotting party members – and even party 'supporters' in some cases – with influence (and possibly even dominance) over the selection process. Due to the lack of appropriate cross-national data, we cannot generalise and say which democratisation usually came first, or whether they generally occurred simultaneously. Yet, we can clearly point to three existing trajectories of intra-party democracy: democratisation of candidate selection long before the democratisation of leadership selection (Canada); simultaneous democratisations (Israel); and democratisation of leadership selection before the democratisation of candidate selection (the Socialists in France, the Italian left).

Why Democratisation? Similar Motives at Different Levels

Changes in leadership and in candidate selection methods, and specifically in the level of the inclusiveness of the selectorates, result from an interplay between three levels: the political system, the party system and the intra-party levels (Barnea and Rahat, 2007). The first level, the political system, affects the direction of reforms and defines their admissible range in any given political system. At this level, long-time cultural, social and political trends are at work – such as 'personalisation' and 'Americanisation'. At the party system level, the party is an actor in a competitive environment. Party-level failures, such as electoral defeat, are likely to ignite change. Indeed, parties tend to reform their selection methods when they are in opposition, and/or after an electoral defeat, as a means of regaining popularity by demonstrating renewal and by presenting a fresh and democratic image (Barnea and Rahat, 2007; Cross and Blais, 2012). The last level is the intra-party one. Here, the party itself is a competitive arena, and within this arena there are different groups that have diverse interests and thus promote or block democratising reform initiatives.

The cartel theory proposes a general theoretical explanation concerning the motivation for democratisation of selection methods, and it fits all three levels presented above (Katz, 2001; Katz and Mair, 1995). The cartel party approach sees a long-term transformation of the relations between parties, society and the state. It argues that parties will try to avoid electoral failure and long stints in opposition. It sees democratisation as a manipulation by the party elite to strip power from the middle layer of the party – party activists who usually play the role of delegates in party institutions. This layer is seen as the more ideological (or radical) in comparison to both party members below and the party elite above (May, 1973). In an era of transformation, when winning elections and holding power have become the most salient objectives of the party, it is necessary to present a moderate policy and to select a pragmatic leader and moderate representatives. These two objectives are much easier to accomplish when the organ that selects leaders and candidates is the party membership. As Mair (1997, p. 149) argued:

> it is not the party congress, or the middle-level elite, or the activists, who are being empowered, but rather the ordinary members, who are at once more docile and more likely to endorse the policies (and candidates) proposed by the party leadership.

The Consequences of Intra-Party Democratisation

Having described possible causes and motivations for democratising leadership and candidate selection methods, we now turn to assessing the consequences of intra-party democracy. In order to achieve this we examine four democratic dimensions: participation, competition, representation and responsiveness.

Participation

The widening of the selectorate in both leadership and candidate selection results in similar changes in political participation. On the positive side, the level of participation increases, from selection by a few individuals to selection involving hundreds and even thousands. Where the selectorate in leadership or candidate selection is the party members or the voters, virtually anyone – with a small investment of time and money – can take part in the selection. While empowering party members did not stop the trend of a decline in party membership in most Western democracies (Mair and van Biezen, 2001; van Biezen et al., 2012; van Biezen and Poguntke, 2014), the empowered yet fewer party members are more demographically representative (except for age) than in the past (Scarrow and Gezgor, 2010).

On the negative side, the incentives that the more inclusive methods create for mass registration bring some undesirable consequences regarding the quality of participation. The easier it is to become a member of the selectorate, the more we are likely to witness phenomena such as 'instant membership' (see, for example, Courtney, 1995; Rahat and Hazan, 2007). Those instant members join the party for a short time and do not create a stable body of members; rather, the opportunity to join, take part in the selection of the party leader or its candidates and leave quickly thereafter might create disincentives for loyal long-term membership. Moreover, registration campaigns open the door for the mobilisation of weaker groups in society on the basis of a patron–client relationship. In short, the quality of participation declines with the increase in its quantity, and the structure of selective incentives within the party organisation is damaged when the rights of long-time loyalists and instant members are equalised. These potential negative side effects of inclusive selectorates are more significant in candidate selection than in leadership selection. This is due to the different scope of each process. In leadership selection tens of thousands of voters produce one winner, and thus the room for manipulation is not wide. In candidate selection there are many winners and often smaller, decentralised selectorates; this opens the door to exploitation.

An additional element relevant to the analysis of participation concerns differences in turnout. Table 2.4 presents data on turnout in 57 party leadership contests held in Canada, Israel and the UK between the early 1960s and 2008.[5] It is evident that the highest turnouts are recorded when the selectorate is the PPG, ranging from 92.8 to 100 per cent. The turnout decreases when the selection is by party agencies (delegates), and falls further when party members are the selectorate. Thus the lowest turnout rates are in party leadership primaries, which is also the case for candidate selection through primaries (Hazan and Rahat, 2010).

Table 2.4   Eligible voters and turnout in 57 leadership contests

Selectorate	Eligible voters	Turnout (%)		N
	Range	Range	Average	
PPG	12–374	92.8–100	98.0	13
Party delegates	296–5,802	59.6–96.7	86.6	20
Party members	39,028–305,000	31.3–79.0	60.1	24

The evidence shows that in both leadership and candidate selection there is a clear negative relationship between the inclusiveness of the selectorate and turnout. This is due to two main reasons. First, in smaller selectorates the impact of each selector is larger, and the incentive to show up and vote is greater, because the selector has a better reason to believe that his/her vote can make a real difference. The cost-benefit equation makes it far more likely for PPG members to show up and vote than party members at large.[6] The second reason is the level of commitment: party delegates, for example, are more involved in the life of the party and have more at stake in its internal elections compared to party members.

Competition

Concerning the influence of the widening of the selectorate on competition, the literature reveals quite different findings. In leadership selection, Kenig (2009a)

---

5   In cases of multiple rounds of voting we considered the first round only. In cases of mixed selectorates we calculated each section separately. For instance, in the 2005 Conservative Party leadership race we calculated separate turnout values for the MPs and for the party members.

6   Voting by telephone or via the internet reduces costs, but these methods have been used only recently by parties.

suggested that inclusive selectorates attract more candidates, but that they produce contests that are likely to be less competitive in terms of the closeness of results. Similarly, Cross and Blais (2012) found only modest effects relating to the type of selectorate used: more inclusive selectorates tend to attract slightly more candidates, but contests are no more competitive in terms of the margin between the top two candidates. In candidate selection, the more inclusive selectorate of party members attracted fewer challengers than when the selectorate was composed of party delegates; party primaries are somewhat less competitive than selection by party delegates; and the rate of success of incumbents is evidently higher in primaries (Rahat, Hazan and Katz, 2008).

It also seems that the party leader is more secure in his/her position when the selectorate is more inclusive. This is mainly because if the selectorate comprises tens of thousands of members, it is practically impossible to mount a quick challenge against the incumbent. This is in contrast to small selectorates that can oust the leader in just a few days. The time needed to mount a challenge in an inclusive selectorate allows the incumbent to prepare. The leader may lose (or resign if he/she sees that they are heading for certain defeat), but he/she is immune to quick 'coups' in the style of Jim Bolger (New Zealand National Party) in 1997 or Kevin Rudd (Australian Labor Party) in 2010.[7] In short, it seems that in both cases of leadership and candidate selection, the more participatory method is not the more competitive one, even though leadership selection through primaries seems to be somewhat more competitive in comparison to candidate selection through primaries.

Representation

The case of leadership selection is substantially different from candidate selection because it is about selecting a single person, which limits the ability to 'represent' the electorate or even just the party voters.[8] Nevertheless, over time and across parties we can gather data on the profiles of the successful candidates. We can then ask if and how different selectorates affect the prospects of, for example, women becoming party leaders. Table 2.5 shows a list of women prime ministers and the selectorate used when they were first selected for party leadership. This exercise produces some very interesting results: only one of the 11 female prime ministers

---

7 A leadership vote may be requested at any time in the main Australian parties by the PPG. When Australian Prime Minister Kevin Rudd was asked by challenger Julia Gillard to set a leadership election, he tabled the vote for the next day. After realising that he was about to lose, he decided to resign. Gillard thus ousted the acting leader and prime minister within 24 hours. Similar circumstances led to Bolger's resignation when he understood that he had lost the support of his PPG.

8 There is an informal pattern of representation in the Liberal Party of Canada. This party's custom is to select, alternately, a French-speaking and an English-speaking leader. This is by no means a formal rule, but it has held since 1919 (see Regenstreif, 1969).

who came to power in the established parliamentary democracies was selected as party leader by an inclusive selectorate – Helle Thorning-Schmidt in Denmark.

Table 2.5   Women prime ministers and their selectorates (as of 2012)

Prime minister	Party	Country	Year	Selectorate
Golda Meir	Labour	Israel	1969	Party delegates
Margaret Thatcher	Conservative	United Kingdom	1975	PPG
Gro Harlem Brundtland	Labour	Norway	1981	Party delegates
Helen Clark	Labour	New Zealand	1993	PPG
Kim Campbell	Prog. Conservative	Canada	1993	Party delegates
Jenny Shipley	National	New Zealand	1997	PPG
Angela Merkel	CDU	Germany	2000	Party delegates
Anneli Jaatteenmaki	Centre	Finland	2002	Party delegates
Helle Thorning-Schmidt	Social Democrat	Denmark	2005	Party members
Mari Kiviniemi	Centre	Finland	2010	Party delegates
Julia Gillard	Labor	Australia	2010	PPG

Note: CDU: Christian Democratic Union of Germany

While this seems to validate the claim that the more inclusive selectorates do not work well for women candidates, this data concerns only those party leaders who became prime minister. If we look at women who won party leadership races in inclusive selectorates but did not become prime minister, we do find a few examples: Manuela Ferreira Leite (Social Democrats, Portugal), Marianne Thyssen (CD&V, Belgium), Joëlle Milquet (CDH, Belgium), Tzipi Livni (Kadima, Israel) and Shelly Yechimovich (Labour, Israel). As Wauters and Pilet (2015) concluded in their study on women as party leaders, perhaps it is not the selectorate that matters but rather the openness to women in the wider context. Female party leaders are more likely to be found in societies and in party systems that are more open to women generally.

Candidate selection selectorates, even wide ones, are clearly neither composed of the whole electorate nor form a representative sample of it (or of the party voters). Moreover, it is harder to guarantee demographically representative candidacies when the selectorate is composed of thousands of uncoordinated voters. Thus, candidate selection – where we have multiple candidacies and where we expect some level of demographic representation – must limit the choice of wide selectorates (for example by adopting quotas) in order to ensure representation (Norris, 2006).

Responsiveness

The cartel school argues that democratisation by the party elite is designed to strip power from the party activists (who are usually the delegates in party institutions) who are more ideological compared to the party members below and the elite above. Following the logic of the cartel school approach the more inclusive the selectorate for party leadership selection, the more space for manoeuvre the leader has because he/she does not have to be responsive to the more radical and attentive elements in the party. Furthermore, leaders who are selected by inclusive selectorates may claim a direct mandate given to them by voters or members. Thus, they may feel less obliged to be more responsive to colleagues in the caucus or cabinet and less committed or attentive to party delegates and activists. In this manner, inclusive selectorates empower party leaders and perhaps encourage the adoption of a 'presidentialised' rather than a collegial leadership style. Finally, regardless of the inclusiveness of the selectorate, party leaders who serve as prime ministers, chief executives or senior cabinet ministers are expected to act 'above party politics' and be responsive to the entire electorate – not only to their party's voters, members or caucus colleagues.

There is a debate regarding the influence of the adoption of more inclusive selectorates in candidate selection. One school claims that when candidate selection is conducted by a wide, unstable and largely passive crowd of party members and voters, the candidates are likely to be dependent on non-party actors (mass media, financial donors, interest groups, campaign professionals) for their selection (Rahat, 2008). This dependency leads them to adopt more individualistic behaviour – at the expense of party-focused conduct. Others argue that a problem is indeed created, but that patronage and some centralisation of the candidate selection method might help solve the problem of party unity (Bolleyer, 2009). Still others claim that expanding the selectorate will not damage party cohesion because of an agreed division of labour between selectors (local members) and policy makers (party in government) within the stratarchical party (Carty, 2004).

There are also several interaction consequences of leadership and candidate selection concerning responsiveness. For example, when candidate selection is the most exclusive the party leader selects the candidates. Regardless of the way he/she was selected, we expect high party/leader responsiveness because the leader is the party. We also expect that parties where both the leader and the candidates are selected by the same selectorate will be more cohesive than parties where the two are selected by different selectorates. The reason is that the agents (party leader and party candidates) will be answerable to the same principal. Furthermore, inclusive candidate selection methods may not only affect the behaviour of the elected representatives but may also decrease the party leader's autonomy vis-à-vis the PPG. For example, the leader's leverage in appointing ministers is constrained when candidates are selected through inclusive measures, because the prime minister/chief executive will take into account the popularity of each MP as reflected in the primary election results. One study points to a close relationship between success in the primary election and being selected to the cabinet, a relationship that was weaker when candidates were selected through more exclusive selectorates (Kenig and Barnea, 2009).

Conclusion

Both leadership (including chief executive) and candidate selection share many commonalities in terms of the relevant dimensions for their delineation, and both are going through a clear process of democratisation exhibiting somewhat similar consequences. However, there are small yet important differences in the two selection mechanisms that highlight their diverse nature:

- The candidacy threshold is likely to be higher in leadership selection.
- The menu of selectorates in leadership selection includes the PPG.
- Leadership selection is by its nature a more centralised process.
- The voting methods for leadership selection are naturally limited to the majoritarian ones (at least in the final stage).

The most important difference, however, regards deselection – which is possible (in principle) at any time when it comes to the party leader. In candidate selection deselection is not a separate dimension, since deselection and selection take place at the same time.

As for the consequences of democratisation, we can identify similar gains and pathologies regarding participation, representation and competition. Yet, the damage is less apparent in leadership selection – for example, when it comes to representation a single leader cannot exhibit this dimension – and the gain in terms of democratic legitimacy could justify some of the costs, especially when it comes to selecting the party's candidate for chief executive. In candidate selection the pathologies are more apparent: democratisation (increased participation) may produce problems in the quality of participation and responsiveness, and lower levels of representation and competition.

Another way to think about leadership and candidate selection methods is by using the concepts of centralising and decentralising personalisation (Balmas et al. 2014). The most centralised personalisation occurs in a party in which the leader is self-acclaimed and is the selector of the party's candidates. In such a case *the party* is the leader. The most decentralised personalisation is when the candidates are selected by an inclusive selectorate – where intra-party personal competition becomes explicit – and they, in turn (as a rather exclusive selectorate) select the leader. When both the leader and the candidates are selected by inclusive selectorates, we can then talk about a mix of both personalisations and of a delicate balance between the leader and the representatives, who can both claim to be selected by a wide, legitimising selectorate.

Chapter 3
The American Experience of Primary Elections in Comparative Perspective

Alan Ware

The United States was the birthplace of party primaries. In some respects, therefore, it has served as an exemplar for their introduction elsewhere; but the context of their use in America is sufficiently different that care must be taken when analysing their relevance to their development in other democracies. This becomes apparent immediately when considering the distinction between primaries for the selection of candidates and their deployment in the selection of party leaders.

Their use in American candidate selection can be stated quite simply: for nearly all offices – from the presidency down to posts in local government – candidates for the two major parties must, by law, be nominated by procedures that involve the use of primaries in some way.[1] Candidates for other parties are exempt from this requirement. For nearly all offices nomination is made through a direct primary; for the presidency, however, a different method is employed. Since 1976 within most states, though not all, a primary has been used to select delegates to their party's National Convention. In theory, it is these delegates who then select the party's presidential candidate; but in practice the dynamics of the primary process are such that one candidate nearly always emerges as the winner before the National Convention convenes. Since the reforms in 1968–76 only one nomination, by the Democrats in 2008, produced such a close contest that it appeared that the nomination might be decided at the Convention itself.

The situation with party leaders is far more complicated, largely because it is confusing as to what constitutes a position of party leadership in the highly decentralised American parties. In some sense the president is the leader of his party – he is the party's figurehead. However, under the separation of powers he is most certainly not in any sense the leader of his party in Congress. Formally, at least, he is also not the head of the national party organisation – his party's National Committee – although informally his appointment of its chair means that it largely operates under his control. Moreover, within a federal system he does

---

1   During the first two decades of the twentieth century some states, especially in the west, prohibited parties from nominating candidates for some offices. Local offices were the ones most affected by such legislation, but two states (Minnesota and Nebraska) had state legislatures that were formally non-partisan. Usually party activists and officeholders acted informally in these contests.

not lead his party in any of the states. State governors, legislators and officials in the party's organisations at state and local level are not answerable to him. With the party that lost the preceding presidential election, the absence of leadership positions is even more striking; after that election the defeated candidate loses the symbolic leadership role acquired following the nomination. For the three months or so between his or her nomination to the presidential election a defeated presidential candidate had had the same 'leadership' role as his or her opponent, but after that defeat 'leadership' within the party is divided still further.

Within the decentralised structures of American parties only the positions at the top and the bottom are filled through the use of primaries. State governors, whose relation to their party in the state is rather similar to that of the president nationally, are chosen in direct primaries – unlike the indirect primaries used for the presidency. Yet, while all these are leadership positions in a sense, it is leadership that derives from their occupants having been *candidates* – candidates who were selected through the use of a primary. At the bottom of the party structures, precinct committee members typically are chosen in a direct primary. But between these levels primaries are absent. Party leadership positions in Congress, state legislatures and city councils are not filled by primaries; nor are the heads of national, state or county committees chosen via primaries. However, all this can be simplified by saying that the distinction between selection of candidates and selection of party leaders, which can be made so clearly in many countries, is difficult to operationalise in the case of America. It is the selection of candidates that is crucial for how parties operate, and this chapter focuses primarily on that.

With respect to the nomination of candidates, it should already be clear from a point made previously (that the process for the presidency is different from that for other offices) that there is no such institution as the 'American primary'. In fact, there are three main types of primary used in the United States, one of which (the direct party primary) is particularly relevant when comparing candidate selection there with its use in other countries. However, to avoid possible confusion, it is necessary to mention briefly the features of the other two types, before turning to the direct primary for most of this chapter.

First, particularly evident in presidential selection, there are a few party primaries in which the primary election does no more than select delegates to a party convention at which – at least formally – candidates will be chosen by those delegates. Formally, therefore, the method introduced in the early 1970s is really no more than a modified version of the caucus-convention system that was widely used by America's parties in the nineteenth century, before the widespread adoption of direct primaries. Yet, while the strategies for obtaining the nomination are now radically different from what they were in the mid-nineteenth century, primaries were actually not one of the initial causes of major long-term change in the conduct of American politics – a change with which they are often linked. The politics of personality in elections that is sometimes associated with the introduction of presidential primaries actually predated their first use (in 1912) – personality politics having been especially notable in the election campaigns of William

Jennings Bryan and Theodore Roosevelt. In seeking a party nomination earlier it was the ability to win over state party politicians that was far more significant than any national profile that the putative candidate might have, but increasingly by the end of the nineteenth century a candidate's personality mattered. The introduction of the first presidential primaries modified the optimal strategies for candidates, but did not revolutionise the process. Between about 1920 and 1968 primaries were used in a few states to select delegates; but while most states continued with caucuses and conventions, the candidate now had to display a greater capacity to appeal to a mass electorate directly, as well as having substantial links with key state politicians. The increased use of primaries from 1972 onwards shifted the balance heavily towards the former, so that primaries can be seen as having a catalytic effect in the 'personalisation' of American presidential elections, by pushing personality politics to the forefront of presidential selection. Yet it was presidentialism itself, rather than primaries,that had driven that transformation.

Secondly, there are American primary elections from which parties are either banned or in which they play no real role. Broadly speaking, these have been of two types:

- Non-partisan primaries. These are elections – usually for local governments – in which party labels cannot appear on the ballot paper and in which parties are banned from formally endorsing any candidates. A variant on this is the non-partisan blanket primary; here all candidates, irrespective of their party identification, are listed on the same ballot. When a candidate secures 50 per cent + 1 of the vote this election is, in effect, a general election because that candidate is deemed elected to the office; when no candidate achieves this share of the vote there is a subsequent runoff election between the two candidates with the most votes, irrespective of their party identifications.[2]
- Cross-filing primaries. Used in California from 1915 to 1959, this method allowed any candidate to run in more than one party primary. Thus, a popular Republican incumbent might run in both his party's and the Democrats' primary, and winning both would result in him or her not having to face major party opposition at the general election.

Having disposed of these other types of primary, the direct party primary can now be discussed. It is a method of nominating candidates in which the immediate result of the primary is the nomination of that party's candidate for an office; there are no further procedures involved after that election. It was widely adopted for most public offices in the United States between the end of the nineteenth century and 1915, although it had been used in some places before then. At the same time as this method was introduced another reform was adopted that has contributed to the unusual characteristics of American candidate selection. From the early

---

2   The non-partisan blanket primary was first used in Louisiana in 1978, and a few other states have tried to adopt it since then.

twentieth century primary elections had to be run by local and state governments, rather than by the parties themselves; they became public elections. Recognising that these two reforms became intertwined is important because there was, and is, no *necessary* link between the two; the decentralised nature of American parties meant that the parties themselves were becoming incapable of enacting and running a complex nomination process. It is a characteristic of these parties that is not shared by most parties in other countries.

The key feature of the direct primary, therefore, was that it took formal decisions over nominations away from party committee rooms and intra-elite negotiations.[3] The remainder of this chapter focuses on three aspects of direct primaries in America, and on how distinctive features of the American political system have shaped the form they take there: (i) the variations of procedure possible within this system; (ii) the possible reasons for a party switching to direct primaries; and (iii) the consequences of their adoption.

The Dimensions of Primary Politics

Who Can Vote in a Primary?

One of the main ways in which the development of American democracy was 'exceptional' was that, relatively early in the process of democratisation (the 1830s), political parties became widely accepted as the key instrument for democracy. Indeed, for most of the nineteenth century the Democratic Party was simply called 'The Democracy' by many of its supporters. A widespread belief was that it was through everyone's participation in parties that democracy would be realised.[4] One consequence of this was a general acceptance that anyone who wanted to be involved in the activities of a particular party should be included. It was assumed that those whose views differed radically from other participants would want to withdraw, and perhaps become active in the other major party. Consequently, the idea that a party was some kind of private club whose membership could be restricted or controlled commanded little support. This meant that when, at the beginning of the twentieth century, most states adopted the direct primary for nomination the widely accepted idea that a broad range of people should be eligible to participate in it encountered virtually no opponents.

Nevertheless, for obvious reasons, most party elites wanted to confine primary participation to those who would likely vote for their party. For that reason, when the direct primary was introduced all but a handful of states opted for a so-called 'closed' primary. In such a primary the electorate is restricted to those

---

3 Whether those kinds of negotiations, conducted on an informal basis, actually became irrelevant in determining who got nominated is an entirely different matter, of course.

4 The form that many thought participation should take, however, was one that would satisfy few democratic theorists.

who declare that they have voted for the party in the past, or will do so at the next general election. Yet, in the era of the secret ballot there was no means of enforcing this. In practice, anyone who wanted to register to vote in the primary of a given party could probably do so, although requiring that registration occur months in advance of a primary election could do much to prevent a party being infiltrated by troublemaking interlopers. This meant that there was still some difference between 'closed' primaries, which required stating party affiliation when registering annually as a voter, and 'open' primaries, in which a voter could decide at the voting booth in which party's primaries they wanted to vote. The core party supporters would have more influence in the former, but the difference between the two systems was not always that great. Over the course of the twentieth century, though, there was a pronounced tendency towards more 'open' primaries. However, even a century ago the *potential* primary electorate was always far larger than the core of individuals who might actively participate in a primary campaign or who were subsequently involved in a party's efforts at the general election.[5] 'Membership' was thus defined broadly.

For those parties in other democracies that formally enrol their members the question of 'who may vote in a primary' is slightly more complex. As a crude approximation, it can be argued that they face three main alternatives:

1. To restrict voting entitlement to formally enrolled fee-paying of the party. This would normally have been regarded as the 'obvious' answer as to who should be included in party decision making, and it is also relatively easy for a party to operate. It has two related disadvantages. First, when a party's members are not a microcosm of its electorate, and often that is the case, then not including the latter in the candidate nomination process in some way may result in important opinions within that electorate not being fully weighted. Secondly, given that membership has been declining in many parties, selection by members alone might reduce the perceived legitimacy of an electoral process; a possible advantage of a primary system is thereby lost.
2. To allow any qualified voter to register as a primary voter some time in advance of the primary election, and to restrict voting rights to those who have registered. This alternative is the equivalent of one version of the American 'closed' primary but, absent a state system of registration, the process would be left in the hands of the party itself. This might require considerable resources for it to conduct registration and could well be open to manipulation by particular party factions, thereby negating the goals of embracing opinions not well represented in the party membership and increasing the legitimacy of the nomination process. As in the US, having the state conduct such elections might be feasible – though engagement

---

5 Between 1928 and 2000 the number of states using 'closed' primaries declined from 44 (out of 48) to 26 (out of 50).

with the state in this way might both be controversial within a party and be opposed by sections of the electorate who object to the use of state resources for partisan purposes.

3. To allow any registered voter to vote in a primary election if they wish to. This third option, akin to an American open primary, could be attractive to a party partly because it conveys an impression of a party acting in a way that appears to be not entirely partisan; the winner can be presented as having a broader legitimacy than would someone nominated wholly within the party.[6] Because it does not require the registration of a *party* electorate it is less costly for a party to undertake than the second alternative. Although infiltration by political opponents is a possible problem with such a process, and there have been some instances of this in American open primaries, the main objection to these kinds of procedure is that they tend to reduce the filtering role played by parties. The more that party insiders are weakened in the nomination process, the more easily can candidates with obvious political weaknesses secure a nomination. Making candidate selection a direct relationship between the would-be candidate and the electorate means that the ability of the nominee to perform well as a legislator or in an executive office is less likely to weigh in the decision process than with a more restricted selectorate.

Who is Eligible to Be a Candidate in a Primary?

The absence of formal party membership in the US affects who may become a candidate in a primary as well as who may vote in it. In the US the only restriction on seeking a nomination is obtaining the minimum required number of voter signatures to do so; without some kind of symbol of attachment to a party that is easily recognisable, a link that formal membership enrolment provides, criteria for seeking a party nomination are necessarily loose. Sometimes, though not that frequently, this is exploited by candidates whose views are more closely allied with those of the other party and who have no record of prior involvement with the party whose nomination they seek. Few parties elsewhere operate under this restriction, and those that do are unlikely to be attracted by a procedure that leaves them vulnerable to exploitation. Parties with formally enrolled members, by contrast, would find it relatively easy to devise criteria for restricting candidacy to members, or to some subgroups of members.

---

6 In 2011 the French Socialists opted for this approach in selecting their presidential candidate for 2012, with those participating paying €1 to do so. As Marino De Luca and Fulvio Venturino discuss in Chapter 7, not only did the Socialists use this kind of process in 2014 for selecting candidates for municipal elections in five major cities, but another party (the UMP) also did so in both Paris and Lyon. At the moment, therefore, open primaries would appear to be gaining increased support in France, despite disadvantages they might otherwise have for parties.

Who Runs the Primary Ballot?

The main factor prompting American parties in the early twentieth century to transfer the running of their direct primaries to state and local governments was the high degree of decentralisation in the American parties. Decentralisation meant that it was increasingly difficult for the parties themselves to run elections, or use other procedures, that were not open to chaos, abuse or corruption. Where there was anarchy or malpractice in specific county parties, the state party would lack the authority to impose fair procedures in those localities. Thus party-run direct primaries could not have provided the antidote to all the problems in the older nominating systems. The only way in which some level of order in the candidate selection procedures could be ensured was to make governments – at local or state level – responsible for administering those procedures.[7]

Few parties elsewhere are as decentralised as America's two major parties. State-run primaries, therefore, would be an option rather than a necessity. Not only could ceding control of primary elections to the state be perceived as evidence of party weakness, but governments may be unwilling to bear the cost of a purely party activity. Thus there is frequently little incentive for this aspect of the American process to be copied in other countries.

When is the Primary Ballot Held?

Three features of American electoral organisation have reduced many of the possible complicating factors in deciding when direct primaries should be held. All general election dates are fixed permanently by law, so that the issue of how soon before an election it would be most advantageous for parties to hold their primaries can, once agreed, be implemented for every future election. Because election dates are fixed – early elections cannot be called – the scheduling of primary elections never has to be altered at short notice. Then again, by comparison with most democracies, legislative terms are brief. The terms of lower houses of both the US Congress and state legislatures are two years; because of this restricted timeframe virtually all American primaries are held between about two and seven months in advance of a forthcoming general election. Primaries for offices with longer tenure – such as most state governorships and the US Senate – fit around this schedule, partly for reasons of cost and partly because historically they did not actually interfere with the schedule for lower chamber primaries.[8] Moreover, in a strictly two-party system both parties are anxious that the opponent does not steal a march in obtaining publicity through

---

7 There were numerous examples of local parties running their own direct primaries in the later nineteenth century, but mostly they were not in urban counties. One exception, generally regarded as a failure by those who experienced it, was in the city of Cleveland in the early 1890s.

8 Most state governorships had two-year terms until the twentieth century, and the Senate was not directly elected until after 1914.

the timing of its primaries, so that it suits the two of them that their primaries are usually held on the same day; a desire not to be seen pushing up the cost to the public of holding primaries also contributes to the stability of this outcome.

The huge number of American public offices subject to partisan elections is exceptional, and this is one respect in which the timing of primaries in other democracies is simplified. But timing could also be more complex for some parties. While some parliamentary systems have fixed terms for their legislature, Britain being one that has recently adopted it, others provide some discretion over this to the legislature itself or to the government on timing. Any uncertainty as to when the general election will be held tends to militate against using primaries. Relatively late nomination of candidates can have the advantage of giving the party momentum immediately before the election, but the calling of an early election might make it impossible for candidates to be selected in time for an effective general election campaign; a primary is also likely to be more complicated to arrange at short notice than a party nominating meeting.

Furthermore, precisely when it would be optimal to select candidates (as with a new party leader) might vary with political circumstances. For instance, following a crushing defeat a party might prefer to select early – to provide a new 'face' or 'faces' to the electorate well in advance of the next general election – so as to have time to develop recognition among the electorate. But in other conditions candidate selection much closer to that election might be preferable – for example, if the party has been internally split over a public issue during the present parliament. Furthermore, within the same election cycle the needs of one party may be very different from those of another, so that there is little incentive for them to use the American model of parties holding their primaries on the same day.

What Role is Played by Parties in 'Filtering' their Potential Nominees?

Because there is no system of formal membership, American parties cannot prevent someone from seeking selection as a candidate; but can they still make it difficult for a particular candidate to succeed in doing so? Today a popular view among foreigners of American direct primaries is that the parties themselves play a small role in the nomination process. Individual candidates run their campaigns to secure the party's nomination, appealing directly to the primary electorate in making their pitch. Those holding senior positions within the party can do little to determine the outcome, except in conjunction with their fellows – in using their personal resources in support of, or in opposition to, a particular candidate. Although this view is broadly correct, there have been variations in some American states that have created a greater role for a party in choosing candidates. One device used by a few states, including Colorado was the pre-primary endorsing convention. There were differences in how this operated in the various states, but the Colorado example illuminates some of its possible features. A would-be candidate would seek support at a convention held some weeks before the primary election:

- Any candidate who obtained at least 15 per cent of the delegates' votes at that convention would be eligible to be placed on the primary ballot.
- The candidate who received the largest share of those votes would be placed at the head of the ballot, with any other candidates who received the minimum necessary share of the vote being placed in rank order according to their vote share.
- Any candidates who failed to meet these conditions could still be placed on the primary ballot providing they obtained a specified number of signatures from Democratic voters supporting them – but at the bottom of the ballot paper.

The effect of this system was considerable in establishing a role for party structures within a primary system.[9] Most primary contests were won by those placed first on the ballot.[10] This was partly because these candidates had established a good organisational base at the beginning of the process; partly because their victories at the convention generated good publicity for them; and partly because, as research from elsewhere in the US has clearly demonstrated, ballot position matters.[11] *Ceteris paribus*, those placed first on an election ballot by a party convention certainly did better than anyone else in an election. While those placed lower down on the primary ballot could (and did) win, and the majority wing of the party elite might fail therefore to get its way, the presence of the convention tended to prevent the complete elimination of party itself as a factor itself in determining who would obtain the party's nomination.

The significance of this discussion of the Colorado model is that the particular rules used for a primary can shape the pattern of results they produce. Yet what that pattern is for any given party will also depend on the differential ability of the members of a particular party faction or the supporters of a particular candidate to mobilise voters. Consider the hypothetical case of a party elite where there is a consensus that the party is not selecting candidates who are attractive to many potential voters. A switch to the use of primaries would have the desired result only if those who were most successful in organising a primary campaign and those who actually voted were more representative of the potential electorate than the selectorate under the previous nominating system. Where, for instance, there is a small but well-organised faction in the party, and also lack of enthusiasm among

---

9 Some discussion of this can be found in Ware, 1979a, chapters 5 and 6. See also Eyre and Martin, 1967. The scheme was sometimes known as the 'Hughes Plan', and had been used also in Idaho, Massachusetts, New Mexico, Rhode Island and Utah.

10 In Denver between 1968 and 1976 one-fifth of candidates who were not designated first at the County Convention went on to win the primary election; between 1948 and 1962, when the state legislators from Denver were selected in a multi-member district, less than 10 per cent of candidates with lower-line designations were subsequently nominated at the primary election; cf. Ware, 1979a, p. 198.

11 There was much literature on the effect of ballot position on voting in American political science journals during the 1960s and 1970s; see, for example, Taebel, 1975.

many potential voters for participating in the primary, the consequence might be the selection of a candidate who could generate even less support at the general election than previously. Manipulating the procedures for candidate selection in order to maximise the chance of victory at a general election depends on making correct assumptions about the structure of opinion of various elements in the party, and their capacity and incentive to mobilise. Switching to a primary system, or modifying an existing primary process, might well not generate the results anticipated previously.

What Restrictions Are There on Expenditures Made by Primary Candidates?

This is one respect in which the American experience is relatively uniform throughout the country. The consistent interpretation by American courts that outright restrictions on expenditures are an infringement of free speech has meant that, in general, there are relatively few limitations on how much a candidate may spend in seeking a nomination. One obvious consequence of this is that it advantages wealthier potential candidates and pushes those who are not wealthy into seeking funds from interest groups and others. This affects both the social composition of the political class in the US and the relationship between private interests and party politicians. It also enhances the position of incumbents in primary contests, since typically they have much greater access to political money than challengers.

However, because American primaries are regulated by law – they are public elections – regulating both the sources of money and how it is spent in a primary campaign would be quite easy. Elsewhere, the ability of a party to regulate the flow of political money and 'in kind' donations hinges on the organisational capacities of the central party units. The lower those capacities are, the more likely it is that special interests will use funding in primary campaigns to further their causes.

The Rationale for Introducing a Primary System

Why might a party consider switching to direct primary elections for the purpose of making specific nominations rather than using other types of procedures? Broadly speaking there are four kinds of advantage that a primary might seem to offer; but whether, in practice, they have any of them is an entirely different matter. The types of problem that primaries might appear to address are:

- chaos and disruptive internal conflict in the party;
- organisational sclerosis of a party that has resulted in incumbent officials having disproportionate influence in preventing reform or the emergence of new leaders;
- lack of legitimacy for the party among a wider public;
- lack of publicity for the party's activities.

The possible advantages can be summarised briefly.

Chaos and Disruptive Internal Conflict

An election usually generates a clear outcome – assuming that the application of the voting procedures themselves does not generate disputes. It produces an end to formal conflict until the next electoral cycle begins. One of the main reasons that 'regular' politicians in the United States supported the switch to direct primaries at the beginning of the twentieth century was that it appeared to offer a solution to the chaos and conflict that had developed in the caucus-convention system during the preceding decades. That chaos had resulted from a vastly increased population in which party meetings were no longer forums where most participants knew each other personally. The informal procedures of candidate selection that had worked quite well in the smaller face-to-face communities of the 1840s tended to produce disorder at party gatherings later that century. That the parties were so decentralised meant that it was difficult to devise ways of acting authoritatively, yet fairly, in these circumstances. A well-run election would circumvent these problems.

Even when chaos is absent from its activities, a party can still experience disruption from factional groups engaged in continual fights for advantage. Obviously, primaries cannot dissolve factionalism; but they usually define clear boundaries for the arenas in which a party's internal rivalries can be conducted. That is, they establish a framework within which intra-party warfare is conducted. A comparison might be made with the introduction of 'Marquess of Queensbury' rules in replacing the older sport of prizefighting; the violence of prizefighting is still present in modern boxing, but the rules constrain that violence so as to limit the damage participants can inflict on each other. The more public nature of a primary contest, by comparison with other procedures for generating outcomes in a party, focuses competition in ways that may constrain how factions interact – to the benefit of the party overall. It does not eliminate intra-party conflict, but it tends to channel it in ways that can make it more manageable.

Important though this problem had been in the American case, it is never likely to be of great relevance in reform of nominating procedures in other countries. Its main causes, the extreme party decentralisation evident in the United States from the very beginning, combined with the high level of participation in its earlier nominating systems, places the US as an outlier among democracies. It is a clear instance of American exceptionalism.

Organisational Sclerosis

Ever since Robert Michels published *Political Parties* a century ago, the issue of how, precisely, control over party organisations generates advantage for party elites has been of central concern both to political scientists and to politicians. One argument traditionally made for primaries is that, by removing politics from backroom deals, it becomes easier for 'out' groups to mobilise against the current elite. That alleged result has been defended both in terms of its supposedly enhancing democracy and also because of its advantages to the organisation itself.

By promoting organisational turnover, the party becomes more aware of, and responsive to, changes in the social environment in which it has to compete at general elections. Formal internal competition is conceived as healthy for a party for that reason. That is the theory, at least, and it was one to which many would-be American reformers who lacked influence in the late nineteenth-century parties subscribed. From their perspective, it was evident that primaries would open up the parties, making them more responsive to popular sentiments and pressure. Unfortunately, for their cause, there was an important qualification to the argument.

Resources – human, financial and so on – are crucial for prospects of success in any kind of election. When, as in most of the eastern United States following the introduction of direct primaries, existing party elites continued to control most of those resources their candidates could still usually win. Indeed, there was a marked difference between the eastern and western United States in the apparent impact of primary reforms. In many western states, direct primaries were one of a number of reforms – including requirements that local government elections be non-partisan – that significantly reduced the power of party organisations (Shefter, 1983). Between them such reforms weakened the role of party elites in candidate selection. In most eastern states these other reforms were not introduced systematically, and the effect on the distribution of power within the parties was much less. The 'regular' party elites in the east retained their influence for decades because of this. In the end they would be undermined by new campaign technologies – especially television – that were available directly to candidates, who could then campaign for a nomination independently of the party organisation (Ware, 1984). However, it was not until the end of the 1960s that this long-term transformation was completed. Moreover, although primaries provide an opening for outsiders, once the outsider becomes an incumbent he or she can then use the advantages of incumbency, especially in fundraising, to consolidate their position. Arguably, primaries can help speed up the demise of insiders who, for whatever reason, are in trouble politically; but otherwise they tend not to weaken the advantages incumbents might otherwise enjoy.

Leaving aside whether organisational sclerosis might be overcome by the introduction of primaries, as a factor actually prompting their use it is likely to be of secondary importance. Party elites are not inclined to support such a radical shifting of power within their party unless either they understand it as being in their own interest to do so or an overturning of their own power by 'outsiders' seems imminent. Such conditions are relatively unusual.

Lack of Legitimacy for the Party among a Wider Public

Because they consist of the type of formal structures usually associated with democracy, primary elections can help legitimise a party that uses them; they are a way of being perceived to 'police' themselves and their actions. Subjecting an official who has been tainted by allegations of corruption or incompetence to re-nomination by a primary pushes the arguments about those allegations into the public domain. Because of this, and subject to the qualification that non-incumbents must have some resources to mount a viable campaign in opposition, a party would have a mechanism for being seen to deal with those who might prove to be a liability for them at a general election. This is the kind of argument that some British politicians, including Labour's deputy leader Harriet Harman, have used in support of introducing primaries.[12] The point is not merely that those who might be a liability can be removed, but that a group of people who are more numerous than the party leadership should have a role in doing so. Again, though, there is the issue of how much in America – the country with by far the longest experience of primaries – the theory does correspond with the reality of political practice.

The vast majority of American incumbents are usually re-nominated by their parties. One of the main reasons for this is their ability to deliver specific resources to their electoral districts, thereby creating a core of personal support for themselves. This does not make incumbents immune from primary challengers, but it does mean that the party can end up reselecting a candidate whose legitimacy among a broader public has been weakened. At issue here is whether the 'mobilisable' primary electorate is sufficiently large that a primary contest can focus on the *party's* interests and not on those of a particular candidate or faction.

Lack of Publicity for the Party's Activities

Elections can be, and are, presented to the public in a manner akin to a horse race. There is a period of parading the contenders in the ring, followed by the 'race' which is held on one day, after which a winner is declared. All this fits well with the presentation of news in the television age. There is an event within a known timeframe, and during the event attention can be focused on it. This is one reason why many US state parties introduced (indirect) presidential primaries between 1968 and 1976. It is an argument that is especially important in explaining their introduction by Republicans; unlike their Democratic counterparts, they were not facing new and complex procedures designed (between 1969 and 1972) to create delegations to the National Convention that were microcosms of a state's electorate. By contrast, internal party decision making that does not involve elections is more continuous and mundane; less frequently can it be portrayed in ways similar to those of a sporting contest. Consequently, primaries are often good sources of publicity for a party.

In many democracies change in recent decades has made the adoption of primaries a seemingly attractive option for some parties. The shares of the vote obtained by the largest parties have typically declined, as have party memberships. Just as they were for some state Republican parties in presidential selection, so primaries can be seen as a means of stimulating activist participation and voter interest in the party. Party self-interest in 'repackaging' itself can always be

---

12   Interview, BBC Radio 4, 9 July 2011.

couched in terms of the party becoming 'more responsible' or 'listening more to the public'. Nevertheless, in one obvious respect primaries for candidates can decrease party responsibility because usually entire slates of candidates are not selected by the same electorate. Instead, smaller groups of party supporters decide each nomination, with the result that the slate may be unbalanced; decentralising decision making is usually not possible in contests for party leaders, but in the case of candidates the danger for a party is that there is no hand on the tiller, as there would be when the central party can exercise some influence over the composition of a slate of legislative candidates.

The Consequences of Introducing Primaries

Finally, what have been the consequences for the parties of introducing primaries in America? In particular:

- Did they contribute to the rise of candidate-centred politics in which personality of individuals is emphasised?
- Did they reduce party organisation influence over the running and ideological direction of the party?
- Did they solidify factionalism parties by providing a formal structure around which competition between factions could be focused?

The Rise of Candidate-Centred and Personalised Politics

Obviously, by allowing party nominations to be contested before an electorate wider than a narrow party elite it becomes more possible for those seeking selection to emphasise their own personal qualities. Direct primaries are likely to be seen by candidates as a system that advantages them individually. Not surprisingly, therefore, research by the historian Jack Reynolds (2006) demonstrates that the rise of the 'hustling candidate' in American politics actually *preceded* the introduction of direct primaries, rather than being a consequence of them. Candidates could take advantage of pressure for reform in the nominating system at the beginning of the twentieth century because the type of reform around which a consensus was emerging was one that would give them greater autonomy in relation to their party organisations. Yet how much candidates can subsequently use the direct primary in this way depends on other factors that can also facilitate a highly personal style of politics.

Southern white demagogues, a widespread feature of electoral politics in that region till the mid-twentieth century, emerged partly because of a complete absence of interparty competition there after the 1890s; primaries actually played a limited role in the development of demagoguery. Similarly, the personalised politics in many of the western states after 1920 came about because of laws that formally reduced the role of parties. As noted earlier, in the east greater candidate autonomy had to await changes in campaign technology which prioritised those resources that candidates could obtain independently of their party organisations. This point is relevant when discussing the impact of introducing primaries elsewhere. In twentieth-century Europe individual candidates, as well as parties, were typically prevented from buying advertising time on television, a restriction that was never present in the US. When candidates are restricted with respect to their ability to use their own finances (and other resources) in a primary election, the full-blown, American style of individual electoral competition is less likely to develop. When there are no such restrictions, primaries can act as a catalyst in speeding up the effects of other factors in freeing candidates from some of the ties of party. Once again, it is the context in which primaries are adopted that is important, and the American context was somewhat atypical.

Reduced Party Influence over its Internal Affairs

To a large degree candidate–party relations are a zero-sum game: the more autonomy the candidates have, the less power over how the party operates is available to those within the party organisation. Yet the American experience, in which parties might be understood today as little more than an aggregation of those individuals who have won primary nominations, is unusual in that the entire party structure is composed of such individuals. Both the sheer number of public offices and the use of primaries for all kinds of positions – both public offices and low-level positions within a party – have brought about this result. Primaries do not have to be used in this way though. More limited use of them – for example, just for nominations to a national legislature or for a party leader – could leave *parties* intact as political actors. Those who contest their party's nomination in a primary mid-career may well have had to spend their earlier political career operating within the party organisation. They would be products of their party's structures in a way that American politicians largely are not and cannot be. Furthermore, devices such as (Colorado-style) pre-primary endorsing conventions can help retain party influence over nominations, even while the opportunities for helping to reinvigorate sclerotic organisations are increased. How you get to be a candidate in a primary election is a significant factor in shaping how independent of your party you will be subsequently. Once again, it is factors other than the introduction of a primary itself that really matter for a party in retaining its role as a significant intermediary in politics.

Increased Factionalism in a Party

It was suggested earlier that one possible effect of primaries is to turn a continuous war between party factions into a more routinised form of competition. However, it might be claimed, there is a less benign effect on parties. By introducing formal competition primaries might actually stimulate internal party division.

Certainly, an election necessarily causes division, but the important question is whether hostility between different party groups is increased by conflict over electoral competition for office or not. Primaries in the US can be divisive in that some supporters of defeated primary candidates do not work for, or even vote for, the winning candidate, thereby diluting party effort at the general election. Firm evidence of this is scant, partly because earlier attempts at obtaining data confused the divisiveness of a primary with the wholly separate point of whether margins of victory in a primary were small or not (Ware, 1979b). In general, most primaries do not seem to create extensive internal division where none existed earlier.

Of course, it might be argued that the candidate-centred, individualised politics of America does not lend itself to the kind of factionalism present in parties elsewhere – whether that factionalised politics is based on differences over ideology or is centred on particular party elites. Nevertheless, even here the American experience can shed light. Party competition collapsed throughout the South after the 1890s; and in the following decade southern states, like their northern counterparts, started to introduce the direct primary within the (dominant) Democratic Party. Did well-organised factionalism then develop among the Democrats in the southern states? In some states, such as Virginia, it did – with a stable form of factional, intra-party competition emerging. But in other southern states, of which Florida was the most extreme example, a highly atomised form of electoral competition was evident throughout the period; there was no tendency towards organised factionalism whatsoever, but instead politics centred on a large number of individual politicians – all of whom were nominally Democrats.[13] Between them the 11 southern states provided a variety of different styles of politics, ranging from Virginia at one extreme to Florida at the other. This suggests two tentative conclusions. First, that, at most, the direct primary by itself was not an especially strong force in generating factionalism.[14] Secondly, the most fruitful lines of future research into the effects of primaries are likely to involve the interaction between the introduction of internal elections and other factors shaping internal party dynamics in particular parties.

Concluding Remarks

For decades primary elections were associated with the distinctive features of American party politics, features that marked a seemingly stark contrast with European politics. Now that primaries are being introduced elsewhere, it is easier to see them for what they really are – particular kinds of rules of the game that are applied within a given context. How these rules interact with other rules – with

---

13   The best account of factionalism in the South during the first half of the twentieth century remains V.O. Key, 1949.

14   However, the kind of primary used could influence how factionalism developed; see, for example, Canon, 1978.

the distribution of political resources within a party, with specific traditions of conducting politics and so on – will depend on the form these other factors take. Consider an analogy. What was the effect of the double ballot voting system during the French Third Republic? Were its effects the same when it was reintroduced at the beginning of the Fifth Republic? They were not. How parties organised themselves in the two Republics was different because other aspects of party politics, and of the social environment in which party politics operated, had changed in the meantime. While we can outline some general consequences of using double ballot systems, context is all-important in any explanation of their impact. So it is with the introduction of primary elections outside the United States. Obviously, comparative analysis will be crucial in developing our theories, but research must be sensitive to how a primary interacts with other factors shaping the nature of party politics. Along the way we may well find significant differences between democratic regimes in the effects seemingly associated with the use of primaries.

Chapter 4
Democratising Party Leadership Selection in Spain and Portugal

Oscar Barberà, Marco Lisi and Juan Rodríguez Teruel

Introduction

Despite their proximity, Spanish and Portuguese political parties have been following two somewhat different paths in terms of the democratisation of their selection procedures. In Spain, party primaries were introduced in the late 1990s and have been mainly restricted to candidate selection. Party leadership selection has remained a party congress affair for the main state-wide Spanish political parties (Barberà et al., 2013). However, from the mid-2000s some regional and new parties introduced direct votes to select their leaders (Barberà and Rodríguez Teruel, 2012), and from the 2010s the PSOE (*Partido Socialista Obrero Español*) and the PP (*Partido Popular*) started to test the use of party primaries for leadership selection purposes at regional level. In this context, the big breakthrough has been the election of the PSOE's new leader in July 2014 through a closed primary election. In contrast, candidate selection in Portugal has remained firmly anchored to the decision of party leadership and national party bodies, whereas the selection of party leaders has experienced a process of democratisation with the introduction of closed primaries. This trend has concerned the main governing parties, while more extreme and anti-government parties have maintained the traditional mechanisms of political recruitment based on the power of the party congress and national organs. In addition, a significant change took place in September 2014 when the PS (*Partido Socialista*) elected the prime ministerial candidate through open primaries.

The broad political context of both countries may account – at least partially – for these different paths, especially when considering some features of the political system and their party systems. Portugal and Spain share an imperial past originating in the fifteenth century, and a long decline during the nineteenth and twentieth centuries. In the twentieth century liberal democratic regimes were introduced in both countries, but were unable to institutionalise and were followed by decades of dictatorship. In the mid-1970s, both Portugal and Spain successfully conducted transitions to democracy. They also have in common several features of political culture, mainly related to religious denomination and to the influence of the Catholic Church on the political system.

Despite this common historical legacy, there are remarkable differences with regard to the pattern of democratisation. The two Iberian countries are often taken as an example of two completely different transition models: the consensual type of the Spanish case, on the one hand; and the revolutionary path followed by Portuguese democratisation after the coup of junior officers, on the other. The different trajectories of state-building and democratisation processes were to establish one crucial difference between the two countries. While the centre–periphery division plays a fundamental role in the Spanish party system, this dimension is much less relevant in Portugal. To address territorial demands for self-government, the new democratic Spain implemented an ambitious devolution process that led to the present multilayered state. In Portugal, both institutional characteristics and the dimensions of competition contributed to strengthening the national character of party organisations and the centralisation of power in party leaders at the national level.

The main features of the Spanish electoral system were designed during the early stages of the transition towards democracy. They were meant to address three key issues: secure stable government; guarantee the representation of the national minorities from the periphery; and strengthen the new and fragile main party organisations. A set of institutional arrangements – such as a restricted vote of no-confidence in the prime minister or a state-funded regime of political parties – was also introduced to protect and enhance both government and parties. In Portugal the new electoral system was designed to guarantee a fair representation of the different social groups and political forces through the adoption of a proportional representation (PR) system based on the D'Hondt method. As in Spain, one of the main objectives was to strengthen the consolidation of party organisations. To achieve this goal, the new constitution established that only political parties had the authority to select candidates for national seats.[1]

Spain's national party system has evolved through three stages. The first period (1977–82) was characterised by two major state-wide parties, the UCD (*Unión de Centro Democrático*) and the PSOE; two medium state-wide parties, the PCE (*Partido Comunista de España*) and the AP (*Alianza Popular*); and several non state-wide parties – notably CiU (*Convergencia i Unió*) and the PNV (*Partido Nacionalista Vasco*). These six parties reached a wide consensus on institutional, economic and welfare policies. However, this party system came to an end at the 1982 general elections, where the PSOE emerged as the dominant party. The current party system started with the 1993 general election and comprises two main state-wide parties: the PSOE and the PP (*Partido Popular*); a medium state-wide alliance, IU (*Izquierda Unida*) which included the PCE and other leftist parties and social movements; and several non state-wide parties – CiU, PNV, the ERC (*Esquerra Republicana de Catalunya*) and others.

Although the Spanish party system remains very much the same as it was in the early 1990s (Oñate, 2008), there are some signs that it may be evolving through a

---

1 Since 1997 independents could be included in party lists for general elections, and they may run autonomously in local elections. Independent lists have assumed growing importance in Portuguese elections.

fourth period. Changes in the public mood, especially since the beginning of the deep economic crisis; the emergence of new state-wide parties such as *Podemos* (*We can*) and *Ciudadanos* (*Citizens*), not included in this chapter, and the UPyD (*Unión Progreso y Democracia*); or the steps taken by some of the political parties to improve their accountability and responsiveness (for example implementing party primaries) might be interpreted as features of this new stage of Spanish politics.

In the case of Portugal, after the Carnation Revolution of 25 April 1974, a stable party system quickly emerged, and by 1976 four parties represented almost 90 per cent of the electorate. Apart from a brief period during the mid-1980s when the centre-left Party of Democratic Renewal (PRD) emerged and disappeared, the party system has remained relatively stable. The general tendency (1987–2005) was for the vote to concentrate on the two centrist catch-all parties: the centre-left Socialist Party (PS, *Partido Socialista*) and the centre-right Social Democratic Party (PSD, *Partido Social Democrata*). These parties have always controlled the government alone or in coalition with the CDS-PP (*Centro Democrático Social-Partido Popular*), with the exception of a short period (1976–78) of presidential government (Freire, 2005; Jalali, 2007).

Since the 1987 realignment elections there has been an increasing concentration of the vote in two major parties. The change from consensual to majoritarian democracy has several features: movement from a fragmented to a kind of bipartisan party system; from coalition (or minority) and unstable governments to single-party majorities (most of the time) and rather stable governments; and from a strong parliament (and president) to a strong government (and prime minister) (Freire, 2005; Bruneau et al., 2001).

The economic and financial crisis that has hit Portugal since 2008 put an end to government stability and single-party majority governments. It is still too early to claim that a new phase began with the 2009 elections and the formation of a socialist minority government; but since then the pattern has been characterised by a decrease in the concentration of votes in the two moderate parties and more unstable government. It should also be noted that the two radical left parties – PCP (*Partido Comunista Português*) and BE (*Bloco de Esquerda*) – have always remained excluded from government, without any coalition potential vis-à-vis the other parties.

Contexts and Rationales for Adopting Primary Elections

The previous section has highlighted some of the main characteristics and transformations of institutional settings in Spain and Portugal. After a synthetic description of the main organisational party features, this section will consider both the strategic rationales and the political context involved in the introduction of party leader primaries using 'one member one vote' (OMOV).

As previous studies have shown, the party in central office is the most important face of both Spanish and Portuguese party organisations, controlling the parliamentary party (Gangas, 1995; Verge, 2007; Oñate, 2008; Lobo, 2003; van Biezen, 2003; Teixeira, 2009). This is mostly the result of the high degree of centralisation invested in the party leader (president or secretary general). In fact, through the main party bodies the party leader usually has the final say on candidate selection and is also directly responsible for choosing the parliamentary leader, who mainly plays an intermediary role between the parliamentary group and the main party bodies. Party discipline is usually very high, strengthening leaders' control over their parliamentary group. In general, party leaders have usually been able to control both the party in central office and the institutional component. The power of party leaders is clear in terms of strategic decisions – related, for example, to governmental alliances or ideological changes – or in the nomination of ministers and other public officials. This is because when the party is in power its leader is usually the prime minister (or equivalent) or the most influential party figure in coalition governments.

Despite these common characteristics, there are differences between Portuguese and Spanish party organisations worthy of examination. The main organisational variances between Spanish parties are the divides between state-wide and non state-wide parties and new and established parties. While the former mainly refers to size and strategy, the latter has so far more organisational consequences. In organisational terms, despite having developed slightly different original models, both the PP and the PSOE have converged towards highly centralised organisation (Méndez, 2000; García-Guereta, 2001). In both state-wide parties the regional party leaders have increased internal influence since the 1990s, especially when they are in office and the national party is in opposition. The IU still remains less centralised due to its original model as an electoral alliance and the more limited power of its regional leaders (Ramiro, 2004). The main differences for the Portuguese parties are mainly related to their original model. Both the PS and the CDS-PP followed a top-down process of penetration, leading to a highly centralised structure. On the other hand, local party structures were extremely important in the formation of the PSD, with notables also playing a significant role at national level (Jalali, 2007, pp. 146–7). This foundational phenomenon has important implications for the party leader position internally. While the leading role of the party chair within the PS and the CDS-PP is evident, within the PSD leaders have essentially been managers rather than uncontested decision-makers. This means that, when in opposition, the party assumes a more stratarchical structure and party leaders have more difficulty asserting their power over local bosses (Jalali, 2006, pp. 368–70). Consequently, the effective role of the party leader can vary according to institutional position and electoral performance.

As stated in the introduction, the main Spanish state-wide parties have been very reluctant to open up their leadership selection methods. Indeed, the implementation of party primaries for leadership started in new or regional parties and party branches. The Catalan ICV (*Iniciativa per Catalunya Verds*) was the first Spanish party to adopt OMOV to select its leader. They were adopted in hard times for the ICV because of its split from the IU, its sister-party. That led to internal division and the formation of a new party that competed against the ICV in the 1999 (regional) and 2000 (general) elections. Although the ICV managed to maintain its representation at both levels the cost was a considerable electoral setback. That fostered criticism of the ICV's leader and the emergence of a challenger. The challenger asked for primary elections to select the leading candidate for the 2000 general election, and shortly afterwards the party leader. This led to the withdrawal of the incumbent party leader. The main rationale for the ICV's implementation of primary elections was to persuade the incumbent party leader to retire. But it was also to invest the challenger with a new and much-needed legitimacy and authority against the potential rebellion of the rest of the party's board.

In the 2003 regional elections, the ERC doubled its share of the vote (from 8 to 16 per cent) and joined the new left coalition government in Catalonia. However, shortly afterwards a scandal led to the resignation of its party leader from government. In a sound tactic, ERC's leader, Josep Lluís Carod-Rovira, decided to run for the 2004 general election and achieved the best results for the party since the 1930s. He then proposed some organisational reforms to restrict the way the party congresses were held. The introduction of primaries was meant to be a sort of deal with dissatisfied party members. But they were also designed to reinforce the power of the party leader and his deputy against the party elites. The first primaries were held at the 2008 congress in a context of poor electoral performance and deep factionalism; on one side a power struggle between the discredited party leader and his deputy; on the other minority factions wanting to withdraw ERC from the regional coalition government. Four teams of candidates ran for the post of party leader and deputy. The deputy leader won the challenge, ERC stayed in government and the minority factions decided to split shortly afterwards (Argelaguet, 2009).

The UPyD was created shortly before the 2008 general election. Born as a reaction against traditional Spanish bipartidism, it relied heavily on its leader, Rosa Díez, who was the only member to achieve representation in the 2008 elections. She promoted primary elections at all levels as a way to differentiate the UPyD from the established parties and, also, to assert its influence over the rest of the party's board and regional elites. However, its early success did not stop internal dissent. At the 2009 congress the party leader was elected through closed primaries. Although another candidate challenged her, she won by a landslide. As stated in the party statutes, the UPyD has implemented primaries ever since. Other new parties, as *Podemos* and *Ciudadanos* (not included in this chapter), have followed the same pattern since their irruption in the national arena in mid 2014.

The PP government in the Balearic Islands lost power in the 2007 regional elections, and the party's leader (Jaume Matas) was then replaced in the 2008 regional congress by Rosa Estarás. However, she resigned just one year after being elected. That led to the appointment of a third leader, José Ramón Bauzá, who was quickly challenged by other party elites. To overcome its democratic deficit the appointed party leader called for a closed primary election in 2010, the first ever held by the PP at the regional level. By implementing party primaries,

Bauzá rightly expected also to overpower the divided local party elites. He won the primary, successfully reunited the party, and shortly afterwards won the 2011 election and regained the regional government.

After losing power in the 2009 regional elections, the PSOE in Galicia elected a new party leader, Pachi Vázquez. The electoral setbacks at the 2011 local and (later) national elections undermined his authority. Things worsened by the 2012 regional congress when he won by a very narrow margin against a former national minister. As expected, the PSOE suffered a new electoral setback in the 2012 Galician elections, which were called early. This forced the emergence of new challengers to the party leader. He then called for a party congress with closed primaries and revealed his intention to relinquish the leadership by 2013.[2] Interestingly, calling for primaries was not only meant to be a way to solve a regional problem; it was also to increase the pressure to reform the national party leadership selection method. A new Galician party leader was elected in September 2013.

However, the most important process of party leadership primaries took place in July 2014. Following a serious electoral setback in the 2014 European elections the PSOE's leader, Alfredo Pérez Rubalcaba, decided to step down. Following the party statutes, Rubalcaba initially called for an extraordinary party congress. However, pressure from challengers forced him to call for a closed primary before the congress. Thus, the national organisation followed the same path initiated by Galicia in 2013. Three candidates fought for the PSOE leadership in July 2014. The PSOE's evolution at national level also forced a change in leadership of the Catalan Socialists' Party (*Partit dels Socialistes de Catalunya*/PSC). The PSC organised another primary on the same date as the PSOE contest, albeit with just one candidate.

In the Portuguese case, recent changes in the method of leadership selection represent a remarkable phenomenon, especially if we consider that party organisational changes are very unusual and that party elites have been mainly concerned with the institutional arena rather than with the improvement of members' participation and inclusion in decision-making processes (Jalali, 2007; Lisi, 2011).

The argument in favour of the adoption of closed leadership primaries emerged first in the PS in 1992 in the context of intra-party conflicts between would-be leaders (Lisi, 2011, pp. 219–21). In this case, democratisation reforms were to a large extent a Trojan horse in the attempt to reinforce internal support and gain party leadership (see also Panebianco, 1988). Yet this attempt failed, and this change remained on paper until the major organisational reform that took place in 1998 (van Biezen, 2003; Lisi, 2009; Coelho, 2014). This time the socialist leader, António Guterres, was forced to reach a compromise with the opposition on the rules for electing the main party bodies and their powers. The final arrangement established the direct election of the party leader by members, while returning

---

2 The PSOE's statutes did not allow party primaries to select the regional party leaders. A legal formula (a multistage method) was found to circumvent the problem.

to the traditional hierarchical structure based on the representative principle for selecting the other party bodies.

On the other hand, both right-wing parties introduced direct leadership elections following the 2005 electoral defeat and their return to opposition. In the case of the PSD, the new leader, Marques Mendes, decided to force the introduction of closed primaries – despite strong internal divergences – in order to enhance party legitimacy and accountability of party leaders, and to boost participation and mobilisation (Lisi, 2010, pp. 137–8). As for the CDS-PP, the adoption of OMOV for leadership selection was due mainly to the weakness of the incumbent leader, Ribeiro e Castro, who was elected by a very tight margin during the previous party congress. Both parties decided to adopt a plurality system, but in 2012 the PSD decided to change to a majority runoff system.

With the partial exception of the PS, which adopted OMOV following major restructuring, the move towards more democratic methods of leadership selection was mainly based on strategic considerations. Therefore, the *raison d'être* for the introduction of direct leadership selection was twofold. On the one hand, this change followed electoral defeats, with the aim of demonstrating party renewal in order to appeal to voters and recruit new party members. On the other hand, democratising reforms were to contest internal power. Opposition leaders often defended the deepening of intra-party democracy to challenge the incumbents, whereas weak leaders (such as Marques Mendes or Ribeiro e Castro) tried to strengthen their position through the use of OMOV. The fact that the same leaders often (and suddenly) changed their opinion on leadership selection procedures according to their circumstances confirms the strategic use of democratisation reforms.

As mentioned above, in Portugal all the main governing parties have recently adopted closed primaries for the selection of leaders. This means that only party members are entitled to participate in choosing the party leader[3]. Two factors are responsible for this decision: first, institutional constraints, given that the new party law (2003) established that the selectorate of official party bodies was formally limited to party members; second, it should be noted that open primaries do not fit the political culture of Portuguese parties. The fact that local notables have controlled the access of party members as a way to influence the election of party cadres and candidates to local and national offices suggests that there are strong opponents of party organisation openness to party sympathisers or independents. Moreover, open primaries are considered detrimental to the image of parties in public opinion and unnecessary given the lack of deep cultural and social divisions.

---

3   An exception to this rule is the new party *Livre* (Free) party, founded in 2014 by ex-MEP Rui Tavares. This party adopts open primaries for the selection of candidates to public offices. In the 2014 European elections it obtained 2.2% of the votes.

The Primary Election Process

This section will focus on the main features of the party leadership primaries. It will analyse both the formal procedures and their real implementation over time in both countries.

It is worth noticing that most Spanish parties have held primaries without introducing these procedures into their statutes. This is especially the case with the PSOE, but also applies to the first primaries held by the ICV, UPyD or the PP Balearic branch. On the other hand, the regulation of party primaries is quite similar for the five Spanish parties selected in this chapter (see Table 4.1). All of them link the selection of the party leader to the celebration of a party congress. The ICV, ERC and PSOE hold their primaries some days before, while UPyD and the PP (Balearic Islands) hold them at the same time as the congress. Some parties link the party leadership election to part of their central board: leader and board are elected on the same ballot in UPyD, while the leader and his/her deputy are elected at the same time (but in different ballots) in the ERC. In all the other cases, the newly elected party leader submits a list of the board for approval by the party congress. In Portugal the election of party leaders takes place sometime before the congress (at least a month).

Almost all Spanish parties use their members as selectorates (closed primaries), with only the ICV using open primaries.[4] This single selectorate ranks quite high (18 out of 24) in Hazan and Rahat's inclusivity continuum (2010, p. 48). It is worth noting that the PSOE and the ICV used a multistage method during their first primary elections: the leader was elected first by all members and then ratified by congress. Portuguese parties have also adopted closed primaries. However, during the campaign to elect a new socialist leader after José Sócrates' resignation in 2011, one of the two candidates, Francisco Assis, defended the need to introduce open primaries for selecting prime ministerial and mayoral candidates. This was mainly a strategic move aimed at increasing support by deepening party democratisation. Yet this issue was a divisive one, as revealed during the congress held in April 2013. In the attempt to neutralise internal opposition and enhance party democratisation, the new socialist leader, António José Seguro, was forced to accept the adoption of open primaries for local offices. Moreover, the new statute approved in March 2012 established the possibility of adopting primaries also for the selection of MPs. Yet direct election can be used only when there is more than one list of MPs at district level, and both the federation (district level) and the national political commission have veto power.

The proposal to adopt open primaries was unexpectedly taken up again by the secretary general after the poor performance at the 2014 European elections. António Costa, the mayor of Lisbon, decided to challenge the incumbent leader by

---

4 The party allows previously registered sympathisers (non-subscribing members) to vote in a different ballot but, apparently, their votes are counted together with those of the members.

demanding a new election for party leadership. Seguro rejected a new contest and decided to introduce open primaries for prime ministerial candidates, to be held in September 2014. This was considered a strategic move of the socialist leader, a rush forward against the challenger's greater popularity and the growing difficulties in controlling the party apparatus. In addition, this decision was criticised not only because it perpetuated the PS's internal crisis for several months, but also because it did not clarify the relationship between the secretary general and the prime ministerial candidate.[5] In the end, Costa won the election by a landslide and Seguro resigned as party leader.

Key differences can be found in Spanish parties on candidacy requirements, ranging from UPyD, where virtually all members can stand, to the PSOE or the ERC where a substantial amount of support is needed (Table 4.1). This is very important because most parties (except the ICV and UPyD) state that if there is just one contestant no election is needed.[6] That is, incidentally, one reason why in Spain many (candidate and leader) primaries are called but not held (with the exception of the PSC primaries in 1999 and 2014). Until 2013 there had been no scandals related to mass enrolment during campaigns. In Portugal, party statutes establish that a candidacy must be supported by a certain number of party members, but this requisite has varied across parties and over time. The most important change took place in the PSD, which requires the submission of 1,500 members' signatures, while this threshold is much lower for the PS (100 signatures). Another requirement for participation in leadership primaries is membership of at least 12–18 months.[7] The open primary recently adopted by the PS also established similar requirements: First, candidacy depends on the support of 1,000 party members and must be presented 45 days before the election. Second, primary rules establish that all members (even non paid-up members) have the right to participate,[8] while all eligible voters who are not members of another party and who sign the declaration of principles are also entitled to vote for a prime ministerial candidate.

All Spanish parties have opted for a plurality formula. The main difference in terms of the electoral system can be found in how many ballot boxes are available during the election. Most parties place one ballot box per local branch. Others, such as the ICV and UPyD, have occasionally allowed the use of electronic voting. The plurality formula is also the most common method adopted by Portuguese

---

5 It is worth noting that this figure is not recognised by any party statutes or by the Portuguese constitution. Usually, party leaders are automatically candidates to the prime ministerial office.

6 UPyD states that, when only one candidate stands, more votes must be cast for him/her than blank votes, otherwise the candidate is rejected. So far this has never happened.

7 It is worth noting that, in general, there has been an increase in the membership period required to run for party positions at national level.

8 Unlike in some other countries, in none of the Portuguese parties is a voting fee required in order to participate.

Table 4.1 Main features of primary election processes in Spain and Portugal

Country (region)	Party	Year	Selectorate	Candidacy	Voting System	Timing[a]	Deselection
Spain (Catalonia)	ERC	2004	Members	5% of party members	Plurality	Non regulated	Non-regulated
Spain (Catalonia)	ICV	2000	Open primaries	50 party members	Plurality	Non-regulated	Non-regulated
Spain (Balearic Islands)	PP	2010	Members	90 party members	Plurality	Non-regulated	Non-regulated
Spain (Galicia)	PSOE	2013	Members	10% of party members	Plurality	Non-regulated	Non-regulated
Spain	PSOE	2014	Members	5% of party member	Plurality	Non-regulated	Non-regulated
Spain (Catalonia)	PSC	2014	Members	10% party members	Plurality	Non-regulated	Non-regulated
Spain	UPyD	2009	Members	Party members	Plurality	Non-regulated	Non-regulated
Portugal	PS	1998	Members	100 party members	Runoff	Non-regulated	Non-regulated
Portugal	PSD	2006	Members	1,500 party members	Plurality[b]	Non-regulated	Non-regulated
Portugal	CDS-PP	2005	Members[c]	Party members	Plurality	Non-regulated	Non-regulated

Notes: [a] Number of months before the general elections. [b] In 2012 the party congress approved the adoption of a runoff majority system, but statutory change and specific electoral rules for leadership selection have not yet been formulated. [c] This rule was adopted between 2005 and 2011. In 2011 the CDS-PP reintroduced election of the party leader by congress.

Source: Authors' own from press and party regulations.

parties. However, there are strong internal divergences regarding the most appropriate method to select party leadership. In particular, strong criticism has emerged within the CDS-PP, leading delegates to reintroduce in 2011 the election of the leader by the congress through plurality voting. The OMOV method for leadership selection is more consolidated within the PS, while in the PSD there are still strong differences of opinion, and in 2012 the leadership decided to change from a plurality formula to a runoff majority system (Table 4.1).[9]

In terms of deselection procedures, the Spanish and Portuguese cases are similar in that party statutes are completely omitted. As a consequence, the only way to punish incumbent leaders is for party delegates or members to call for a new congress.[10] Funding of the party leadership election is also omitted from Spanish and Portuguese party regulations. The only mentions of this topic establish that all candidates must have at their disposal party structures on equality bases, as well as equal access to membership files.

So far, the main areas of analysis have been the rules. The rest of this chapter will focus on processes rather than rules. This will give a more detailed account of what has happened in each party beyond that stated in their regulations. However, it must be noted that in Spain not all parties have held the same number of processes. In fact, there is a high disproportion between the number of party leader primaries held by UPyD (75 per cent of processes) and the other parties (ICV, PP, ERC, PSOE). There is also a disparity regarding the level at which the primaries are held. Almost all of them are organised by regional parties or regional branches of state-wide parties.[11] Only the PSOE and UPyD have organised leadership primaries at national level. In Portugal, closed primaries have taken place exclusively to select party leaders at national level. Besides this, from 2003 the PS adopted closed primaries to select party leaders at district level.[12] However, these elections are internal by nature, with no visibility outside the party. Moreover, these middle-level leaders have a marginal role in the party's functioning, and their influence on the decision-making process is secondary. Recently, the PS also held closed

---

9   According to a 2011 survey of socialist party delegates, 68 per cent of PS activists support the selection of the leader by party members, while 20 per cent would prefer an open ballot for sympathisers and voters (less than 10 per cent support the previous procedure based on party delegates). There are no similar data for the PSD, but in both the 2010 and 2012 congresses an intense debate took place about the opportunity to return to the election of leaders by party delegates.

10   This is indeed what happened in the PS after the 2014 European elections when the conflict between Seguro and Costa emerged.

11   Some party primaries have also been held at the local level, mainly to select local party candidates (Ramiro, 2013).

12   The requirements for candidacy are 2 per cent of signatures of party members at district level, or 80 members.

primaries for the election of candidates to local offices, but these concerned only a very small number of municipalities (10 out of 308).[13]

Democratisation of the party leadership selection has indeed increased the number of party members involved in both countries, but data on participation and mobilisation must be interpreted with caution because party membership figures are highly unreliable in both countries (see below). That said, participation rates have fluctuated substantially between parties and elections both in Spain and Portugal (Table 4.2). In Spain, turnout has ranged from 29 to 81 per cent. Average turnouts for each party are quite close to the overall mean (49.8 per cent). The ICV has the lowest mean (35.3 per cent) and the PSOE the highest (57.6 per cent). In Portugal, the level of mobilisation in closed leadership primaries also varies greatly, ranging from 14 to 66 per cent. On average, the PSD displays the highest rate of participation (52.6 per cent), while members of the CDS-PP are less likely to participate (23.8 per cent). The PS falls between these two (40.4 per cent). These figures are not significantly different from data on internal participation before the reform of leadership selection methods.[14] Overall, the Portuguese experience shows that only a small portion of the parties' supporters actually participate in these contests.

On the other hand, party primaries have not always meant competition between two or more contestants. In Spain, less than half (40 per cent) of the primaries had two or more candidates; the rest have been uncontested races. The ICV and the PSC have never had a contested party leader primary. Nevertheless, contested primaries have far higher competition rates than party congresses (Barberà et al., 2013). In this respect, party primaries have represented a change. The overall picture of Portuguese parties is the low number of candidates and relatively high proportion of uncontested races. The evidence suggests that in the PS there has been a decrease in the number of candidates after the adoption of OMOV, while in the PSD this change has been associated with more centrifugal dynamics and lower levels of party cohesion. The limited experience of the CDS-PP displays a mixed trend, with the alternation of both highly competitive elections and uncontested races for party leaders. If the institutional position is a key factor for explaining this different pattern, the degree of competitiveness is also associated with a leader's popularity or electoral challenges (Lisi and Freire, 2013). This is especially true for the PSD, while CDS-PP party leaders seem less vulnerable, showing greater capacity to insulate themselves from electoral pressure.

Regardless of the party, when competition has taken place the number of contestants has remained low. In Spain only 5 out of 50 processes have had three or more contestants, while in Portugal this proportion is slightly higher (4 out of 19 contests). Despite the number of non-contested primaries in the Spanish case,

---

13   OMOV elections took place especially when deep intra-party divisions emerged. From this viewpoint, the adoption of primaries aimed mainly to solve internal divergences.

14   Data from internal referenda show the stability of turnout rates. The CDS-PP called for a referendum in 1992, in which 26 per cent of party members participated (Lisi, 2011). Turnout in the socialist referendum in 1982 was 30 per cent (Lisi, 2009).

the winner's mean share of the votes is slightly higher in Portugal than in Spain (83.7 and 80.5 per cent respectively). This phenomenon can be explained by the plebiscitary nature of leadership contests when the party is in office. This means that incumbency is always associated with very low levels of competitiveness, while the shift to opposition fosters more competitive contests. Nevertheless, if we only take into account the share of votes of the contested elections the mean drops to 70 per cent in Portugal and 65 per cent in Spain. The mean results of the runner-up are 33.6 per cent for Portuguese parties and 30.9 per cent for Spanish ones. This indicates that even when competition does take place the runner-up hardly represents a serious threat to the winner(s).

As a conclusion, it should be pointed out that the introduction of primaries to select party leaders has certainly strengthened the personalisation of politics and enhanced candidate-centred campaigns. Although party leaders have always played a central role in the electoral arena and have been an essential link between party image and voters (Oñate, 2008; Lobo, 2006), the democratisation of leadership selection has led the media to increasingly focus on party candidates and marginalise intra-party debates on policies and strategic orientations that usually take place during the party congress. This is especially true in Portugal, where all mayor parties have adopted closed primaries as their leadership selection method, but can also be applied with caution for Spanish parties. One important indicator of this increasing personalisation is the greater professionalisation of party leadership campaigns. Since the 2004 election of the PS leader – the first competitive contest –, internal party campaigns have attracted widespread attention from the mass media and have been organised as electoral campaigns with campaign staff and external consultants, raising the costs normally associated with internal elections.[15] On a smaller scale this is also true for the PSOE and the regional branches of both the PP and the PSOE, but is less relevant for UPyD, the ERC or the ICV.

And yet, Portuguese leadership contests have not displayed high levels of negativity. Generally speaking, candidates prefer to highlight the divergences between the different programmatic and strategic options rather than stressing the negative aspects of their opponent(s). Two main reasons can explain this phenomenon. One is related to the political culture, which has always rejected personal attack as an instrument to increase a leader's popularity. It is also worth noting that the mass media do not usually rely on this type of communication, in the belief that it fosters demobilisation and mistrust of politics. On the other hand,

---

15 All main Portuguese newspapers started to conduct or publish opinion polls from the first competitive contest in 2004. In general, the greater the competitiveness, the higher is the visibility and the coverage of leadership elections in the media. The candidates from the two main parties usually form ad hoc teams for the organisation of internal campaigns. Unfortunately, no data or estimates are available for the funding of leadership contests and internal campaigns. A similar phenomenon happened with the primary election of the PSOE leader in Spain. Data on the funding of this campaign is not available either.

Table 4.2 Main features of primary elections in Spain and Portugal

Country (region)	Party	Year	Turnout	Number of candidates	Incumbent running	Incumbent winner	Winner's votes	Runner-up's votes	Women running	Women winners	Winner's age	National seniority
Spain (Catalonia)	ERC	2008	70.9	4	No	n.a.	37.4	27.7	No	n.a.	42	Yes
Spain (Catalonia)	ERC	2011	41.0	1	No	n.a.	u.r.	n.a.	No	n.a.	42	No
Spain (Catalonia)	ICV	2004	29.0	1	Yes	Yes	u.r.	n.a.	No	n.a.	54	Yes
Spain (Catalonia)	ICV	2000	38.4	1	No	n.a.-	u.r.	n.a.	No	n.a.	50	Yes
Spain (Catalonia)	ICV	2008	38.5	1	Yes	Yes	u.r.	n.a.	No	n.a.	58	Yes
Spain (Catalonia)	ICV	2013	-	11	No	n.a-	u.r.	n.a.	Yes	Yes	42	Yes/No
Spain (Balearics)	PP	2010	48.3	2	No	n.a.	69.2	30.8	No	n.a.	40	No
Spain (Balearics)	PP	2012	33.8	1	Yes	Yes	u.r.	n.a.	No	n.a.	42	No
Spain (Galicia)	PSOE	2013	60.0	2	No	n.a.	77.0	21.0	No	n.a.	46	No
Spain	PSOE	2014	65.9	3	No	n.a.	48.7	36.2	No	n.a.	42	Yes
Spain (Catalonia)	PSC	2014	47.0	1	No	n.a.	u.r.	n.a.	No	n.a.	54	Yes
Spain	UPyD	2009	37.9	2	First time	n.a.	81.0	19.0	Yes	Yes	57	Yes
Spain (Asturias)	UPyD	2010	65.0	2	No	n.a.	70.8	29.2	No	n.a.	35	No
Spain (Aragón)	UPyD	2010	-	3	No	n.a.	-	n.a.	Yes	Yes	47	No

Region	Party	Year									
Spain (Balearics)	UPyD	2010	-	2	First time	n.a.	-	n.a.	No	n.a.	60	No
Spain (Euskadi)	UPyD	2010	-	1	No	n.a.	u.r.	n.a.	No	n.a.	34	No
Spain (C. León)	UPyD	2010	43.0	1	Yes	Yes	u.r.	n.a.	No	n.a.	55	No
Spain (C. Mancha)	UPyD	2010	60.0	2	No	n.a.	69.7	30.3	No	n.a.	-	No
Spain (Cantabria)	UPyD	2010	50.0	1	First time	n.a.	u.r.	n.a.	Yes	Yes	-	No
Spain (Valencian C.)	UPyD	2010	-	2	First time	n.a.	-	n.a.	No	n.a.	46	No
Spain (Murcia)	UPyD	2010	55.0	2	Yes	Yes	69.5	26.8	No	n.a.	50	No
Spain (Extremadura)	UPyD	2010	49.0	1	Yes	Yes	u.r.	n.a.	No	n.a.	-	No
Spain (Madrid)	UPyD	2010	-	-	No	n.a.	-	n.a.	-	n.a.	-	No
Spain (Navarre)	UPyD	2010	40.7	1	First time	n.a.	u.r.	n.a.	No	n.a.	44	No
Spain (Catalonia)	UPyD	2010	60.0	2	First time	n.a.	70.4	29.6	Yes	Yes	-	No
Spain (Canary I.)	UPyD	2010	46.8	2	Yes	No	50.0	n.a.	No	n.a.	-	No
Spain (Andalusia)	UPyD	2010	-	3	Yes	Yes	45.0	n.a.	No	n.a.	-	No
Spain (Galicia)	UPyD	2010	-	1	First time	n.a.	u.r.	n.a.	No	n.a.	66	No
Spain (Euskadi)	UPyD	2011	-	-	No	n.a.	-	n.a.	-	n.a.	-	No
Spain (Madrid)	UPyD	2011	29.0	-	-	n.a.	59.0	n.a.	-	n.a.	52	No
Spain (C. Mancha)	UPyD	2012	72.1	2	No	n.a.	53.0	n.a.	Yes	Yes	-	No
Spain (Catalonia)	UPyD	2012	-	2	No	n.a.	-	n.a.	Yes	No	-	No

Table 4.2 Main features of primary elections in Spain and Portugal continued

Country (region)	Party	Year	Turnout	Number of candidates	Incumbent running	Incumbent winner	Winner's votes	Runner-up's votes	Women running	Women winners	Winner's age	National seniority
Spain (Andalusia)	UPyD	2012	47.1	2	No	n.a.	-	n.a.	No	n.a.	36	No
Spain (Extremadura)	UPyD	2012	81.0	1	No	n.a.	u.r.	n.a.	No	n.a.	-	No
Spain (Aragón)	UPyD	2012	33.0	1	Yes	Yes	u.r.	n.a.	No	n.a.	43	No
Spain (Rioja)	UPyD	2012	-	1	No	n.a.	-	n.a.	No	n.a.	-	No
Spain (Galicia)	UPyD	2012	-	1	No	n.a.	u.r.	n.a.	No	n.a.	-	No
Spain (Euskadi)	UPyD	2013	n.a.	n.a.	No	n.a.	-	n.a.	Yes	1	59	No
Spain	UPyD	2013	n.a.	1	1	1	u.r.	n.a.	Yes	1	61	Yes
Spain (Asturias)	UPyD	2014	n.a.	1	No	n.a.	u.r.	n.a.	No	n.a.	56	No
Spain (Cantabria)	UPyD	2014	46.0	1	1	1	u.r.	n.a.	No	n.a.	-	No
Spain (C. León)	UPyD	2014	40.0	1	1	1	u.r.	n.a.	No	n.a.	47	No
Spain (Navarre)	UPyD	2014	47.0	1	1	1	u.r.	n.a.	No	n.a.	48	No
Spain (Balearic I.)	UPyD	2014	n.a.	1	1	1	u.r.	n.a.	No	n.a.	-	No
Spain (Catalonia)	UPyD	2014	n.a.	1	No	n.a.	u.r.	n.a.	No	n.a.	-	No
Spain (Galicia)	UPyD	2014	n.a.	1	No	n.a.	u.r.	n.a.	No	n.a.	-	No
Spain (Murcia)	UPyD	2014	n.a.	2	1	No	56.4	43.6	Yes	1	35	No
Spain (Valencian C.)	UPyD	2014	70.0	3	No	n.a.	51.2	44.1	No	n.a.	-	No

Spain (Aragón)	UPyD	2014	n.a.	n.a.	1	No	1	-	-	n.a.	n.a.	45	No
Spain (Madrid)	UPyD	2014	n.a.	2	No	-	Yes	66.3	32.9	Yes	1	37	No
Mean Spain			49.8	1.6	38.6	87.5	-	80.5[a]	30.9	22.0	20.0	47.7	16.0
Portugal	PS	1999	65.0	1	First time	Yes	u.r.	-	n.a.	No	n.a.	50	Yes
Portugal	PS	2001	43.0	1	Yes	Yes	u.r.	n.a.	n.a.	No	n.a.	-	Yes
Portugal	PS	2002	15.0	2	No	n.a.	96.4	n.a.	n.a.	No	n.a.	53	Yes
Portugal	PS	2004	48.0	3	No	n.a.	80.1	15.7	n.a.	No	n.a.	47	Yes
Portugal	PS	2006	27.0	1	Yes	Yes	u.r.	n.a.	n.a.	No	n.a.	-	Yes
Portugal	PS	2009	36.0	1	Yes	Yes	u.r.	n.a.	n.a.	No	n.a.	-	Yes
Portugal	PS	2011	37.0	4	Yes	Yes	93.3	3.3	n.a.	No	n.a.	49	Yes
Portugal	PS	2011	30.4	2	No	n.a.	68.0	32.0	n.a.	No	n.a.	-	Yes
Portugal	PS	2013	62.1	2	Yes	Yes	96.5	3.5	n.a.	No	n.a.	-	Yes
Portugal	PSD	2006	37.0	1	First time	Yes	u.r.	n.a.	n.a.	No	n.a.	49	Yes
Portugal	PSD	2007	61.0	2	Yes	Yes	u.r.	42.7	n.a.	No	n.a.	54	Yes
Portugal	PSD	2008	59.0	4	No	n.a.	96.4	31.1	Yes	Yes	n.a.	68	Yes
Portugal	PSD	2010	66.0	4	No	n.a.	80.1	38.3	n.a.	No	n.a.	46	Yes
Portugal	PSD	2012	40.2	1	Yes	Yes	u.r.	n.a.	n.a.	No	n.a.	48	Yes
Portugal	PSD	2014	38.0	1	Yes	Yes	u.r.	n.a.	n.a.	No	n.a.	50	Yes
Portugal	CDS-PP	2005	14.0	1	First time	n.a.	u.r.	n.a.	n.a.	No	n.a.	52	Yes
Portugal	CDS-PP	2007	21.0	2	Yes	No	74.9	24.9	n.a.	No	n.a.	45	Yes
Portugal	CDS-PP	2008	31.0	1	Yes	n.a.	u.r.	n.a.	n.a.	No	n.a.	-	Yes
Portugal	CDS-PP	2011	29.0	1	Yes	n.a.	u.r.	n.a.	n.a.	No	n.a.	-	Yes
Mean Portugal			40.0	1.8	68.7	90.9	85.7[a]	33.6	5.3	5.3	5.6	50.9	100

Notes: u.r. – uncontested race; [a] taking into account the share of votes of the uncontested races; 1 collegial/collective leadership (a man and a woman).
Source: Authors' own from press and party official sources.

negative campaigns are considered detrimental to party image, and leaders tend to downplay internal conflicts. There is very little evidence of negativity of the campaigns involved in party leadership primaries in Spain. Most media coverage has until now focused on the results, not on the internal campaigns, because this has mainly concerned small state-wide and regional parties and some regional branches of the PP and PSOE. Fair play between the contestants dominated the PSOE party leadership campaign of 2014.

Political Consequences for Parties

The literature has identified several factors that can be influenced by the use of party leadership primaries: continuity of the incumbent leader; leader's profile (women, age, seniority); the number of party members; and, eventually, the party's electoral results. This section discusses the main consequences for and outcomes of this kind of primary on Portuguese and Spanish parties.

So far, party leadership primaries seem to have led to a low rate of incumbent stability in Spain (Table 4.2). Less than 40 per cent of incumbents do not contest the next primary.[16] However, it has to be taken into account that a great number of processes came from UPyD, a state-wide party formed in 2007. This means that instability has probably more to do with the formation of a new party than with the primaries themselves. Portuguese parties display a higher level of stability, with an average of 62.5 per cent of contests where incumbents compete for re-election (52.6 per cent if we also consider the first primaries). Usually incumbents do not contest party leadership when they suffer electoral defeats or are not able to increase party popularity when they are in opposition. Regardless of the party, the chances of an incumbent winning the competition are very high. Up to now, only two incumbents out of 14 (14.3 per cent) have lost a primary in Spain, while in Portugal the percentage is even lower (8.3).

In the Portuguese and Spanish case, party leadership has been dominated – if not monopolised – by men. In Spain, only 11 women (22 per cent) have been encouraged to contest party leadership primaries, all but one of them from UPyD (Table 4.2). This is probably because the UPyD national party leader is a woman – Rosa Díez. But also seems to point out another divide between UPyD and the other parties, as women there represent almost one quarter of the contestants (26.3 per cent). In Portugal, the only woman elected as party leader (PSD) was selected through closed primaries, but this case can be considered an exception to the rule.

Party leaders in Spain are generally younger than their Europe-wide counterparts, with the average age of the winners being about 48. There are no big differences between parties in this regard, not even with the age of party leaders elected through party congresses (Barberà et al., 2013). In Portugal the average

---

16   First-time primaries are excluded, otherwise the rate would be even lower (30 per cent).

age of party leaders elected under closed primaries is 50.9, which is slightly above the average for party leaders under a democratic regime (Lisi and Freire, 2013). Despite this apparent continuity, it is worth noting that the introduction of direct elections shifted the emphasis from intra-party conflicts to the personal aspects of the candidates. After the first and second generations of leaders more directly associated with the consolidation of the democratic regime, a new young generation – especially within the PS and PSD – with no connections to the transition period assumed power. Therefore, it can be argued that this change facilitated the adoption of OMOV – and vice versa – because it broke with the traditional mechanisms based on the election of party delegates to the congress.

This generational turnover also has relevant consequences in terms of political background. From this viewpoint, two considerations are crucial for understanding the Portuguese case. The first is that party leadership has followed a process of professionalisation based on the occupation of important positions within the party. This means that a good partisan curriculum is a prerequisite for contesting the leadership at the national level. All the leaders elected through closed primaries are experienced politicians with a strong background within the party – for example previous leaders of its youth organisation – or at institutional level (as MPs). In other words, there is little room for outsiders or leaders with a more technocratic profile. As shown in Table 4.2, all leaders in Portugal elected through closed primaries – with no exceptions – have held a national position. In contrast with the Portuguese figures, in Spain the number of senior party leaders elected via primaries is very low (16 per cent) because most of them are leaders of non state-wide parties, regional branches of the main state-wide parties and the newly created UPyD. Although it may seem paradoxical, the regional ICV is the party with most senior leaders elected through primaries. This is mainly because of the career paths of its last two leaders (serving first as MP and then as party leader).

As already stated, ICV is the only Spanish party that allows registered sympathisers to vote in party leadership primaries. In our understanding, disagreement on this issue by paying-fee members has not been reported so far. As closed primaries formally empower party members, they are usually expected to boost membership. However, the literature has warned of some *pathologies* such as 'multi-speed membership' – members enlisted just for a race (Scarrow, 2015) – and the existence of 'vote contractors' (Kenig, 2009; Cross and Rahat, 2012). In the case of Spain and Portugal it is worth noting that parties do not keep accurate enrolment files, and membership figures are likely to be inflated. Therefore, it is extremely hard to assess the real impact of direct leadership selection on the evolution of party membership (see Table 4.3). The still very limited evidence from Spanish parties shows that membership is usually higher on election day than it was one year earlier. The number of missing cases does not allow much further comment, but this seems consistent, nonetheless, with two other pieces of evidence: the growing number of members recorded in comparative studies of party membership (Mair and van Biezen, 2001; van Biezen et al., 2012) and the steady growth of UPyD since its origins. One year after the primaries the (limited)

Table 4.3 Effects of primary elections on political parties in Spain and Portugal

Country (region)	Party	Year	Members			Electoral performance (Votes)			Change (Votes after primaries % - votes before primaries %)
			Year before primaries (N)	Year after primaries (N)	Change (%)	Before primaries (N)	Before primaries (%)	Before primaries (%)	
Spain (Catalonia)	ERC	2008	9,923	9,878	-0.45	291,532	7.2	7.2	-0.8
Spain (Catalonia)	ERC	2011	7,257	n.a.	-	291,532	7.2	7.2	-0.8
Spain (Catalonia)	ICV	2000	4,053	n.a.	-	119,290	5.9	5.9	2.3
Spain (Catalonia)	ICV	2004	4,800	5,721	19.18	234,790	5.0	5.0	-0.9
Spain (Catalonia)	ICV	2008	5,464	5,340	-2.26	183,338	8.2	8.2	3.2
Spain (Catalonia)	ICV	2013	5,224	n.a.	-	280,152	-	-	-
Spain (Balearic I.)	PP	2010	n.a.	22,201	-	208,246	50.5	50.5	6.0
Spain (Balearic I.)	PP	2012	19,000	22,201	16.84	217,327	-	-	-
Spain (Galicia)	PSOE	2013	11,317	11,550	2.05	457,633	27.8	27.8	-
Spain	PSOE	2014	197,480	201,000	1.8	7,003,511	28.8	28.8	-
Spain (Catalonia)	PSC	2014	20,658	n.a.	-	922,547	26.7	26.7	-
Spain	UPyD	2009	5,000	6,363	27.26	306,079	4.8	4.8	3.6
Spain (Asturias)	UPyD	2010	150	208	38.66	9,485	4.0	4.0	2.6
Spain (Aragón)	UPyD	2010	n.a.	64	-	8,728	5.9	5.9	4.7
Spain (Balearic I.)	UPyD	2010	n.a.	150	-	3,107	4.3	4.3	3.6
Spain (Euskadi)	UPyD	2010	n.a.	135	-	10,636	1.8	1.8	0.8
Spain (C. León)	UPyD	2010	n.a.	384	-	25,504	6.2	6.2	4.7
Spain (C. Mancha)	UPyD	2010	n.a.	246	-	13,230	5.0	5.0	3.9
Spain (Cantabria)	UPyD	2010	n.a.	90	-	5,094	3.6	3.6	2.2
Spain (Valencian C.)	UPyD	2010	600	610	1.6	19,294	5.7	5.7	5.0

Spain (Murcia)	UPyD	2010	n.a.	212	-	7,172	6.3	5.4
Spain (Extremadura)	UPyD	2010	71	72	1.4	5,366	3.5	2.7
Spain (Madrid)	UPyD	2010	n.a.	n.a.	-	132,095	10.4	6.6
Spain (Navarre)	UPyD	2010	30	21	-30	2,608	2.1	1.3
Spain (Catalonia)	UPyD	2010	300	202	-32.66	6,252	1.2	1.0
Spain (Canary I.)	UPyD	2010	n.a.	198	-	3,577	2.7	2.3
Spain (Andalusia)	UPyD	2010	n.a.	1383	-	40,568	4.8	3.9
Spain (Galicia)	UPyD	2010	n.a.	140	-	10,110	1.2	0.6
Spain (Euskadi)	UPyD	2011	n.a.	135	-	10,636	1.8	0.8
Spain (Madrid)	UPyD	2011	1,844	301	22.35	132,095	10.4	6.6
Spain (C. Mancha)	UPyD	2012	246	n.a.	-	58,224	-	-
Spain (Catalonia)	UPyD	2012	202	n.a.	-	39,650	-	-
Spain (Andalusia)	UPyD	2012	1383	n.a.	-	207,923	-	-
Spain (Extremadura)	UPyD	2012	72	n.a.	-	22,913	-	-
Spain (Aragón)	UPyD	2012	64	n.a.	-	41,032	-	-
Spain (Rioja)	UPyD	2012	50	n.a.	-	10,367	-	-
Spain (Galicia)	UPyD	2012	140	150	7.14	19,969	-	-
Spain (Euskadi)	UPyD	2013	135	200	48.14	10,636	1.0	-
Spain	UPyD	2013	6,068	6,115	0.8	1,143,225	4.7	-
Spain (Asturias)	UPyD	2014	n.a.	250	-	24,721	3.9	-
Spain (Cantabria)	UPyD	2014	81	n.a.	-	12,614	3.6	-
Spain (C. León)	UPyD	2014	500	n.a.	-	93,197	6.1	-
Spain (Navarre)	UPyD	2014	n.a.	n.a.	-	6,829	2.1	-
Spain (Balearic I.)	UPyD	2014	n.a.	n.a.	-	18,525	4.2	-
Spain (Catalonia)	UPyD	2014	n.a.	n.a.	-	39,650	1.2	-
Spain (Galicia)	UPyD	2014	150	n.a.	-	19,969	1.2	-
Spain (Murcia)	UPyD	2014	n.a.	n.a.	-	45,984	6.3	-

Table 4.3 Effects of primary elections on political parties in Spain and Portugal continued

Country (region)	Party	Year	Members		Change (%)	Electoral performance (Votes)		Change
			Year before primaries (N)	Year after primaries (N)		Before primaries (N)	Before primaries (%)	(Votes after primaries % - votes before primaries %)
Spain (Valencian C.)	UPyD	2014	730	900	23.28	146,064	5.6	-
Spain (Aragón)	UPyD	2014	n.a.	n.a.	-	41,032	5.9	-
Spain (Madrid)	UPyD	2014	n.a.	n.a.	-	347,354	10.3	-
Portugal	PS	1999	90,062	124,611	29.65	2,583,755	43.8	0.3
Portugal	PS	2001	124,611	122,548	-1.65	-	43.8	-6.3
Portugal	PS	2002	122,548	66,917	-45.4	2,385,922	37.8	7.2
Portugal	PS	2004	74,949	90,629	20.9	2,068,584	37.8	7.3
Portugal	PS	2006	90,629	105,232	16.11	2,588,312	45.0	-8.4
Portugal	PS	2009	n.a.	n.a.	-	-	45.0	-8.4
Portugal	PS	2011	n.a.	n.a.	-	2,077,238	36.6	-8.6
Portugal	PS	2012	105,232	133,058	26.44	1,566,347	28.0	-
Portugal	PS	2013	133,058	84,443	-36.4	-	28.0	-
Portugal	PSD	2006	116,000	142,673	22.9	1,653,425	28.8	0.3
Portugal	PSD	2007	142,673	140,000	-1,87	-	28.8	-0.3
Portugal	PSD	2008	140,000	153,361	-	-	28.8	-0.3
Portugal	PSD	2010	n.a.	n.a.	-	1,653,655	29.1	9.6
Portugal	PSD	2012	153,361	112,009	-26.9	2,159,181	38.7	-
Portugal	PSD	2014	n.a.	n.a.	-	-	38.7	-

Portugal	CDS-PP	2005	32,571	34,744	6,67	416,415	7.2	3.2
Portugal	CDS-PP	2007	34,744	34,353	-1,13	-	7.2	3.2
Portugal	CDS-PP	2008	34,353	17,500	-49,06	-	7.2	3.2
Portugal	CDS-PP	2011	23,345	29,655	27,03	592,778	10.4	-

Source: Authors' own from press and party official sources.

data show mixed results. In some cases the membership figures rise far beyond 10 per cent, and yet in others there is a small decline. Whether this has to do with the existence of instant membership pathologies still seems unclear.

In Portugal there is almost no relationship between party membership figures and leadership contests: numbers go up and down regardless of the election of new leaders. Usually, party membership increases when the party is in power; while in opposition these data are revised, leading to the exclusion of a significant proportion of members (especially those who do not pay party fees regularly). Moreover, enrolment files are not updated regularly and membership figures fall drastically when member lists are cleaned up. This has been a problematic issue in the two main parties (PS and PSD) due to the manipulation of files by local notables. There have been several cases of mass enrolment in the period immediately preceding the election of party leaders. Usually, incumbents have used the rules to make it more difficult for non-members to join and participate in the leadership contest, while challengers have favoured the possibility of registering new members until a few days before the election.

This section concludes with an analysis of changes in the electoral performance of parties, and a preliminary assessment of whether they can be connected to the use of primaries. At first sight it is worth noting that the Spanish parties do improve their electoral performance in the subsequent national election after holding a primary. The ERC is the only exception to this pattern. However, other factors have to be taken into consideration, the most important being the long gap between the primary election and the subsequent national election (almost two years on average). That time span makes it difficult to ascertain a direct relation between the two figures. Another factor is that most of the selected party leaders discussed here did not actually take part in the national elections. This is because they are mainly regional party leaders (the exception being UPyD's Rosa Díez) and thus compete as top candidates in the regional elections.[17] The last factor concerns the very low media profile of the party leadership primaries held by the selected parties. That said, there may be indirect effects derived from the legitimacy of the process and, of course, from the performance of those party leaders.

Moving to the Portuguese case, we can see that there is almost no correlation between electoral performance and leadership contests. As noted above, strategic considerations were crucial for the introduction of OMOV procedures for right-wing parties. This followed the successful example of the 2004 election of the socialist leader, which contributed to increasing the party's performance in the 2005 elections. However, closed primaries do not display any systematic effect in terms of electoral results. Although there may be short-term benefits with regard to party popularity and leader visibility, the performance of the main governing parties has fluctuated regardless of the timing of leadership contests.

---

17   Few of UPyD's regional party leaders stood as top candidates in both the 2011 regional (May) and national (November) elections.

Due to the relatively limited experience of closed primaries in Portugal, it is difficult to analyse their effect on the relationship between leaders and members. In the case of the PS, the evidence suggests that this procedure has strengthened the degree of centralisation, with a marginalisation of both local party branches and congress (Lisi, 2006). It has also reduced programmatic divergences, leading to more pragmatic and flexible intra-party alignment. On the other hand, the power of local notables is greater in the case of the PSD, which has displayed significant territorial division in terms of party organisation. This means that the conflict between centre and periphery may reach higher levels of salience, especially if closed primaries tend to enhance the centralisation and the concentration of power in the national party elite. Even if there are signs of this tension, it is still too early to make a definitive assessment of the impact of OMOV on intra-party dynamics. As in Portugal, party primaries in Spain do seem to have enhanced party centralisation, but again the Spanish experience is not really conclusive on the impact of primaries on leader–member relationships. To some extent they have diminished the power of party congress delegates (still relevant for programmatic matters), yet little media attention makes it unclear whether this has downplayed or enhanced the role of local party elites. More research is needed to assess whether they are still needed to mobilise support at local level or whether they have been bypassed.

Conclusions

This chapter had two main objectives: to examine the rules and processes of party leadership primaries in Spain and Portugal; and to investigate the impact of leadership contests and compare the two countries, highlighting the main similarities and differences. The first point worth mentioning is that in both southern European democracies the adoption of primaries has shown a low level of institutionalisation. This means that this method of leadership selection is still a controversial issue in several parties, with party elites divided on the pros and cons of OMOV procedures. Moreover, party statutes lack clear and well-defined rules for primary contests. The absence of accurate regulations and the fact that few contests have taken place are two relevant indicators of this low level of institutionalisation.

Overall, in both Portugal and Spain only party members have been eligible to vote in leadership selection. Although there have been some exceptions, party elites seem to consider open primaries potentially dangerous for the cohesion and stability of the leadership. There has also been an overwhelming preference for the adoption of a plurality formula, with no significant experience of innovation (for example mixed methods). Yet primaries in Spain have been adopted for the selection of leaders at regional level, while in Portugal this process has concerned mainly national party elites.

What are the consequences of leadership primaries in Portugal and Spain? First, the evidence suggests that their introduction had no impact on the representation and responsiveness of political parties. If we look at gender, age or political background, we found small or no differences before and after the adoption of OMOV. In Spain the only exception seems to be UPyD, a new party that has been able to attract disaffected voters from the mainstream parties. Second, there are mixed trends with regard to the evolution of party membership and electoral performance. It is hard to draw definite conclusions, due to the reliability of party membership figures on the one hand, and the time span between leadership contests and national elections on the other. Finally, there are some examples of increased centralisation, thus strengthening the role of party leaders vis-à-vis members. However, these conclusions must be taken with a note of caution due to the limited experience of primaries in both countries.

Chapter 5

Democratising Party Leadership Selection in Belgium and Israel

Bram Wauters, Gideon Rahat and Ofer Kenig

Introduction

Belgium and Israel are worlds apart in terms of geostrategic situation. The former is located in the centre of a rather peaceful and unified Europe, while the latter is in the troubled Middle East. Yet both countries share many political features: both are somewhat veteran parliamentary democracies; both have a consensus regime with a highly proportional PR electoral system, a multiparty system, wide coalition governments and a relatively equal balance of power between parliament and government (Lijphart, 2012). Belgium and Israel are also quite similar in population (10.4 and 7.8 million inhabitants as of 2014) and area (30,000 and 20,000 sq km); and are closely ranked globally in terms of GDP per capita (20th and 25th) and Human Development Index (17th and 16th).[1] Both societies are heterogeneous, and many sociopolitical divisions (national, religious, linguistic, socioeconomic) are reflected in their party systems, resulting in many parties. Indeed, parties in both countries democratised their leadership selection processes similarly in the 1990s and adopted primaries. Yet, while almost all parties in Belgium followed this trend, in Israel it was almost limited to the major parties, which leads us to point out some more differences between the two political systems.

Belgium has a consensus regime in the sense that it is a federal state with considerable competences for territory-based regions and language-based communities. Conversely, Israel is a unitary state, and while there are some aspects of sociological decentralisation that fit the consociational model, it is a highly centralised state, especially in the territorial sense. In addition, Belgium's legislative branch is bicameral (we should note, however, that the second chamber has lost a considerable part of its power in recent years), while Israel has a unicameral parliament.

Another remarkable feature of the Belgian party system is that, in practice, it is split into two quite autonomous systems: Flemish (or Dutch-speaking) parties and French-speaking parties. On both sides of the language divide are two sets of three traditional parties: Christian Democrats (CD&V and CDH), Social Democrats

---

1 See CIA World Factbook, 2014; International Monetary Fund, 2013; UN 2013 Human Development Report.

(sp.a and PS) and Liberal Democrats (OpenVLD and MR).[2] Despite recent uncertainty about traditional parties due to electoral volatility, in general a long-term stability could be noted for the Belgian party system(s) (Deschouwer, 2009). This corresponds to what Lipset and Rokkan (1967) have called the 'freezing' of the party system. Thus, the six traditional parties are in decline in electoral terms, but are still present and continue to play a significant role in Belgian politics. Apart from these traditional parties, there are other parties whose entry to parliament is facilitated by the PR electoral system. New parties come and go (such as the social-liberal party 'Spirit', which was created in 2001 and has now ceased to exist). The Green parties, such as the Flemish Greens (Groen) and Ecolo in French-speaking Belgium; the regionalist parties New Flemish Alliance (N-VA) and the Francophone Democratic Federalists (FDF); and the extreme right Flemish party Vlaams Belang appear to have become constant factors over time.

Almost all Belgian parties adopted closed party primaries to select their leaders. In this chapter, we discuss primaries that have taken place in all parties that were represented at least once in the Belgian parliament. A number of parties – (in particular Groen, Ecolo and the FDF) have taken advantage of the small size of Belgium (and its regions) and of their own limited numbers of members to organise leadership contests in party conferences open to all members. Since attending a conference clearly involves much more effort for the rank and file (Rahat and Hazan, 2006) and since the absolute number of participants in these contests is generally much lower than in the 'standard' primaries of other parties, they are omitted from the present analysis.

Israeli society is also highly heterogeneous, and many sociopolitical divisions (national, ethnic, religious, veterans vs immigrants) are reflected in its party system, resulting in many parties representing different political subcultures (Kimmerling, 1999). Each subculture has its own menu of legitimate leadership selection methods, based on different notions of authority (traditional, charismatic, and rational-legal). This means that even if each subculture does not develop its own typical leadership selection method, Israeli parties are more resilient than those in more homogenous societies to the contingency effect, i.e. pressure to imitate other parties. In this chapter, we examine leadership primaries in the three main parties that have led coalition governments: Likud (seven cases between 1993 and 2012), the Labour Party (eight cases between 1992 and 2013) and Kadima (two cases, 2008 and 2012). Labour and Likud have origins in pre-state politics, while Kadima was a young party that was born out of a split in Likud in 2005. We also consider leadership primaries in Meretz (two cases, 2004 and 2008) – an alliance of left-wing social democratic parties established in the 1990s – and Jewish Home (one case, 2012), a right-wing religious party based on the veteran National Religious Party (NRP).

---

2   In order not to confuse the reader, we will always use the most recent name of the parties. Parties in Belgium tend to change their name from time to time.

This chapter compares leadership primaries in Belgium and Israel, starting with an analysis of the contexts and reasons for their adoption. We then discuss how primaries are conducted, both in terms of formal rules – for example selectorate, candidacy, voting system – and in practice (participation, competition). This is followed by an analysis of the consequences of primaries regarding the parties' electoral performance in general elections and membership recruitment.

Contexts and Rationales for Adopting Primary Elections

Before discussing the introduction of primary elections for party leadership selection, we must first clarify the role of party leaders in the Belgian and Israeli systems. A party leader in Belgium – usually called the party president or chairman – could be defined as the person formally empowered as such by party statutes (Pilet and Wauters, 2014). The position of party chairman is important and his power is considerable, in terms of policy determination and coordination, and government formation and selection of political personnel (Deschouwer, 2009). They are also, in most cases, the electoral leader of the party; but, unlike the case in many other Western democracies (including Israel), the function of party leader does not coincide with that of leader of the parliamentary party (or parties, as there are several assemblies in the federal state) (Pilet and Wauters, 2014). As Belgian parties apply an incompatibility rule between the position of party president and member of a government, also the role of leader of the party in government is not exercised by the party leader. When a party leader (chair/president) becomes a member of a government, he must in principle resign his position as party president. All in all, party leader is a very powerful position in Belgian politics, only trumped by the prime minister or regional government leader.

Unlike several countries where leadership positions (electoral, organisational, parliamentary) are divided between several individuals, party leaders in Israel combine these functions. They are the undisputed 'number one' in the party. They top the list of candidates for the Knesset elections; they are the recognised candidates for prime minister; and they usually have the authority to pick the politicians who will represent their party in the cabinet (Kenig and Barnea, 2009). Israeli party heads are often just called 'leaders', although the formal title in most parties is chairman (*yoshev rosh*).

In the 1970s and 1980s almost all Belgian and Israeli parties designated their leader at a party conference where delegates could vote. In Belgium only the Christian Democratic PSC, the predecessor of the Humanist Democratic Centre (CDH) organised at that time selections with the participation of all members. In Israel, a one-shot centre party, the Democratic Movement for Change (DMC), selected both its leader (as number 1) and candidates by using party primaries in 1977.

Yet, in both countries primaries started to become the norm for leadership selection during the 1990s (albeit in Israel only for the major parties). At the beginning of the 1990s, the radically transformed liberal party, Flemish Liberals and Democrats (VLD), was the first party in the Flanders region to introduce internal elections to designate the party leader. Soon, most others followed, and by the early 2000s all Belgian parties – except for the extreme right Flemish Interest/ Vlaams Belang (VB) – had introduced full members' vote to select their leader in their statutes. In Israel, the Labour Party adopted leadership primaries in 1991, followed by Likud in 1992, and these parties (usually perceived as contenders for leading coalitions) have continued to use primaries to select their leader. Other parties, such as Kadima, which was a government alternative for a while, and even some minor parties, also used primaries from time to time. The factors and motivations that explain these developments can be found at three levels: the political system, party system and intra-party (Barnea and Rahat, 2007).

Political System Factors

At the system level, interestingly, in both countries the adoption of primaries may be seen as an answer to a political crisis. In Belgium, party transformation – including the introduction of far-reaching participatory procedures in the 1990s – was a direct response to the crisis of the political system, particularly the breakthrough of the extreme right in 1991 ('Black Sunday'). These elections provided a shock, prompting parties and governments to consider change. New initiatives such as referenda, ombudsmen, government transparency and party renewal were high on the political agenda at that time. Traditional parties (often also involved in government) were faced with the erosion of their loyal voting base. In attempts to remedy this electoral dealignment, parties looked first and foremost to their own internal organisation (Deschouwer, 2004). By reforming and opening up their internal procedures, they hoped to bridge the widening gap between politicians and citizens and regain voters' confidence. However, owing to resistance by middle-level elites, it took some time to adopt these changes (see below).

In Israel, Labour's adoption of primaries can be seen as part of its attempt to rebuild its image as a reformist party after its failed attempt to oust the Likud government through coalition manoeuvres that are remembered in Israel political history as the 'stinking trick'. Beyond these events, other general developments at the system level explain reformist democratising moves. They can be understood as adaptations to the *Zeitgeist*, and more precisely to overall trends of democratisation, Americanisation and personalisation of Israeli politics and society. These, combined with the decline of parties and the overall decline of trust in them (and in politics in general), created fertile ground for the promotion of reform.

Interparty Factors

In Israel, what particularly ignited change at the interparty level was the replacement of the dominant party system with a competitive bipolar party system in 1977. In the context of the close competition between Labour and Likud, democratisation was perceived as a tool for achieving electoral leverage. Indeed, as could be expected (Cross and Blais, 2012), Labour and Likud both adopted party primaries after experiencing electoral defeat and while they were in opposition. Yet, the contagion was limited in Israel for reasons mentioned above, and mainly affected only the parties that saw their leaders as potential candidates for leading a coalition as a prime minister. In Belgium, on the other hand, contagion was more far-reaching and primaries became the norm, resisted only by Vlaams Belang (where the party council holds a vote and the preferred candidate is subsequently acclaimed by a party conference). At the beginning of the 1990s, OpenVLD set the political agenda in Flanders with a highly mediatised party renewal operation, including a new name; the attraction of senior party figures from other parties; and the introduction of leadership primaries (De Winter, 2000). As such, the radically transformed OpenVLD was the first in Flanders to introduce real internal elections (with polling booths in every local section). This radical transformation attracted much media attention, and the party also topped the opinion polls. The CD&V promptly followed OpenVLD's example by introducing leadership primaries in December 1993. The Flemish Socialist Party – Differently (sp.a), the French-speaking Socialist Party (PS) and the Flemish regionalists Volksunie – now New Flemish Alliance (N-VA) – followed a bit later (Pilet and Wauters, 2014).

Intra-Party Factors

The Belgian parties and the major Israeli parties seem to have in common the motivation of intra-party forces to adopt and preserve primaries as a way to somewhat neutralise mid-level activists and certain organised internal interests. That is, instead of facing active, dedicated delegates at party conferences, leaders now have more space to manoeuvre, facing largely passive, atomistic crowds of party members (Katz and Mair, 1995; Wauters, 2014). Therefore, party elites in both countries were the driving force in introducing leadership primaries. Especially in Belgium, middle-level party elites (either representatives of regional branches or social organisations) were rather reluctant about or even opposed to these reforms, as these would remove the power they could exert at party conferences or other occasions. Consequently, the link between electoral defeat and the introduction of primaries is less straightforward in Belgium (Wauters, 2014). A reinforced position of the party elite (following an electoral victory such as in the case of sp.a) or a further deep crisis rendering reform inevitable was needed in order to overcome resistance of middle-level elites and finally implement the reform.

In sum, the explanations for the timing of the adoption of primaries and also some of the motivations for adopting them share similarities, but are also somewhat different when we look at Belgium and Israel and also when focusing on particular parties within each system. Yet it seems that the introduction of the method can be explained in the creation of a new power equilibrium that seems to enjoy the aura of (direct) democracy and at the same time to serve the party leaders by weakening the middle-level elites (Mair, 1994).

The Primary Election Process

We will now focus on the election process itself. We first discuss the formal rules and then indicate how they function in practice.

Formal Rules

In terms of the *inclusiveness of the selectorate*, we can see that the selectorate comprised party members in all the leadership primary contests in Belgium and Israel (Table 5.1). No party has looser or weaker categories of affiliation that are allowed to vote in leadership primaries, and proposals to open the primaries to non-members were always rejected. Party membership in both countries must be obtained before the day of the primaries. Waiting periods ranged from a few weeks to more than a year, and changes sometimes reflected the interests of the contester(s) and sometimes the interest of the party, for example in building a long-term membership base rather than a short-term selectorate. It should be noted that in both countries members are the sole selectors of the party leader. This is different from systems used in some parties in other democracies (for example the Labour Party and the Conservatives in the UK) which mix selection by members with that of other selectorates, either in multistage selection or using an electoral college.

With regard to *candidacy*, requirements for party leadership in Belgium include support from party actors and seniority within the party. First, candidates for the leadership must be nominated by a coalition of party organs. In particular, leadership candidates must be supported by a number of provincial branches (which typically groups a few dozen local sections) and/or by a number of local sections (and even by a number of individual members in OpenVLD). The general trend (compared to the 1970s) is an upgrading of the role of local sections and of unorganised members in the certification process. It is striking that while in the past the support of one arrondissemental federation[3] was sufficient, nowadays a number of party sections at the same level must express their support (for instance at least 10 local sections from at least two provinces, who together count at least 5,000 members in sp.a). The rationale for this requirement is twofold: excluding irrelevant candidates without support in the party and ensuring a regional spread of the support of candidates. A new factor in comparison with the 1970s is

---

3 A terrirorial organisational level below the provincial level, typically involving about ten local communities.

seniority as a condition for leadership candidates. Whereas in the 1970s this was not mentioned in any of the party statutes, now most parties expect candidates for party presidency to have been a member for some time – ranging from two years in OpenVLD to five years in the PS (Pilet and Wauters, 2014). All in all, it seems that because of the increase in inclusiveness of the selectorate (see above), this filtering function, which is spread over a larger number of party actors, has become more important.

In Israel, candidacy rules are quite similar in the sense that they include a minimum length of membership before one can present her candidacy (usually from six months to three years), and having the support of a minimum number of party members and/or delegates. An additional requirement is payment of a candidacy fee of about €800–2,000. As can be expected from a territorially centralised political system, there are, in contrast to Belgium, no requirements for regional or local support. Like in Belgium, candidacy rules are basically intended to somewhat restrict the contest to serious candidates, a reasonable motivation due to the high price of managing primary contests.

The most common voting system in both countries is the two-round *runoff* system. In Belgium, the two frontrunners contest a second round if no candidate obtains an absolute majority, while in most Israeli parties (except for Meretz in 2008) a second round takes place only if no candidate obtains 40 per cent of the votes. It should be noted, however, that a second round was seldom used, as most of the time a candidate had already obtained the required majority in the first round. Only two of the 20 leadership primaries in Israel needed a second round, both in the Labour Party (2007 and 2011). In Belgium in only one of the 55 leadership primaries included in our analysis was a second round required to come up with a winner, that of the OpenVLD in 2009, when the runner-up in the first round, Alexander De Croo, eventually won in the second round.

The *plurality* system, which was often used earlier at Belgian party conferences, is now used only for selecting leaders of the CDH and N-VA. The Flemish Greens select their leader through elimination ballots with majority requirements, which is why their members must attend a party congress to vote (and therefore leadership selection in this party is not included in this analysis). Such a system cannot realistically be used if selection of the party leader is conducted in polling stations around the country.

As for the *timing*, in all three main Israeli parties (Likud, Labour and Kadima) leadership selection is expected to take place a few months before each general election. In case the party did not win the general election, Labour's constitution also allowed for selection to take place within 14 months after the general election. However, in some cases, party rules have been bent or changed to allow contests at other times: sometimes due to the wishes of a leader whose interests in keeping his position were served by the timing; and sometimes because challengers were strong enough to force an early contest. In fact, only eight out of 20 leadership primaries were conducted within six months of a general election. In Belgium (except for CDH), there are no formal requirements for the timing of leadership contests, but

Table 5.1 Main features of primary election processes in Belgium and Israel

Country	Party	Year	Selectorate	Candidacy	Voting system	Term (years)	Timing	Deselection
Belgium	CD&V	2013	Party members	Endorsed by at least one provincial, two regional or three local sections	Runoff	4	Not regulated	Not regulated
Belgium	CDH	2002	Party members	Party member for at least three years	Plurality	4 (max two terms)	In principle within six months of the national elections; in any case not six months before national or regional elections or during government formation process	Regulated (party bureau)
Belgium	sp.a	2002	Party members	Endorsed by at least 10 local sections from at least two provinces, who together count at least 5,000 members	Runoff	4	A few weeks before the quadrennial administrative conference	Regulated (party council)
Belgium	PS	2013	Party members	Party member for at least five years, and member of a party committee at arrondissemental level	Runoff	4	Not regulated	Regulated (party council)
Belgium	Open VLD	2011	Party members	Party member for at least two years; nominated by at least two regional sections from different provinces, at least one local section in every province or by 500 members	Runoff	4	Not regulated	Regulated (party council)

Country	Party	Year	Selectorate	Candidacy requirements	Electoral system	Term	Timing of contest	Spending limits
Belgium	MR	2005	Party members	Member of the General Council	Runoff	4 (max two terms)	Not regulated	Not regulated
Belgium	N-VA	2012	Party members	No conditions	Plurality	3	Not regulated	Not regulated
Israel	Likud	2012	Party members	Three years' membership; 500 signatures of party members in support of candidacy; NIS (New Israeli Shekel) 10,000	Runoff if no candidate wins 40% of votes in the first round	4–5[b]	At least six months before general election[b]	Regulated (party members)[c]
Israel	Kadima	2012	Party members	13 months' membership; 300 signatures of party members in support of candidacy; NIS 10,000	Runoff if no candidate wins 40% of votes in the first round	4–5[b]	2–3 months[b]	Regulated (party members)[c]
Israel	Labour Party	2012	Party members	Six months' membership[a]; signatures of 500 party members in support of candidacy; NIS 10,000	Runoff if no candidate wins 40% of votes in the first round	4–5[b]	Not regulated	Regulated (party members)[c]
Israel	Meretz	2008	Party members	n.a.	Runoff if no candidate wins 50% of votes in the first round (2008)	4–5[b]	Not regulated	Regulated (party members)[c]
Israel	Jewish Home	2012	Party members	One month's membership; signatures of 300 party members in support of candidacy	Runoff if no candidate wins 40% of votes in the first round	4–5[b]	Not regulated	Regulated (party members)[c]

Notes: [a] The formal constitutional rule was that the right to select and be selected was granted after a six-month wait, but for each selection event the actual waiting period was different. [b] There is no formal fixed term; terms are correlated to the legislative term, formally 4–5 years but typically (due to early elections) 3–4 years. In Labour, incumbent leaders may be challenged twice during the legislative term should the party not form a government. [c] Party leaders are removed when and if they lose the leadership contest to a challenger.

Sources: Pilet and Wauters, 2014; Kenig and Rahat, 2014.

in practice they are often held after general elections, and in any case preferably long before new general elections. In the event of unsuccessful elections, the party leader is usually replaced; after winning an election, it might be that the party leader enters a (coalition) government and then has to be replaced as leader of the party.

As for the leader's *length of term*, in Belgium and Israel it typically coincides with the parliamentary term – that is about four years.[4] In some Belgian parties, the number of terms is limited to two, meaning that, in principle, party presidents can serve for no more than eight years, but exceptions are possible and do indeed occur. In Israel there is no limit on party leaders' terms.

In Belgium, in contrast to selection rules, *deselection* procedures are not extensively described in party statutes (if at all). In those parties which do define procedures to deselect the party president, it is striking that in general the 'deselectorate' tends to be more exclusive than the selectorate (Pilet and Wauters, 2014). While leaders are generally selected by all party members, according to the party statutes they are deselected by party councils or executives ('party bureau'). The Israeli parties are different in this sense. There are no formally defined deselection rules. It is the norm, however, that party leaders can only be challenged and deselected through party primaries.

Functioning in Practice

On the basis of some indicators, we will now give an idea about how leadership primaries function in practice (Table 5.2). Concerning the *degree of participation*, average turnout rates in leadership primaries are much lower in Belgium (less than 39 per cent) than in Israel (56.5 per cent). This is remarkable as, due to the system of compulsory voting, turnout in Belgian parliamentary elections is about 90 per cent, among the highest in the world. Even when we put aside uncontested primaries, which are very common in Belgium, turnout is low (40.7 per cent on average for the 26 contested primaries). A possible explanation concerns the low levels of competitiveness that characterise even the contested Belgian primaries (Wauters, 2015), as will be demonstrated below. Yet there is also high variance within each country. The range in Belgium (14.5–67.6 per cent) is larger in comparison to Israel, where turnout ranges from 31.3 to 77.4 per cent. The differences at party level has to do not only with the level of competition but also, as the Israeli experience teaches us, with the administration of the contest, such as the number and geographic spread of polling stations (Rahat and Sher Hadar, 1999). And, as the Belgian experience teaches us, with mobilisation efforts by the party (Wauters, 2015).

---

4 Recently, a decision to extend the parliamentary term at the national level to five years has been taken in Belgium (in order to be congruent with the parliamentary term for the European and regional parliaments). It remains to be seen, however, whether and to what extent this principle decision will be kept in practice and whether and when parties will subsequently adapt the length of term for their party leader.

Table 5.2 Main features of primary election competitions in Belgium and Israel

Country	Party	Year	Turnout (%)	Number of candidates	Incumbent running	Incumbent winner	Winner's votes (%)	Runner-up's votes (%)	Women running	Women winner	Winner's age	National seniority
Belgium	CD&V	1993	36.0	1	Yes	Yes	88.4	n.a.	No	n.a.	39	Yes
Belgium	CD&V	1996	34.1	1	No	n.a.	92.5	n.a.	No	n.a.	47	Yes
Belgium	CD&V	1999	20.7	1	No	n.a.	96.4	n.a.	No	n.a.	48	Yes
Belgium	CD&V	2002	24.8	1	Yes	Yes	91.2	n.a.	No	n.a.	51	Yes
Belgium	CD&V	2003	23.1	1	No	n.a.	93.1	n.a.	No	n.a.	43	Yes
Belgium	CD&V	2004	50.6	3	No	n.a.	53.8	35.3	No	n.a.	46	Yes
Belgium	CD&V	2008	27.3	1	No	n.a.	96.6	n.a.	Yes	Yes	52	Yes[a]
Belgium	CD&V	2010	35.2	1	No	n.a.	98.7	n.a.	No	n.a.	36	Yes
Belgium	CD&V	2013	26.6	1	Yes	Yes	98.7	n.a.	No	n.a.	39	Yes
Belgium	CDH	1970	47.7	2	Yes	Yes	74.6	24.3	No	n.a.	63	Yes
Belgium	CDH	1972	53.4	4	No	n.a.	45.9	22.5	No	n.a.	36	Yes
Belgium	CDH	1977	29.3	1	Yes	Yes	92.8	n.a.	No	n.a.	42	Yes
Belgium	CDH	1979	39.4	2	No	n.a.	65.5	35.5	No	n.a.	60	Yes
Belgium	CDH	1982	36.6	3	No	n.a.	77.6	18.4	No	n.a.	38	No
Belgium	CDH	1988	40.7	2	Yes	Yes	60.7	39.3	No	n.a.	44	Yes
Belgium	CDH	1994	45.5	3	Yes	Yes	51.1	39.0	No	n.a.	50	Yes
Belgium	CDH	1996	63.9	3	No	n.a.	47.9	47.8	Yes	No	60	Yes
Belgium	CDH	1998	44.9	1	No	n.a.	90.2	n.a.	No	n.a.	50	Yes
Belgium	CDH	2003	67.6	4	Yes	Yes	62.6	28.3	Yes	Yes	42	Yes

Table 5.2 Main features of primary election competitions in Belgium and Israel continued

Country	Party	Year	Turnout (%)	Number of candidates	Incumbent running	Incumbent winner	Winner's votes (%)	Runner-up's votes (%)	Women running	Women winner	Winner's age	National seniority
Belgium	CDH	2009	36.6	2	Yes	Yes	87.1	12.9	Yes	Yes	48	Yes
Belgium	MR	1990	16.6	2	No	n.a.	80.7	29.3	Yes[b]	no	49 and 36	Yes (2)
Belgium	MR	1992	19.5	1	No	n.a.	93.7	n.a.	No	n.a.	50	Yes
Belgium	MR	1995	14.5	1	Yes	Yes	92.7	n.a.	No	n.a.	53	Yes
Belgium	MR	1997	40.0	1	No	n.a.	96.3	n.a.	No	n.a.	49	Yes
Belgium	MR	1999	37.0	1	No	n.a.	94.2	n.a.	No	n.a.	43	Yes
Belgium	MR	2003	31.0	1	No	n.a.	94.3	n.a.	No	n.a.	62	Yes
Belgium	MR	2004	50.7	1	Yes	Yes	93.1	n.a.	No	n.a.	46	Yes
Belgium	MR	2008	36.2	1	No	n.a.	90.8	n.a.	No	n.a.	50	Yes
Belgium	MR	2011	59.6	2	No	n.a.	54.8	45.2	No	n.a.	35	Yes
Belgium	OpenVLD	1993	43.8	2	Yes	Yes	62.5	28.7	No	n.a.	40	Yes
Belgium	OpenVLD	1995	34.7	11	No	n.a.	49.5	28.5	Yes	No	58	Yes
Belgium	OpenVLD	1997	40.6	15	Yes	No	52.1	27.5	No	n.a.	44	Yes
Belgium	OpenVLD	1999	26.7	9	No	n.a.	68.1	29.2	No	n.a.	45	Yes
Belgium	OpenVLD	2001	32.8	2	Yes	Yes	86.1	13.9	Yes	n.a.	47	Yes
Belgium	OpenVLD	2004	37.3	5	No	n.a.	50.5	38.3	Yes	No	40	Yes
Belgium	OpenVLD	2008	23.6	3	Yes	Yes	69.3	22.7	Yes	No	44	Yes
Belgium	OpenVLD 1st round	2009	30.7	3	No	n.a.	36.5	35.7	Yes	No	n.a.	n.a.

Country	Party	Year										
Belgium	OpenVLD 2nd round	2009	32.2	2	No	n.a.	54.9	45.1	No	n.a.	34	No
Belgium	OpenVLD	2012	30.7	2	No	n.a.	59.4	40.6	Yes	Yes	37	Yes
Belgium	PS	1999	38.7	4	No	n.a.	71.4	16.9	Yes	No	48	Yes
Belgium	PS	2003	35.0	1	Yes	Yes	93.9	n.a.	No	n.a.	52	Yes
Belgium	PS	2007	24.9	2	Yes	Yes	89.5	10.5	No	n.a.	56	Yes
Belgium	sp.a	1997	63.1	1	Yes	Yes	83,9	n.a.	No	n.a.	59	Yes
Belgium	sp.a	1999	48.9	1	No	n.a.	81,6	n.a.	No	n.a.	43	No
Belgium	sp.a	2001	56.4	1	Yes	Yes	82,5	n.a.	No	n.a.	45	No
Belgium	sp.a	2003	48.5	1	No	n.a.	95,5	n.a.	No	n.a.	49	Yes
Belgium	sp.a	2005	48.6	1	No	n.a.	93,4	n.a.	No	n.a.	50	Yes
Belgium	sp.a	2007	44.6	2	No	n.a.	66,4	32.8	Yes	Yes	32	Yes
Belgium	sp.a	2011	37.8	1	No	n.a.	96.7	n.a.	No	n.a.	42	Yes
Belgium	N-VA	2000	59.0	2	Yes	No	53.9	46.1	No	n.a.	51	Yes
Belgium	N-VA	2008	52.0	1	Yes	Yes	98.9	n.a.	No	n.a.	38	Yes
Belgium	N-VA	2011	57.6	1	Yes	Yes	99.4	n.a.	No	n.a.	41	Yes
Mean Belgium			39.2 (52)	2.4 (52)	42.3% (22/52)	90.9 (20/22)	77.9 (52)	30.6 (26)	23.1 (12/52)	41.7 (5/12)	46.3 (50)	92.2 (47/51)
Israel	Labour	1992	71.4	4	Yes	No	40.6	34.8	Yes	No	70	Yes
Israel	Labour	1997	69.2	4	No	n.a.	50.3	28.5	No	n.a.	55	Yes
Israel	Labour	2001	54.8	2	No	n.a.	51.2	47.3	No	n.a.	65	Yes
Israel	Labour	2002	60.0	3	Yes	No	53.5	38.3	No	n.a.	58	No
Israel	Labour	2005	63.9	3	Yes	No	42.3	40.0	No	n.a.	54	Yes
Israel	Labour 1st round	2007	65.2	5	Yes	No	35.6	30.6	No	n.a.	n.a.	Yes

Table 5.2 Main features of primary election competitions in Belgium and Israel concluded

Country	Party	Year	Turnout (%)	Number of candidates	Incumbent running	Incumbent winner	Winner's votes (%)	Runner-up's votes (%)	Women running	Women winner	Winner's age	National seniority
Israel	Labour 2nd round	2007	65.4	2	No	n.a.	51.2	47.8	No	n.a.	65	Yes
Israel	Labour 1st round	2011	66.0	4	No	n.a.	32.2	30.9	Yes	n.a.		Yes
Israel	Labour 2nd round	2011	62.1	2	No	n.a.	53.8	45.5	Yes	Yes	51	Yes
Israel	Labour	2013	52.3	2	Yes	No	58.5	41.5	Yes	No	53	Yes
Israel	Likud	1993	67.1	4	No	n.a.	52.1	26.3	No	n.a.	43	Yes
Israel	Likud	1999	31.3	2	Yes	Yes	81.7	18.3	No	n.a.	49	Yes
Israel	Likud	1999	34.8	3	No	n.a.	53.0	24.0	No	n.a.	71	Yes
Israel	Likud	2002	46.2	3	Yes	Yes	55.9	40.1	No	n.a.	73	Yes
Israel	Likud	2005	43.3	4	No	n.a.	44.6	33.1	No	n.a.	55	Yes
Israel	Likud	2007	39.3	3	Yes	Yes	72.4	23.3	No	n.a.	57	Yes
Israel	Likud	2012	50.4	2	Yes	Yes	77.0	23.0	No	n.a.	62	Yes
Israel	Kadima	2008	53.9	4	No	n.a.	43.1	42.0	Yes	Yes	50	Yes
Israel	Kadima	2012	42.2	2	Yes	No	61.9	37.1	Yes	No	63	Yes
Israel	Meretz	2004	77.4	3	No	n.a.	53.3	46.4	No	n.a.	56	Yes
Israel	Meretz	2008	72.8	3	No	n.a.	54.5	27.1	Yes	No	68	Yes
Israel	Jewish Home	2012	69.3	3	No	n.a.	67.1	32.6	No	n.a.	40	No
Israel Mean			57.2 (22) 56.5 (20)	3.2 (20)	50.0 (10/20)	40.0 (4/10)	54.0 (20)	33.3 (20)	30.0 (6/20)	33.3 (2/6)	57.9 (20)	90 (18/20)

Notes: [a] Seniority in the European Parliament. [b] A leadership contest in which teams of two candidates competed with each other; one person of the losing team was a woman.

Table 5.2 reveals a substantive difference in the *levels of competition* between Belgian and Israeli parties. In all respects, primaries in Israel are more competitive. First, all primaries in Israel involve two or more contestants (and more than three on average). Yet, as we can see, this does not mean that leadership primaries are less frequent than in Belgium, and thus the number of candidates is indeed a valid index for comparing the two countries. About half of Belgian primaries are uncontested (a single candidate is put before the members for approval or disapproval), which gives an average of 2.4 candidates, even though there are outliers such as competitions with 11 and 15 candidates. Second, the gap between winner and runner-up is generally larger in Belgian parties, 32 per cent)on average) compared to about 21 per cent in Israel.

Finally, incumbents' success rate in Belgium is much higher, about 91 per cent in comparison to only 40 per cent in Israel. This is true even if we look at the contested primaries in Belgium, where in 10 out of 12 cases incumbents won (83.3 per cent). A small part of the difference may stem from the fact that incumbents in Belgium refrain from competition more than their Israeli counterparts. Only 42.3 per cent of the primaries in Belgium involve incumbents, in comparison to 50 per cent in Israel. Belgian party leaders could possibly save themselves from defeat in some cases by not running, but it may be more plausible to point to the fact that Belgian party leaders who have taken up a government position can no longer remain leader (see above). Yet, we should be cautious about the low success rates for incumbents in Israel: this may not be a characteristic of Israeli primaries, but rather of one single party, Labour, in which all five leadership contests that involved the incumbent ended in their defeat.

This gap in the level of competitiveness might illuminate a difference in political culture. In Israel, parties do not conduct primaries when there is a single candidate, while in Belgium about half of the primaries included only one contestant. The Israeli notion is that there is no point bothering members in a non-competitive situation. If such a move was initiated, it might end in loss of legitimacy. This is not the case for Belgium, which may point to a more deeply grounded consensual culture. In line with the consociational tradition of symbolic mobilisation (Luther, 1999), it has historically been important for the bargaining position of elites to show their ability to mobilise supporters (an indication of the strength of their subculture); but at the same time their goal was not to challenge the elite's autonomy to make decisions. The introduction of primaries fits this tradition as they are, foremost, a means to present a good image of the party to the outside world without diminishing the party elite's power (Wauters, 2014). Thus, even if Belgium and Israel share institutional features of consensus democracy, their cultures at this time are quite different.

In both countries, *women* candidates took part only in a minority of the contests. The success rate for women candidates in those few contests in which they took part was, in Belgium, 41.7 per cent, compared to just 33 per cent in Israel. This success rate was lower than that of men. This seems to indicate that women's representation at the top level is still far from the ideal of gender equality, and that it will take many more years until progress made in women's politics in general will be pronounced at the top of the party. We should note, however, that the number of women party leaders (selected through primaries) in Belgium has risen enormously in recent years (Pilet and Wauters, 2014).

As for *age*, it is very interesting to note that Belgian winning candidates are on average 11 years younger than their Israeli counterparts (46.3 versus 57.9). This is even more fascinating if we remember that Israel's population is much younger than Belgium's. A partial explanation could be the incompatibility of senior government position and party leadership that exists in Belgium. While in Israel politicians can combine both functions, Belgian politicians often become party leader first before entering government, and then give up their mandate as leader once in government. The average age of government ministers in the Belgian postwar period is 50.7 (Dumont et al., 2009), which is older than Belgian party leaders but still much younger than Israeli party leaders. Hence, this incompatibility rule can only provide a partial explanation for the difference.

Yet, at the same time, it seems that the *political background* of the selected leaders is quite similar in the sense that almost all of them have some background in national politics. It should be stressed that in Israel, even the two selected leaders with no 'national seniority' had a background that made them prominent on the national scene: one was a military general and was later elected mayor of the country's third largest city, while the second headed a semi-official organisation of settlements in the occupied territories. In Belgium, on three occasions a candidate without parliamentary experience has been selected in party leadership primaries: OpenVLD in 2009; sp.a in 1999 (re-elected as party leader in 2002 still without a parliamentary mandate); and CDH in 1982. These were all cases in which the party was in deep crisis and was hoping to make a fresh start by launching a new, not well-known face. Although these candidates had no parliamentary experience, they were asked to stand and were backed either by the party elite itself (sp.a) or by senior party figures unhappy with the current leadership (OpenVLD and CDH). When asked by the elite, the newcomer was the only candidate and very easily obtained the position of party leader. For those inexperienced leaders challenging the elite, selection was tougher, and even a second round was needed in OpenVLD. All candidates without parliamentary experience had relevant experience from other fields, but were not necessarily known by the general public. For example, they were active in advertising (sp.a), as a head of ministerial staff (CDH) and running his own business while having a well-known father active in national politics (OpenVLD).

Political Consequences on Parties

It is difficult to connect the *electoral performances of the parties in general elections* to the fact that their leader was selected through primaries because there are many other variables that affect voter's behaviour. It is nevertheless undeniable that Belgian parties like to spotlight their internal democratic character to the voters. Internal democratic functioning is clearly used as an element of electoral competition between parties (Punnett, 1992), especially in the early days following its introduction. In communicating the results of their internal democratic procedures, parties always exaggerate how well they functioned (Wauters, 2009). In 1993, when OpenVLD introduced party leadership elections, the party spokesman, Guy Vanhengel, wrote:

> Last month, Frank Vandenbroucke was elected party leader of sp.a. He obtained 294 of the 394 expressed votes. Only 0.3 per cent of the 98,000 sp.a members were entitled to vote. We, as party of the citizen, on the contrary, invite all the 80,000 OpenVLD members to express their vote. [cited in Wauters, 2009]

The question arises whether the introduction of internal democratic procedures has really produced any effect in electoral terms. A condition for such an electoral effect is voters' awareness of these intra-party democratic procedures. As the internal functioning of parties often remains hidden from the general public, this condition seems not to be met. This is confirmed by a survey of the entire Flemish population, which proved that most voters could not distinguish between parties using leadership primaries and parties not using them (Wauters, 2009).

In the case of the Israeli Labour party, it can be argued that its adoption of primaries for selecting its leader and candidates in 1992 contributed the party's attempt to create an image of a renewed party, and thus helped it win the elections. The fact that the primaries enabled the highly popular Yitzhak Rabin to win the intraparty leadership contest also contributed to this victory. This might also be the case for Benjamin Netanyahu's first victory in the first primaries conducted by Likud (1993). Yet, in the long run, leadership primaries seem to contribute their fair share to the weakening of the parties that use them, as they enhance the process of centralised personalisation of politics (Rahat and Sheafer, 2007; Balmas et al. 2014). While primaries may look like a method that would democratically legitimise leaders and strengthen their position, in comparison to the past, leaders are actually challenged more frequently and also lose their position more frequently. However, this appears not to be the case in Belgium, where the party elite (including the leader) has firmly kept control of the selection process in its own hands.

The adoption of leadership primaries may also affect the nature of *membership recruitment*. In Israel, we usually witnessed wide recruitment campaigns before the contests (Since 2005 Likud's regulations allows only relatively veteran members, i.e. with tenure of 16 months or more, to participate in the selection, but Likud did not always follow this rule). Thousands of new members were recruited, sometimes doubling and even tripling party membership. Once the leadership contest was over, many left the parties simply by not renewing their subscriptions. The size of the selectorates in the 20 Israeli primaries contests ranged from about 10,000 to 305,000, with an average of about 115,000 members. Recruitment campaigns were part of the game from the time that Israeli primaries were adopted. The candidates themselves made efforts to recruit as many supporters as they could. Other actors – heads of interest groups, local activists and vote contractors – also took part in the game, registering members and offering their support to candidates in return for defending/promoting their interests. The number of party members indeed rose temporarily as a result of recruitment campaigns. Yet in the long run we can see a decline in party membership, even when we look only at the seasonal peaks that followed the campaigns (Kenig et al., 2013).

In Belgium, in contrast, there have never been massive membership recruitment campaigns before primaries, in large part because competitiveness in leadership primaries is generally low. When there is only a single candidate, or a senior candidate who has only to struggle with some minor candidate(s), the risk of losing the contest is low, and hence there is simply no incentive to set up large membership registration campaigns. Indeed, bending declining membership figures has been one of the goals when adopting primaries. Yet, attracting new members was only a subordinate goal and definitely not the central driving force behind their introduction (Wauters, 2014).

The introduction of leadership primaries has not been able to stop the gradual decline in membership figures in Belgium. In 1990, at the eve of the wave of the adoption of primaries, Belgian parties in total counted 543,023 members. The most recent numbers (2012) indicate that there are now only 388,579 party members (Van Haute, 2013). This means a decrease of about 30 per cent between 1990 and 2012 despite the introduction of leadership primaries, which were expected to attract new members and stop the decline.

Conclusion

The political systems of Belgium and Israel share many features, such as a multiparty PR system that reflects its heterogeneous societies and ensures their political representation. Therefore, we expected to find similarities in the rules and use of leadership primaries in both countries. Our comparative analysis reveals that while the formal rules of primaries and the reasons for their adoption are indeed similar for both countries, there are some distinct differences in the practice of primaries and in their political consequences.

Parties in both countries introduced primaries when they were in crisis (electoral defeat or being in opposition functioned as triggers to consider party renewal). Their selectorates include members only; they use a runoff system in which a second round is only seldom used; candidacy rules in both countries include support from party actors and a minimum tenure as a party member; and, when selected, party leaders have, in most cases, prior political experience at the national level.

Despite these similarities, we also discovered some marked differences. First of all, while leadership primaries are used by all Belgian parties expect one, in

Israel they are almost all confined to the major parties with ambitions to lead the government. A general contagion effect as in Belgium did not take place. A second difference lies in the degree of competitiveness. Israeli primaries are much more competitive than Belgian ones. Israeli party primaries have more (viable) candidates, that win closer shares of the vote. Belgian parties often only present a single candidate to the selectors, who can only approve or disapprove the candidate. Consequently, participation rates in Belgian (non-competitive) primaries are much lower than in Israel. Thirdly, there are differences in the profile of the selected party leaders: in Belgium they are generally about 10 years younger, and women are selected more frequently than in Israel. Finally, the effect on membership numbers is very pronounced in Israel, but only in the short term due to the widespread practice of instant membership. In both countries, decline in membership numbers continued after the adoption of primaries.

We can point to two major explanations for these differences: the position of the party leader and the consociational tradition. In Israel, leadership of a major party and prime ministership is a normal combination, while in Belgium these two functions are incompatible. Hence, party members selecting a leader are at the same time selecting a government leader in Israel. Consequently, this position is more difficult to reach, which could explain why party leaders in Israel tend to be older and why the gender gap is more pronounced in the Israeli case. These differences may also account for the highest levels of participation and competition that were found in Israel. The stakes of party primaries in Israel are higher because they are, many times, about the selection of the candidate for prime ministership. A second explanation refers to the consociational tradition that has historically secured stability in these divided societies. This legacy appears to be more pronounced in Belgium, where parties operate according to one of the basic principles of consociationalism: showing their ability to mobilise a large group of supporters, while at the same time keeping power in their own hands. In Israel, consociationalism has declined (Hazan, 2000) and hence primaries are more like competitive elections in which incumbents are challenged, and often even lose the contest.

Chapter 6
Democratising Party Leadership Selection in Japan and Taiwan

Yohei Narita, Ryo Nakai and Keiichi Kubo[*]

Introduction

As interest in the causes and consequences of party primaries has been growing in the literature, there have been various studies on this topic for East Asian cases such as Japan and Taiwan. However, most of these studies focus on a single country, and few analyses have been conducted from a comparative perspective. Furthermore, most studies in the literature focus on specific parties or periods, and comprehensive data on primaries for leadership selection has not been gathered and presented systematically. In order to fill the gap, therefore, this chapter attempts to make a comparative analysis of Japan and Taiwan based on a newly constructed dataset[1] covering all major parties that have used primaries for leadership selection.[2] The chapter consists of four parts.

The first section, by way of introduction, addresses the political context in the two countries, focusing on their political and party systems. The second section then examines the rationales for adopting the primary at individual party level. The third section analyses and explores the primary processes as a whole, taking into account both the rules governing internal elections and their actual functioning.

---

[*] The present chapter is based on findings of the research project 'Data collection and comparative analysis of the primary in democratic countries', funded by Waseda University, Research Grant for Special Project A (2012A-501). We would like to express our gratitude for their generous assistance. We would also like to thank Professor Mitsutoyo Matsumoto, Mr Yuki Tsuruzono and Mr Tsun-yen Wang for their valuable assistance in the case of Taiwan.

1 The empirical data on primaries presented here is based on the dataset of leadership selection of major political parties in Japan and Taiwan that we constructed using primary sources. The sources will not be presented here, but the whole dataset with information on the relevant sources is available on Keiichi Kubo's personal website: www.k-kubo.jp/data.

2 This chapter adopts the definition of primary elections described in Chapters 1 and 2 of this volume. As we discuss below, in Japan primary elections are often part of a mixed method of selection which also entails a second phase of voting by the incumbent parliamentarians (and other party elites) to select the party leader. We use the term 'internal election' to refer to the entire election process, of which the primary election can be part and can constitute one of the phases of selection.

The fourth section then examines the impact of the primary on political parties, focusing on party support among the general public and membership recruitment. We conclude with a brief recapitulation of the main findings.

The Political Context: Political and Party Systems

Japan and Taiwan differ markedly in terms of political system, but share commonalities in terms of party system. This section will describe these commonalities and differences, and examine how they might affect the rationales for the adoption of primary elections and various aspects of their implementation.

Political System

Japan has adopted the bicameral parliamentary system, while Taiwan uses the semi-presidential system.[3] In Japan, the chief executive is the prime minister, and his cabinet is responsible to the Diet. If the House of Representative (lower house) adopts a vote of no confidence in the cabinet, it has to resign, unless the lower house is dissolved by decision of the cabinet.[4] The upper house, the House of Councillors, cannot be dissolved by the cabinet, and its members serve a fixed term of six years. By contrast, in Taiwan, executive power is shared by the president, who is directly elected by the people, and the president of the Executive Yuan (prime minister), who is appointed by the president (with the consent of parliament, the Legislative Yuan) but is responsible to the Legislative Yuan. Even though the Executive Yuan is formally 'the highest administrative organ of the State' according to the constitution, the prime minister practically acts as chief of the president's administrative team (Matsumoto, 2013). Although the prime minister must resign if the Legislative Yuan passes a motion of no confidence against him, he can petition the president to dissolve parliament in these cases.[5]

Does this difference have any impact on the subject of the present chapter? As discussed below, as for the rationale for adoption of primaries, Japan and Taiwan demonstrate the importance of similar factors. As for the participation and competitiveness of the primary, there is no clear-cut difference between Japan and Taiwan: turnout and competitiveness vary significantly across the cases, but

---

   3   The local Taiwanese often call this a 'dual leadership system' (*shuang shouzhang zhi*) (Wu, 2007, p. 214).

   4   More precisely, the constitution of Japan stipulates that the emperor dissolves the House of Representatives 'with the advice and approval of the Cabinet'. However, the emperor does not play a politically active role: he can dissolve the House of Representatives only on the basis of a Cabinet decision, and he never rejects its decision or actively seek its approval. Therefore, one can safely say that the lower house is dissolved by decision of the cabinet.

   5   These rules were introduced after the amendment of the constitution in 1997.

the variance is not correlated with country. Thus, the system-level difference discussed here does not appear to have an impact on these aspects of the primary.

One aspect of the primary that may be affected by the political system is the formal rules of the primary. The Japanese political parties tend to give more weight to the preferences of the party elites (especially incumbent parliamentarians) and reduce the impact of voting by the ordinary members. By contrast, the Taiwanese parties have adopted a 'one man one vote' (OMOV) system, giving no privileged status to the elite. This difference may well be affected by the different selection methods of the chief executive in the two countries.

Party System

Japan and Taiwan share some commonalities regarding party system. First, both countries had a dominant conservative party after WWII. While Japan was institutionally under a democratic system, it was dominated by the Liberal Democratic Party (LDP), which was established in 1955 and remained in power for several decades until 1993. Taiwan had been under a one-party dictatorship of the Nationalist Party (Kuomintang, KMT) since it lost the civil war on mainland China and moved its central government to Taiwan in 1949. Even after martial law was lifted in 1987 and full multiparty elections were held at the beginning of the 1990s, the KMT remained in power until 2000, when the major opposition party, the Democratic Progressive Party (DPP), won the presidential elections.

Second, in both countries, party system change (that is, the end of the dominant party system) was triggered by a split in the dominant party. In Japan, one reformist faction abandoned the LDP and established a new party on the eve of the 1993 general election, which led to the formation of an eight-party coalition government to oust the LDP from power. In Taiwan, when Lien Chan was nominated as the KMT's presidential candidate, James Soong Chu-yu – a powerful and popular politician within the party – decided to run as an independent candidate in the 2000 presidential elections. This led to a split in the KMT votes and victory for Chen Shui-bian of the DPP.

Third, both countries now have a system with two major parties. In Japan, during the era of LDP dominance, the Social Democratic Party of Japan (SDPJ) was the main opposition party,[6] but it was too weak to defeat the LDP. After the LDP split in 1993, attempts were made to create a more viable party against the original LDP, which led to the establishment of the New Frontier Party (NFP). Although the NFP was rather short-lived and soon split into several smaller groups, some of them – along with other ex-LDP members and those who left

---

6 The Japanese name is *Nihon shakaito*, literally Socialist Party of Japan, and indeed some scholars use the term SPJ or JSP – Japanese Socialist Party – as its English translation. However, at its founding convention it was decided that the English name should be the Social Democratic Party of Japan (SDPJ, 1986, p. 17), so here we follow the official terminology and use the abbreviation SDPJ.

the SDPJ – founded the Democratic Party of Japan (DPJ) in 1998. The DPJ kept expanding and finally took power after winning the elections in 2009. In Taiwan, the DPP (founded in 1986) gradually grew to emerge as a viable rival to the KMT, and won the presidency in the 2000 and 2004 elections.

This similarity in terms of party system seems to explain similar tendencies observed in the two countries regarding primary elections. The factors behind their adoption are associated with the types of political party. In both Japan and Taiwan the dominant party (the LDP and the KMT) adopted the primary after electoral defeat and due to the initiative of the less powerful leaders within the party. The challenger parties – those that have challenged the dominant 'conservative' party (that is, the SDPJ, NFP and DPJ in Japan and the DPP in Taiwan) – adopted it to present a better public image to attract votes from various segments of society. As for the formal rules, the challenger parties tend to adopt more democratic rules than the dominant conservative party, as they tend to be more liberal in value orientation. As for actual implementation, it is these challenger parties that allow women to be selected as chairpersons. These similar tendencies will be examined in the following sections.

Contexts and Rationales for Adopting Primary Elections

In analysing factors that explain organisational reforms to grant ordinary party members greater influence in the choice of leader, Cross and Blais (2012) demonstrate that these kinds of reform tend to be adopted by parties that are (1) in the aftermath of the electoral setback, (2) in opposition, (3) newly established. They also observe a strong 'contagion effect' within party systems. These factors also seem important in the case of Japan and Taiwan.

Electoral Setback

For the two dominant parties in Japan and Taiwan in particular, electoral defeat was a crucial factor which compelled the parties to introduce primaries for leadership selection. As for the LDP, the move to adopt the primary was initiated after the 1976 elections, which were considered a defeat because the party could not achieve an outright majority in parliament due to the Lockheed bribery scandals. After the elections, the outgoing party president, Takeo Miki, proposed reforms to adopt the primary in the leadership selection process to reduce the influence of factionalism and tackle the sources of corruption (Tsurutani, 1980; Ishikawa, 1995, p. 142). Thus the rules were changed in April 1977 and the first primary was conducted in 1978. As for the KMT, its party elite were reluctant to introduce the primary in the 1990s because of bitter experience of its earlier use for candidate selection,[7]

---

7 In 1989, the KMT decided to adopt a closed party primary to select candidates for the Legislative Yuan elections, but its results were disastrous for the party as it led to

but they then introduced the primary for leadership selection in 2001. Clearly, the shock of defeat in the 2000 presidential election played a critical role in pushing the KMT to adopt the primary as an election machine (Hsieh, 2010; Matsumoto, 2010). Electoral defeat was also an important factor for the SDPJ, which decided to adopt the primary after 'defeat' in the upper house elections in July 1977.

Opposition and Newly Established Parties

These two factors tend to be correlated: newly established parties are typically in opposition, and they tend to adopt primary elections. In Japan, the NFP and DPJ decided to adopt primaries for leadership selection soon after their foundation. In Taiwan, the DPP decided to use the primary for candidate selection soon after foundation, and some years later for leadership selection. In the context of single-party dominance, one of the main purposes of the adoption of the primary by newly established opposition parties was to present a better, 'open and democratic' public image to attract votes against the elite-dominated ruling party.

Contagion Effect

This effect within the party system is also observed: when one party conducts a primary, it sometimes compels others in the party system to also adopt it. A typical example here is the NFP in 1995, which was forced to adopt the primary to compete with its main rival, the LDP. Indeed, one MP told the NFP party caucus in August 1995 that the party should have clear rules to select its leader 'because the attention will be concentrated on the LDP party president elections in August and September'.[8]

In addition to the four factors discussed above, we observed one important internal factor, namely the influence of the *less powerful* leaders within the party. Especially within the dominant parties in Japan and Taiwan, the leadership selection used to be dominated by a small circle of the top party elites. Those who are dominant in these elites have no incentive to introduce primary elections because the status quo fits their interests. The less powerful leaders, on the other hand, have much smaller chances of being selected as party leader, and therefore have a greater incentive to introduce primaries in order to improve their position vis-à-vis the more powerful elite or to reduce the latter's influence. Takeo Miki, who advocated primaries in the LDP in the 1970s, was leader of a smaller faction. In the KMT, the adoption of the primary to select the party leadership was first advocated by Ma Ying-jeou, who was much younger than Lien Chen, the leader

---

the severe division and conflict within the party and the weakened party discipline (Baum and Robinson, 1999; Wu, 2001). Thus, the KMT soon abandoned the pure closed primary system and adopted a mixed primary in which the results of ordinary member voting counted for 50 per cent and cadre vote for the other 50 (Fell, 2012, p. 94). In 1993, the KMT completely abandoned the primary.

8   *Asahi Shinbun*, 19 August 1995.

at that time, but was already quite popular among the general public as the mayor of Taipei (Matsumoto, 2010). This intra-party factor is also important for some challenger parties. In the NFP, advocates of the open primary had the intention to limit and reduce the influence of Ichiro Ozawa, a dominant figure within the party (Uekami, 2011b, p. 88). In the DPP, the emergence of several new, less powerful factions in the 1990s led to the increased fluidity of intra-party power relations between the factions, which resulted in the adoption of the primary as a compromise (Hsu and Chen, 2007).

This section has pointed out the importance of five factors in the adoption of primaries: electoral setback; status of the opposition; 'newness' of the party; the 'contagion effect' within party systems; and the influence of the less powerful leaders within the party. This brief comparative analysis suggests that the rationale deemed important for the adoption of primary elections depends on the type of political party. Both in Japan and Taiwan, the main rationale for the dominant conservative parties (the LDP and the KMT) was electoral defeat, combined with the influence of the less powerful leaders within the parties. The latter may be strengthened by the former: the less powerful leaders are not so influential under normal circumstances, but their influence may be increased instantly due to electoral setback, which tends to weaken the authority of the mainstream leaders. In contrast, key factors for challenger parties seem to be their oppositional status and newness, which compel them to adopt primaries to demonstrate that they are more open and democratic. In terms of the connection between rationales and political party, therefore, Japan and Taiwan appear remarkably similar. As discussed above, this similarity seems to be due to the similar party system in the two countries.

The Primary Election Process

This section analyses the main features of the primary in Japan and Taiwan. First, we examine the formal rules on internal elections for leadership selection, and then analyse aspects of the actual implementation in the two countries.

Formal Rules for Internal Elections

These demonstrate a considerable difference between Japan and Taiwan. As for the two parties in Taiwan, the formal rules are fairly simple (see Table 6.1). Here both parties adopted a simple closed primary in which only party members can vote to select a leadership based on majoritarian principles. There are only a few minor differences between the two parties. One difference concerns the type of electoral system: the KMT uses the two-round system, while the DPP uses simple plurality. This difference may lead to the lower number of candidates for primaries in the KMT (see Table 6.2), as this system requires the candidate to gain an outright majority to win. Another difference is in the candidacy criteria. In the KMT, only party members who have served as members of the Central Committee or Central Standing Committee, with the signature of more than 3 per cent of total members, can run for primary selection. In contrast, in the DPP, anyone who held party membership for more than one year could run for a primary until 2013, when this requirement was changed to two years. Although the candidacy criteria in the DPP thus became slightly tougher, the DPP still imposes virtually almost no restrictions, whereas the KMT only allows the party elite to run for primaries. Therefore, one can say that the challenger party have adopted more democratic rules than the dominant party regarding candidacy criteria.

By contrast, the rules governing internal elections in Japan are extremely complicated and vary considerably (see Table 6.1), so here we will just enumerate some general features. First, concerning candidacy, most parties require the candidate to be an incumbent MP and to receive a certain number of recommendations by other incumbents. This allows only the party elite to enter the chairmanship race. Thus, Japanese parties generally tend to allow for the domination of the elite. The only exception to this tendency is the SDPJ, which allows any party member to stand if they have been a member for at least five years and receive recommendations from more than 100 party members. Here again, the challenger parties seem to be more open, at least formally, to those outside the central elite, and thus more democratic.

Second, all Japanese political parties examined here have adopted a two-round electoral system, and in most cases the primary is conducted in the first round but not in the second. In the overwhelming majority of cases, only incumbent MPs are allowed vote in the runoff elections. This means that the party elite can overturn the results of the primary in second-round voting. Internal elections in the LDP held in September 2012 demonstrated that this can indeed happen: Shigeru Ishiba gained the largest number of votes in the first-round elections, but Shinzo Abe won the runoff elections as a majority of the MPs voted for him.

Third, the two major parties in Japan (the LDP and the DPJ) tend to adopt a mixed system for the first round, in which some points are distributed to the candidates based on the results of the closed primary and other points are allocated based on the votes of the incumbent MPs. One vote cast by an ordinary member counts for much less: for example, 1 point for every 10,000 votes in the primary (as in LDP internal elections in 1995 and 1999) compared to one vote cast by an incumbent MP (usually one MP, one point). This system gives significant room for manoeuvre to limit the impact of the primary by changing the *share* of the points distributed via the primary in the first round. The actual share of the points determined by the primary in the total points in the first-round elections varies from 20 to 60 per cent in the LDP after 1991 and is around 20–30 per cent for the DPJ. However, this tendency is not shared by other challenger parties. The SDPJ adopted a simple closed primary system: 'one man one vote'. The NFP adopted a quasi-open primary in which anybody above 18 years old and paying the required fee (1,000 yen, or around US$10 as of December 1995) can participate in the primary. Therefore, here again the challenger parties tend to be more willing to give power to ordinary members or citizens.

Table 6.1 Main features of primary election processes in Japan and Taiwan

Country	Party	Year	Selectorate	Candidacy	Voting system	Timing	Deselection
Japan	LDP	1978	Mixed: members[a] and MPs	Party member; MP; recommendation by 20 MPs from the party	Runoff: first round by primary; second round by MPs only	Not regulated	Not regulated
Japan	LDP	1982	Mixed: members[b] and MPs	Party member; MP; recommendation by 50 MPs from the party	Runoff: first round by primary;[c] second round (fought by the leading three candidates) by MPs only	Not regulated	Not regulated
Japan	LDP	1991–99	Mixed: members[d] and MPs	Party member; MP; recommendation by 30 MPs from the party	Runoff: first round by mixed system;[e] second round by MPs only	Not regulated	Not regulated
Japan	LDP	2001	Mixed: members[d] and MPs	Party member; MP; recommendation by 20 MPs from the party	Runoff: first round by mixed system;[f] second round by MPs only	Not regulated	Not regulated
Japan	LDP	2003–12	Mixed: members[d] and MPs	Party member; MP; recommendation by 20 MPs from the party	Runoff: first round with mixed system;[g] second round by MPs only	Not regulated	Not regulated
Japan	SDPJ	1978–96	Members	Party member for at least five years; recommendation of party prefectural headquarter or 100 members	Runoff	Not regulated	Not regulated
Japan	NFP	1995	Mixed: members; anybody paying the 1,000 yen fee; MPs	Party member; MP; recommendation by 20 MPs from the party	Runoff: first round by primary; second round by MPs only	Not regulated	Not regulated

Japan	DPJ	2002	Mixed: members and supporters; local councillors; party-approved parliamentary candidates for the next elections; MPs	Party member; MP; recommendation by 20 MPs from the party	Runoff: first round by mixed system;[h] second round by MPs, party-approved candidates and representatives of prefectural branches	Not regulated	Not regulated
Japan	DPJ	2010	Mixed: members and supporters; local councillors; party-approved parliamentary candidates for the next elections; MPs	Party member; MP; recommendation by 20 MPs from the party	Runoff: first round by mixed system;[i] second round by MPs	Not regulated	Not regulated
Japan	DPJ	2012	Mixed: members and supporters; local councillors; party-approved parliamentary candidates for the next elections; MPs	Party member; MP; recommendation by 20 MPs from the party	Runoff: first round by mixed system;[j] second round by MPs and party-approved candidates	Not regulated	Not regulated
Taiwan	KMT	2000–2014	Members	Party member who have served on the Central Committee or the Central Standing Committee; support by signatures of 3% of total membership	Runoff	Not regulated	Not regulated
Taiwan	DPP	1998–2013	Members for at least one year	Party member for at least one year	Plurality	Not regulated	Not regulated
Taiwan	DPP	2013–14	Members for at least two years	Party member for at least two years	Plurality	Not regulated	Not regulated

Notes: For Notes, see following page.

Notes: [a] Party members, party supporters and members of the People's Political Association (PPA: the LDP's political funding organization) who pay more than 10,000 yen annually to the party.
[b] Party members, supporters and members of the PPA, paying membership fees for two consecutive years.
[c] Primary is held only when there are more than four candidates or, in case of only two or three candidates, if one-third of the party's MPs request the primary and two-thirds of all MPs and local councillors approve the request.
[d] Party members, supporters and members of the PPA, paying membership fees for three consecutive years (in 1996, it was rephrased into 'in the last two years before the year of party-president elections').
[e] Each MP has one vote, while results of the voting by party members and supporters are translated into some votes (1–4) at prefectural level.
[f] Each MP has one vote, with three votes allocated to each prefecture; the headquarters of each prefecture can decide whether to hold a primary to determine the winner of the votes allocated to the prefecture.
[g] Each MP has one vote, while 300 votes are allocated to prefectures (three votes are allocated to each of the 47 prefectures; in addition, 159 votes are allocated to prefectures based on the D'Hondt method); within each prefecture, the number of votes won by candidates is determined according to voting by party members and supporters, based on the D'Hondt method.
[h] Each MP has two votes; each party-approved candidate has one; 47 votes are distributed to candidates based on the voting of local councillors; 320 votes are distributed to candidates based on the voting of party members and party supporters.
[i] Each MP has two votes; each party-approved candidate has one; 100 votes are distributed to candidates based on the voting of local councillors; one vote is allocated to each electoral district, which is distributed to the candidates by plurality based on the voting of party members and supporters.
[j] Each MP has two votes; each party-approved candidate has one; 141 votes are distributed to candidates based on the voting of local councillors; 409 votes are allocated to the prefectures, which are distributed to the candidates by the D'Hondt method based on the voting of party members and supporters within the prefecture.

Participation and Competitiveness

Let us now turn to features of the actual implementation of primaries. As regards the degree of participation, turnout varies considerably across the cases, as shown in Table 6.2. There is no clear pattern associated with the type of party or the country: there is a significant variance both within a party and within a country. For example, turnout for LDP primaries varies from 46.6 per cent in 2009 to 93.2 per cent in 1982. For the DPP it varies from 20 per cent in 2006 to 68.9 per cent in 2012, even when considering competitive (multi-candidate) cases only. Therefore, turnout seems to be determined mostly by the political context of each primary.

In order to demonstrate competitiveness, Table 6.2 presents the number of candidates and the share of votes of the two leading candidates. It shows that competitiveness also varies significantly across the cases. Why are some primaries competitive while others are not? One might think that the presence or absence of the incumbent candidate has an effect. An incumbent seeking re-election in a primary might enjoy considerable advantages vis-à-vis other candidates, which may lead to a lower degree of competition. One can see this impact by comparing the average margin between the first and second candidates in the primaries. Out of a total 28 *competitive* primaries, 10 included incumbent candidates, and the average margin between winner and runner-up is 43.1 percentage points, while that of primaries without incumbents is 36.9 per cent. Thus, on average, the margin is indeed wider (that is, the primary is *less* competitive) when there is an incumbent candidate. However, whether or not this difference is statistically significant should be examined more rigorously, and is outside the scope of this chapter. The data in Table 6.2 also suggests that incumbents tend to win chairmanship races: incumbent candidates won nine out of 10 competitive primaries.

Table 6.2 also clearly demonstrates that intra-party competition is still dominated by elderly, male and experienced politicians both in Japan and Taiwan. The average age of the winner is around 60 years in both countries, and women contested only seven primaries out of a total 34. There were only four cases in which female candidates won the election – and the same candidate in Taiwan, Tsai Ing-wen, won in three out of the four primaries. In other words, in six major political parties in Japan and Taiwan, there have been only two women chairpersons elected internally. As for seniority, out of the 34 cases, there was only one in which the winner did not hold a political position at national level,[9] although this is quite normal in the case of Japan as candidates in most parties there must be incumbent MPs. One can point out that the challenger parties tend to be more liberal: all cases of the election of female candidates and candidates with no experience at national level took place in the challenger parties, namely the SDPJ in Japan and the DPP in Taiwan.

---

9   A 'political position at national level' means cabinet minister or member of the Diet in Japan; president, vice president, chief secretary for the president, or members of the Executive or Legislative Yuan in Taiwan.

Table 6.2 Main features of primary election competitions in Japan and Taiwan

Country	Party	Year	Turnout (%)	Number of candidates	Incumbent running	Incumbent winner	Winner's votes (%)	Runner-up's votes (%)	Women running	Women winner	Winner's age	National seniority
Japan	LDP	1978	87.4	4	Yes	No	42.0	36.1	No	n.a.	68	Yes
Japan	LDP	1982	93.2	4	No	n.a.	57.6	27.3	No	n.a.	64	Yes
Japan	LDP	1991	55.0	3	No	n.a.	49.5	32.5	No	n.a.	72	Yes
Japan	LDP	1995	53.7	2	No	n.a.	81.1	18.9	No	n.a.	58	Yes
Japan	LDP	1999	49.3	3	Yes	Yes	67.9	19.9	No	n.a.	62	Yes
Japan	LDP	2001	61.5[a]	4	No	n.a.	58.0	30.2	No	n.a.	59	Yes
Japan	LDP	2003	69.3	4	Yes	Yes	57.3	24.8	No	n.a.	61	Yes
Japan	LDP	2006	61.5	3	No	n.a.	60.2	25.0	No	n.a.	51	Yes
Japan	LDP	2008	53.9	5	No	n.a.	66.5	12.0	Yes	No	68	Yes
Japan	LDP	2009	46.6	3	No	n.a.	53.2	36.9	No	n.a.	64	Yes
Japan	LDP	2012	62.5	5	No	n.a.	47.5	28.6	No	n.a.	58	Yes
Japan	SDPJ	1978	83.1	1	Yes	Yes	98.0	n.a.	No	n.a.	62	Yes
Japan	SDPJ	1981	92.8	3	Yes	Yes	68.5	25.6	No	n.a.	66	Yes
Japan	SDPJ	1986	84.7	2	No	n.a.	83.3	16.7	Yes	Yes	57	Yes
Japan	SDPJ	1991	71.7	2	No	n.a.	56.0	44.0	No	n.a.	69	Yes
Japan	SDPJ	1993	66.5	2	No	n.a.	78.4	21.6	No	n.a.	69	Yes
Japan	SDPJ	1996	66.2	2	Yes	Yes	84.7	15.3	No	n.a.	71	Yes
Japan	NFP	1995		2	No	n.a.	66.4	33.6	No	n.a.	53	Yes
Japan	DPJ	2002	51.3	4	Yes	Yes	35.8	26.1	No	n.a.	55	Yes
Japan	DPJ	2010	66.9	2	Yes	Yes	60.5	39.5	No	n.a.	63	Yes
Japan	DPJ	2012	33.7	4	Yes	Yes	65.6	19.3	No	n.a.	55	Yes
Japan Mean			*65.5*	*3*	*42.8*	*88.8*	*63.7*	*26.7*	*9.5*	*50*	*62*	*100*

Country	Party	Year										
Taiwan	KMT	2001	57.9	1	Yes	Yes	97.1	n.a.	No	n.a.	64	Yes
Taiwan	KMT	2005	50.2	2	No	n.a.	72.4	27.6	No	n.a.	55	Yes
Taiwan	KMT	2007	53.8	2	Yes	Yes	87.2	12.8	No	n.a.	67	Yes
Taiwan	KMT	2009	57.0	1	No	n.a.	93.9	n.a.	No	n.a.	59	Yes
Taiwan	KMT	2013	57.9	1	Yes	Yes	91.9	n.a.	No	No	63	Yes
Taiwan	DPP	1998	55.3	5	No	n.a.	63.4	29.9	Yes	n.a.	56	No
Taiwan	DPP	2000	11.4	1	No	n.a.	98.7	n.a.	No	n.a.	54	Yes
Taiwan	DPP	2005	19.7	1	No	n.a.	99.7	n.a.	No	No	57	Yes
Taiwan	DPP	2006	20.0	3	No	n.a.	54.4	36.1	Yes	Yes	57	Yes
Taiwan	DPP	2008	51.6	2	No	n.a.	60.2	39.8	Yes	Yes	51	Yes
Taiwan	DPP	2010	59.1	2	Yes	Yes	90.3	9.7	Yes	n.a.	53	Yes
Taiwan	DPP	2012	68.9	5	No	n.a.	50.5	21.0	No	n.a.	64	Yes
Taiwan	DPP	2014	65.1	2	No	n.a.	93.7	6.3	Yes	Yes	57	Yes
Taiwan Mean			*48.3*	*2*	*30.7*	*100*	*81*	*22.9*	*38.4*	*60*	*58*	*92.3*

Note: a Estimate based on turnout and number of votes won by the candidates in 45 prefectures in which primaries took place.

Political Consequences for Parties

This section briefly analyses the consequences of the primary in Japan and Taiwan. Two types of dependent variable are considered here: membership of the political parties; and their electoral performance and party support.

Impact on Party Membership

Table 6.3 shows the number of party membership in the years before and after the year when primary elections were held.[10] Overall, it presents a mixed picture and does not show any consistent pattern regarding the impact on party membership. The effect of a primary on membership may change depending on time. For example, LDP membership increased significantly when the primaries were held in 1978, 1982 and 1991, but this positive impact cannot be seen after 1991. Indeed, Uekami (2008) concluded that the primary had a positive impact on membership until 1991 even when one controls for the general upward trend of LDP membership, but that this positive impact cannot be observed after 1991.

In any case, we cannot make a proper inference of the impact of primaries on party membership here, because Table 6.3 contains only the years the primaries were held, and has no information on the years they were not held (that is, there is no variance in the independent variables). In order to estimate the effect of primaries on party membership, one should examine the overall membership trend across time and the degree of increase/decrease when primaries did not take place,[11] as well as other control variables that would also affect the membership, such as whether or not the party is in power. This will be a task for our future research.

Impact on Electoral Performance and Party Support

Table 6.3, following the common format, presents the percentage of votes won by parties in general elections before and after primaries were held. However, as for the cases of Japan and Taiwan, using general election results to evaluate the effects of primary elections is methodologically problematic, primarily because party leadership selection is not synchronised with general elections, unlike candidate selection. More concretely, one faces two methodological problems.

---

10 For some parties, especially the KMT in Taiwan, it is difficult to acquire consistent time-series data because the parties do not disclose information on membership in a regular and systematic manner. Therefore, Table 6.3 lacks data for some cases.

11 For example, if one examines the long-term trend of DPP membership, it kept rising until 2006 whether or not there was a primary, and the rate of increase in this period does not seem to be affected by the occurrence of primaries. Therefore, even though there were more cases that saw increased membership in the DPP, it may have been simply because there were more cases in the period of upward trend of the membership.

First, two or more primaries are sometimes held between general elections, which makes it impossible to evaluate the effect of each primary on the electoral performance due to the lack of one-on-one correspondence. If one uses the results of different types of election – lower and upper house elections in Japan; presidential and parliamentary elections in Taiwan – this problem can be partly (but not entirely) solved; but then the issue arises of the comparability of two different types of election, conducted with different electoral systems.[12]

Second, even when one-to-one correspondence between the primary and the general election results exists, the timing of the primaries vis-à-vis general elections varies considerably across the cases. In some cases, the primary was held just several months before the general elections, while in other cases it was held several *years* before the general elections. Given these varying intervals between primary and general elections, it is not appropriate to simply compare election results before and after primaries across the cases. For these two methodological reasons, we would like to refrain from making any inference of the impact of the primary on electoral performance based on the information presented in Table 6.3.

As a remedy to the problems discussed above, we propose to use the party support data instead of election results. In Japan, Jiji Press has published a long series of opinion poll data on the level of party support, taken monthly for many years.[13] We believe that one can estimate the effects of primary elections on party support more appropriately by using this data and comparing the change in levels of support before and after primaries with roughly the same time interval. Table 6.4 in the Appendix presents the level of party support from monthly opinion polls in prior and subsequent to the party leader selection and the magnitude of change of party support for all parties in Japan. It demonstrates that, at least for the LDP, the impact of the primary on party support is somewhat larger than that of other selection methods. On average, party support when a primary was held increased by 1.8 percentage points; without a primary but with multi-candidate elections (voted only by the MPs) there was an increase of 1.0 percentage points; and without any contest the increase was 1.3 percentage

---

12 When one uses two types of election, and both results are usable for one case of a primary, one faces the question whether to prioritise the comparability (choose the same type of election before and after the primary) or the time interval (closer elections before and after the primary). In Table 6.3, we used both the lower and upper house elections in Japan and the presidential and the Legislative Yuan elections in Taiwan. When both election results were available, we used the same type of results (lower house elections in Japan and Legislative Yuan elections in Taiwan are prioritised) unless the other type of election took place more than one year closer to the primary.

13 Jiji Press (established in 1945) is one of two major private news agencies in Japan which provide domestic and foreign news and information to various organisations such as commercial banks and financial institutions.

Table 6.3 Effects of primary elections on political parties in Japan and Taiwan

Country	Party	Year	Members			Electoral performance (Votes)			Change
			Year before primaries (N)	Year after primaries (N)	Change (%)	Before primaries (N)	Before primaries (%)		(Votes after primaries % - votes before primaries %)
Japan	LDP	1978	517,040	1,113,190	115,3	23,653,626	41.8		2.8
Japan	LDP	1982	1,200,592	2,450,000	104,1	28,262,442	47.9		-2.1
Japan	LDP	1991	2,206,026	3,827,553	73,5	30,315,417	46.1		-9.5
Japan	LDP	1995	2,791,760	1,683,673	-39,7	11,096,972[a]	27.3[a]		5.5[a]
Japan	LDP	1999	3,984,366	1,914,126	-52,0	14,128,719[a]	25.2[a]		3.1[a]
Japan	LDP	2001	1,914,126	1,169,951	-38,9	16,943,425	28.3		10.3[a]
Japan	LDP	2003	1,169,951	1,066,197	-8,9	21,114,728[a]	38.6[a]		-3.6[a]
Japan	LDP	2006	1,062,687	1,081,059	1,7	25,887,798	38.2		-10.1[a]
Japan	LDP	2008	1,081,059	871,871	-19,4	16,544,761[a]	28.1[a]		-1.4[a]
Japan	LDP	2009	1,041,846	851,137	-18,3	18,810,217	26.7		-2.6[a]
Japan	LDP	2012	811,137	800,936	-1,3	14,071,671[a]	24.1[a]		3.5[a]
Japan	SDPJ	1978	50,695	54,109	6,7	11,713,009	20.7		-1.0
Japan	SDPJ	1981	56,557	65,617	16,0	11,400,748	19.3		0.2
Japan	SDPJ	1986	72,838	86,209	18,4	10,412,585	17.2		7.2
Japan	SDPJ	1991	140,380	167,488	19,3	16,025,472	24.4		-9.0
Japan	SDPJ	1993	167,488	130,372	-22,2	9,687,589	15.4		1.5[a]
Japan	SDPJ	1996	129,921	57,454	-55,8	6,882,919[a]	16.9[a]		-10.5[a]
Japan	NFP	1995	n.a.	n.a.	-	12,506,322[a]	30.8[a]		-2.8[a]
Japan	DPJ	2002	n.a.	86,108	-	15,067,990	25.2		12.2
Japan	DPJ	2010	263,700	303,219	15,0	29,844,799	42.4		n.a.
Japan	DPJ	2012	303,219	218,508	-27,9	n.a.	n.a.		n.a.

Taiwan	KMT	2001	952,835	n.a.	-	2,925,513[a]	23.1[a]	5.5[a]
Taiwan	KMT	2005	1,117,000	n.a.	-	3,190,081	32.8	n.a.
Taiwan	KMT	2007	n.a.	n.a.	-	n.a.	n.a.	n.a.
Taiwan	KMT	2009	n.a.	n.a.	-	5,010,801	51.2	-6.7
Taiwan	KMT	2013	n.a.	n.a.	-	5,863,279	44.5	n.a.
Taiwan	DPP	1998	137,968	200,476	45,3	3,132,156	33.2	-3.6
Taiwan	DPP	2000	200,476	406,611	102,8	4,977,697[a]	39.3[a]	-5.9[a]
Taiwan	DPP	2005	508,056	544,515	7,2	3,471,429	35.7	n.a.
Taiwan	DPP	2006	531,355	510,669	-3,9	n.a.	n.a.	n.a.
Taiwan	DPP	2008	510,669	458,551	-10,2	3,610,106	36.9	n.a.
Taiwan	DPP	2010	458,551	n.a.	-	n.a.	n.a.	n.a.
Taiwan	DPP	2012	n.a.	251,049	-	4,556,424	34.6	n.a.
Taiwan	DPP	2014	251,049	n.a.	-	n.a.	n.a.	n.a.

Note: [a] Calculation based on the Election for the House of Councillors (Japan) or presidential election (Taiwan).

points.[14] However, for the other parties, the impact of primaries on party support is actually smaller than that of other selection methods, and even negative in the case of the DPJ. These results seem to confirm the findings of McElwain and Umeda (2011), who analysed the effect of primaries on party support for two major parties and concluded that primaries had a positive impact for the LDP but not for the DPJ.

Unfortunately, we cannot make a similar analysis for the case of Taiwan, as we do not have equivalent data, taken so frequently and regularly, of the party support. However, some authors do suggest that the introduction of the primary had a positive impact for the political parties. For example, Fell (2010) argued that the first competitive primary in the KMT and the election of popular candidate Ma Ying-jeou as party chairman had a significant impact on the increase in electoral support for the KMT. Fell points out that, after Ma's election as chairman in July 2005, the level of party identification for the KMT increased from 32 to 47 per cent in December of that year, when local elections were held and Ma pledged to resign if the party failed to win half the seats (Fell, 2010, p. 938). It remains to be examined whether primaries generally had such a positive impact on support for the Taiwanese political parties.

Conclusion

We have examined the causes, processes and consequences of the primary for party leadership selection in Japan and Taiwan. Despite their obvious difference regarding political system, these two countries do show some commonalities. As for the rationales for the adoption of primaries, we pointed out the importance of five factors, and that the major rationale seems to be associated with the type of political party in both countries in a similar manner. Concerning formal rules, we pointed out that the challenger parties tend to adopt more democratic rules; and in the actual implementation of the primary, both countries present similar features, such as the dominance of elderly, male and experienced politicians. As discussed in the first section, these commonalities may be due to the two countries' similar party systems.

As for party support among the general public and the party membership, there are some empirical indications that primary has some positive impacts on political parties, but these indications are only preliminary due to various limitations, and further research is required for a more conclusive argument. Also, due to the limitations of time and space, we could not elaborate the impact of the primary on intra-party politics, such as inter-factional relations and relations between leaders,

---

14 Of course, whether or not this difference is statistically significant should be examined by more rigorous statistical tests with proper control variables, which is outside the scope of this chapter.

cadres (elites) and ordinary members. This could be an interesting topic, given the importance of the issue of factions for political parties in both Japan and Taiwan, and will be the subject of our future research.

Appendix

See Tables 6.4a, 6.4b, 6.4c and 6.4d on the following pages.

Source: created by the authors, based on Jiji Press (1981); Jiji Press (1992); Jiji Press (1992–2013

Table 6.4a The level of party support before and after the leader selection in Japan: LDP

	year/mo	78.nov	82.nov	91.oct	95.sep	99.sep	01.apr	03.sep	06.sep	07.sep	08.sep	09.sep	12.sep			average
full-member	before	29.3	30.7	39.0	22.9	25.5	21.4	21.5	27.0	20.3	20.9	16.6	12.8			
	after	32.7	31.4	40.1	23.5	23.9	25.5	22.2	29.3	23.4	23.4	17.7	16.8			
	change	3.4	0.7	1.1	0.6	-1.6	4.1	0.7	2.3	3.1	2.5	1.1	4.0			1.8
	change (%)	11.6	2.3	2.8	2.6	-6.3	19.2	3.3	8.5	15.3	12.0	6.6	31.3			9.1

	year/mo	60.jul	62.jul	64.jul	66.dec	68.nov	70.oct	72.jul	89.aug	93.jul	98.jul					average
caucus	before	34.4	37.6	37.2	36.7	33.3	36.7	28.2	20.3	25.6	19.7					
	after	34.9	36.4	40.4	31.5	34.6	35.9	33.2	26.5	25.6	20.8					
	change	0.5	-1.2	3.2	-5.2	1.3	-0.8	5.0	6.2	0.0	1.1					1.0
	change (%)	1.5	-3.2	8.6	-14.2	3.9	-2.2	17.7	30.5	0.0	5.6					4.8

	year/mo	64.nov	74.dec	76.dec	80.jul	80.oct	84.oct	86.sep	87.oct	89.jun	89.oct	93.sep	97.sep	00.apr	01.aug	average
no contest	before	37.6	21.6	26.1	36.8	36.1	35.5	37.6	33.6	22.1	29.4	23.9	26.5	22.4	27.9	
	after	42.7	27.1	28.8	35.3	38.1	34.0	35.6	33.1	21.4	31.3	23.2	27.9	27.0	29.1	
	change	5.1	5.5	2.7	-1.5	2.0	-1.5	-2.0	-0.5	-0.7	1.9	-0.7	1.4	4.6	1.2	1.3
	change (%)	13.6	25.5	10.3	-4.1	5.5	-4.2	-5.3	-1.5	-3.2	6.5	-2.9	5.3	20.5	4.3	5.0

Source: created by the authors, based on Jiji Press (1981); Jiji Press (1992); Jiji Press (1992–2013)

Table 6.4b The level of party support before and after the leader selection in Japan: SDPJ

full-member

year/mo	81.dec	86.sep	91.jul	93.sep	96.jan	average
before	7.9	7.5	10.0	7.2	5.3	
after	8.9	10.1	8.9	6.6	5.1	
change	1.0	2.6	-1.1	-0.6	-0.2	0.3
change (%)	12.7	34.7	-11.0	-8.3	-3.8	4.8

caucus

year/mo	66.dec	70.dec	average
before	19.3	11.8	
after	18.3	14.7	
change	-1.0	2.9	0.5
change (%)	-5.2	24.6	5.6

no contest

year/mo	61.mar	62.jan	62.nov	64.feb	64.dec	65.may	67.aug	68.oct	73.feb	74.dec	77.feb	77.dec	78.feb	80.jan	83.aug	85.nov	87.dec	90.mar	91.nov	93.jan	average
before	20.1	20.0	21.5	15.8	15.2	19.1	16.6	17.4	15.5	12.0	10.8	10.6	9.2	10.9	10.3	8.6	11.0	12.3	7.4	9.2	
after	22.3	19.4	21.0	20.4	18.0	21.7	17.4	16.8	17.0	11.6	10.3	10.0	11.5	10.1	8.8	7.8	8.9	14.3	8.7	8.6	
change	2.2	-0.6	-0.5	4.6	2.8	2.6	0.8	-0.6	1.5	-0.4	-0.5	-0.6	2.3	-0.8	-1.5	-0.8	-2.1	2.0	1.3	-0.6	0.6
change (%)	10.9	-3.0	-2.3	29.1	18.4	13.6	4.8	-3.4	9.7	-3.3	-4.6	-5.7	25.0	-7.3	-14.6	-9.3	-19.1	16.3	17.6	-6.5	3.3

Source: created by the authors, based on Jiji Press (1981); Jiji Press (1992); Jiji Press (1992–2013)

Table 6.4c The level of party support before and after the leader selection in Japan: DJP

		02.sep	10.sep	12.sep							average
	year/mo										
full-member	before	5.0	20.6	7.4							
	after	2.8	20.0	7.3							
	change	-2.2	-0.6	-0.1							-1.0
	change (%)	-44.0	-2.9	-1.4							-16.1
	year/mo	99.jan	99.sep	02.dec	05.sep	06.apr	09.may	10.jun	11.aug	12.dec	average
caucus	before	4.9	4.2	2.1	10.2	8.8	14.2	17.0	10.1	5.9	
	after	5.7	4.1	3.5	11.4	10.0	15.5	20.0	12.4	5.3	
	change	0.8	-0.1	1.4	1.2	1.2	1.3	3.0	2.3	-0.6	1.2
	change (%)	16.3	-2.4	66.7	11.8	13.6	9.2	17.6	22.8	-10.2	16.2
	year/mo	00.aug	04.may	04.aug	06.sep	08.sep				12.dec	average
no contest	before	8.7	7.6	15.7	9.2	15.0				5.9	
	after	8.9	10.3	13.8	10.8	12.8				5.3	
	change	0.2	2.7	-1.9	1.6	-2.2				-0.6	2.8
	change (%)	2.3	35.5	-12.1	17.4	-14.7				-10.2	57.1

Source: created by the authors, based on Jiji Press (1981); Jiji Press (1992); Jiji Press (1992-2013

Table 6.4d The level of party support before and after the leader selection in Japan: NFP

		year/mo	95.dec	average
full-member		before	5.9	0.4
		after	6.3	6.8
		change	0.4	
		change (%)	6.8	

		year/mo	94.dec	average
caucus		before	4.9	2.8
		after	7.7	57.1
		change	2.8	
		change (%)	57.1	

Source: created by the authors, based on Jiji Press (1981); Jiji Press (1992); Jiji Press (1992-2013

Chapter 7
Democratising Candidate Selection in Italy and France

Marino De Luca and Fulvio Venturino

Introduction

The socio-economic structure of Italy has several features in common with that of France. Both Italy and France are large countries with nearly 60 million inhabitants; both feature advanced and industrialised economies; and both were founding members of the European Economic Community (EEC), a predecessor of the European Union (EU). Moreover, they are culturally similar, as both Italy and France are homogeneous societies lacking substantial linguistic minorities, and the predominance of Catholicism prevents the existence of other sizeable religious groups. Even after World War II Italy and France also shared similar political attributes. In the years following the war, both were parliamentary regimes with a proportional representation (PR) electoral system; a multiparty system affected by ideological antagonism (Sartori, 1976); unstable coalition governments; and strongly centralised centre–periphery relationships.

However, the two countries took different paths in 1958. At that time, Italy proceeded to consolidate its dysfunctional form of parliamentarianism, while reforms enforced by General Charles de Gaulle converted the troubled French polity into a semi-presidential system. The Gaullist reforms also entailed changing the electoral system from PR to a two-round system which, with some differences, is still used today to elect either the president or the parliament.[1] In contrast, in Italy all the institutions remained unchanged until the first half of the 1990s. Then, to help the political system recover from an unparalleled crisis, PR was substituted in 1993 (and again in 2005) by two mixed systems. Although the newly adopted electoral laws were different in both countries – majority in France, mixed in Italy – their effects on the party systems were quite similar. Immediately after the reforms, both countries evolved towards a two-bloc competition where, unlike most North European democracies, each bloc is composed of several parties. In the case of Italy, the reshaping of the party system has also been related to an endless instability for all the parties as organisations.

---

1 The first presidential election was held in 1962, while the 1986 parliamentary election was disputed using PR. The two-round system was restored shortly after (Lewis-Beck et al., 2011).

Via different paths, both Italy and France entered the 2000s facing recurrent problems which affect long-term consolidated democracies. The most important among them was the need to ensure parties' organisational renewal in order to avoid sclerosis and to circumvent populist criticism. To do so, many parties resolved to democratise their internal life by relying on their members and sympathisers to select their political personnel. As we discuss at length in the next section, Italy and France, like most other countries, today offer an increasing number of primary elections. In this chapter, we prefer to focus on the selection of the candidates to the role of chief executive. It is not difficult to justify such a choice. In all democratic political systems, governments wield the greatest power, and their leaders – presidents, prime ministers or chancellors – are, without exception, the top rulers. They have substantial authority over ministerial appointments and policy agenda, and are prominent in the mass media. Moreover, they are usually the leaders of their own parties, even if this does not happen in the cases dealt with here. Recently, following the advancement of presidentialisation in most democracies, they have even enhanced their roles (Poguntke and Webb, 2005).

Here we take into account all five cases of the democratic selection of chief executive candidates that have so far occurred in Italy and France. In Italy the selections took place in 2005 and in 2012; were promoted by the (changing) left coalition; and, for the first time outside the United States, they took the form of open primaries, where all citizens were eligible to vote regardless of whether they were enrolled in the parties involved. In France we look at three cases of primaries to select the leader. In 1995 and 2006 they were closed primaries reserved to members of the Socialist Party (PS). In 2011, using the Italian primaries as an example, the PS promoted for the first time open primaries which, because of the participation of a small leftist party, should at least formally be considered coalition-shaped.

Before proceeding, it should to be underlined that the Italian primaries' aim is to select a candidate for prime minister entering a parliamentary election, while in France primaries are used to select a presidential candidate. According to the rules of semi-presidential systems, the nominee, once elected, is the French head of state and one of two chief executives besides the prime minister. As the president – coalition apart – is usually the main leader, a comparison between Italy and France is, from this point of view, practicable without question.

Contexts and Rationales for Adopting Primary Elections

After the upheavals of the 1990s, survival was the main problem that Italian parties had to face. Detested by a large part of the general public and challenged by mounting anti-party movements, all the parties were concerned about maintaining the classical advantages guaranteed by the cartel parties: public funding and access to government-controlled mass media (Katz and Mair, 1995). Additionally, all parties were involved in a hectic process of merging, splitting and coalition-making, preventing the party system as a whole from reaching a new equilibrium.

Personalisation was the most important tool employed by centre and right parties to implement their survival strategies. On the right, Forward Italy (FI) and the Northern League (LN) have until recently been examples of leader-centred organisations. For decades they were led by their respective founding fathers – Silvio Berlusconi and Umberto Bossi – and both leaders were unquestionably the parties' main electoral asset (Venturino, 2010).

The foundation of personal parties was an unfeasible strategy for politicians on the left. This inaptitude was due to several factors, such as the legacies of the mass parties, the well-entrenched attitudes of left-wing voters and the predominant cultural orientation of the political class (Mulé, 2007). Yet left-wing parties could refer to another principle shared by their leaders and followers: participation. Moreover, large numbers of formally enrolled members were still available for mobilisation. This condition allowed left-wing parties to discover an innovative strategy for Italian politics, namely the opening up of leader and candidate selections.

The practice of primary elections was inaugurated by left-wing parties in the mid-2000s. This method was then unfamiliar in Italy. At national level, only the Democrats of the Left (DS) had adopted a one member one vote (OMOV) system to select their leader, in 2001. In 2004 open primaries were used to select mayors in a few small towns, but their introduction at that time went completely unnoticed by the media. Nevertheless, they paved the way for the first case of primary elections which were certainly noticed and debated in public opinion. The elections were held in January 2005, when Nichi Vendola – a post-Communist and underdog candidate from a weak party – unexpectedly defeated the frontrunner endorsed by the main parties of the leftist coalition, and then subsequently the incumbent rightist governor of an important region in southern Italy. After this case, and approaching the 2006 parliamentary elections, the parties comprising the leftist coalition chose Romano Prodi as candidate chief executive using open primaries. Rather than answering any demand for increased party democracy from citizens or the grassroots, the first Italian primaries were above all used to resolve partisan quarrels among leaders. Nevertheless the turnout reached an astounding peak of more than 4 million voters.

The success of the Prodi primaries brought several consequences. Created in 2007 (Bordandini et al., 2008), the Democratic Party (PD) adopted a statute whereby open primaries are assumed to be the standard process to select candidates to all representative roles. Moreover, it has so far selected three leaders (out of five) using a multistage method where an open primary election is the critical phase (Pasquino, 2009; Pasquino and Venturino, 2010, 2014). After a pause in the 2008 early parliamentary election, the centre-left coalition again used primaries in 2012 to select Pier Luigi Bersani as its chief executive candidate (Gelli et al., 2013). Under the same circumstances, three other parties – the PD, the post-Communist Left Ecology Freedom (SEL) and the populist Five Star Movement (M5S), led by the comedian Beppe Grillo – have also democratically selected their candidates to parliament, the latter using a pioneering closed and online primary election.

To summarise, since the second half of the 2000s, open primary elections have become the standard method for selecting all candidates fielded by most left-wing parties at local and national level, and also the basic rule for selecting the leader of the largest left-wing party. Consequently, the right-wing coalition entered an electoral crisis in 2010–11, and Berlusconi's leadership was contested. The primaries successfully operated by the left were also considered an option by some rightist politicians. In fact, this new case of contagion from the left fuelled a hot debate about the succession to Berlusconi as both party leader and coalition-maker; but the right promoted only a limited number of open primaries at local level, and the ageing Berlusconi remained candidate chief executive for the 2013 parliamentary election.

The scope of the contagion is more remarkable when party leader selections are considered. In 2013 Italy of Values (IDV) – a centre-left personal party led for 15 years by its founder, the renowned former judge Antonio Di Pietro – chose its new leader through closed (OMOV) primaries. After his involvement in a financial scandal, the long-standing Northern League leader Umberto Bossi was beaten by the young challenger Matteo Salvini in a two-candidate, non-competitive closed primary. Finally, in 2014 the far-right Brothers of Italy (FDI) – after splitting from the People of Freedom (PDL) – selected its first (female) leader by an open and uncontested primary.

In France, after a debate dating back to the 1970s, the first socialist primaries took place in the 1995 presidential election. At that time, President François Mitterrand had completed his second term, and the various factions of the Socialist Party were quarrelling over the selection of a new candidate. The party elites managed to find a traditional solution 'behind closed doors', but their efforts were frustrated by the successive withdrawal of two viable candidates. The popularity of the former Prime Minister, Michel Rocard, had plummeted after the defeat of the PS in the 1994 European elections; and the economist Jacques Delors refused to stand because of his disagreement with the party's policies under the leadership of Henri Emmanuelli. At this point, the lack of experimentation notwithstanding, an opening up of the selectorate was considered the only way to solve the internal conflicts. Lionel Jospin first announced his candidacy for the closed primaries, followed by Emmanuelli few days later. Then, for the first time, party members chose the presidential candidate, replacing the *Conseil National* (National Council) which had held the responsibility until this point.

During the approach to the 2002 presidential election, while the Greens promoted their first closed primaries to select a presidential candidate, the Socialist Party preferred to avoid them. At this time, Jospin was the outgoing prime minister after five years of cohabitation with Jacques Chirac, thus he appeared to be the only candidate capable of challenging the incumbent. However, in the presidential election Jospin unexpectedly failed to pass the second round, beaten by Chirac himself and by the populist leader of the National Front (FN), Jean-Marie Le Pen (Lewis-Beck, 2004; Dolez and Laurent, 2007). Chirac easily succeeded in winning against Le Pen, but the temporary success of the xenophobic and radical right evoked a sense of shock not just in France but in all European countries. Chirac's success quickly restored the state of affairs in the French political system, but the disastrous performance of the Socialist candidate remained as the worst blow in the party's history.

In the run-up to the 2007 presidential election, the Greens again selected their candidate by consulting their members. Also the Union for a Popular Movement (UMP) organised an uncontested internal vote to confirm Nicolas Sarkozy's candidacy (Ivaldi, 2007; Grunberg and Haegel, 2007). Like many parties that use primaries to recover after an unsuccessful election, the Socialists turned once more to their members after the 2002 flop. In 2006 Ségolène Royal entered the competition as the frontrunner and easily won the nomination, largely because she was the most electable Socialist candidate according to the polls. For the first time ever a woman was considered electable to the French presidency. As is well known, the final result was not favourable for the Socialist candidate, but in any case the 2006 closed primaries marked a turning point. In contrast to the low profile of the 1995 precedent, Royal's highly visible nomination through primaries ensured that they would be acknowledged as an accepted tool both for leadership selection and grassroots public participation.

In the years to come closed primary elections were used by the Socialists to elect Martine Aubry as party leader, and by the UMP to select several candidates for local elections, including the 2008 mayoral election in Paris. An innovative debate aimed at promoting a more inclusive method of selection began in 2009, when a report significantly named *Pour des primaires ouvertes et populaires* was issued by the Secretary of the National Renewal of the Socialist Party, Arnaud Montebourg. This document was subsequently approved in a vote by 68 per cent of the party members, paving the way for open primaries to be used to select the Socialist presidential candidate. The reformers deplored the weak support for the candidates when selected by the party members alone. In their view, a competitive nominee had to be chosen by the voters at large through open primaries, and they quoted the Italian case to advance their argument (Ferrand and Montebourg, 2011). The reformist position attained a notable level of attention. The newspapers close to the left presented the debate among Socialists as a confrontation between conservatives and modernisers. The case for open primaries enjoyed the support of prominent personalities such as the sociologist Alain Touraine.[2] Particularly valuable to accelerate the adoption of open primaries was the public endorsement by the Terra Nova think tank. At that point, as stated by Laurent Fabius, one of the most influential Socialist leaders, favourable or not, the open primaries had become unavoidable (Lefebvre, 2011). Thus the modernisers succeeded in promoting the first open presidential primaries in 2011.

After the victory by François Holland and his subsequent success in the 2012 presidential election, primaries for selecting both candidates and leaders have

---

2 Touraine was among the signatories of the petition in support of open primaries; cf. *Libération*, 29 August 2009.

definitely become a key factor in French politics. Besides the 2011 (and third) closed presidential primaries organised by the Greens, the FN and the UMP also used a full member vote to select new party presidents, in 2011 and 2012 respectively. Following the model of the presidential primary, the PS organised open primaries in five major cities for the 2014 municipal elections. At the same time, the UMP organised open primaries in Paris (via internet voting) and Lyons.

In the last analysis, both in Italy and France the adoption of primaries to select the chief executive candidates is the consequence of a long and complex process involving national and local levels. Moreover, in both countries an extraordinary episode contributed to promoting primaries as standard practice. In Italy, it was the high turnout (4 million voters) of the 2005 primaries won by Romano Prodi. In France, the success of the primaries was mainly linked to the defeat of Lionel Jospin in the 2002 presidential election, when the Socialist Party preferred to select its candidate in a 'smoke-filled room'.

The Primary Election Process

Inclusiveness of the Selectorate

In 2005, concomitant with the first use of primaries to select their prime ministerial candidate, the Italian left-wing parties also made a controversial decision. Moving on from the full member vote briefly used by the Democrats of the Left to select their leader, voting rights were extended to all Italian citizens, regardless of their enrolment in the promoting parties (see Table 7.1). By so doing, the Italian parties paved the way for the utilisation of open primaries in Europe. Remarkably, participation was also permitted for two groups excluded from voting in general elections, namely 17-year-olds and resident foreigners. Voters did not need to pre-register – only a written endorsement of the coalition manifesto and a fee of €1 were requested at the polling stations on election day.

Following the extraordinary turnout in 2005, all the primaries organised by the left since then to select both candidates and party leaders have adopted the same benchmark. A few changes were implemented in 2012 during the second open primaries for the candidate Prime Minister. At that time, the challenger, Matteo Renzi – the 37-year-old mayor of Florence – was aggressively criticising the top leadership of the Democratic Party, meaning that competitiveness and negativity affected the campaign. To disadvantage him, the 2012 primaries were again opened to all Italian citizens and to resident foreigners, but voters under 18 years old – supposed to be Renzi's sympathisers – were excluded. For the same purposes, a complicated pre-registration system was set up and the fee was doubled to €2 with the aim of hindering non-member potential voters.

The 1995 French primaries were reserved to Socialist members, without additional requirements. Formally at least, the same rules were repeated in 2006. In this case, however, in the months preceding the primary the party launched a

Table 7.1 Main features of primary election processes in Italy and France

Country	Party	Year	Selectorate	Candidacy	Voting system	Timing[d]	Deselection
Italy	Centre-left coalition[a]	2005	All citizens	10,000 signatures of voters	Plurality	6	Not regulated
Italy	Centre-left coalition[b]	2012	All citizens	20,000 signatures of voters	Runoff	3	Not regulated
France	Socialist Party	1995	Party members	Authorisation by the National Council	Runoff	3	Not regulated
France	Socialist Party	2006	Party members	Endorsement by 30 members of the National Council	Runoff	5	Not regulated
France	Socialist Party[c]	2011	All citizens	Endorsement by 5% of MPs; or 5% members of the National Council; or 5% regional councillors; or 5% mayors	Runoff	6	Not regulated

Notes: [a] The coalition comprised Democrats of the Left (DS), Democracy is Freedom – The Daisy, the Communist Refoundation Party (RC), the Union of Democrats for Europe (UDEUR), Italy of Values (IDV) and the Greens.
[b] The coalition comprised the Democratic Party, Left Ecology Freedom (SEL) and the Democratic Centre (CD).
[c] The Radical Party of the Left (PRG) participated in the primary.
[d] Number of months before the general elections.

recruitment campaign through the offer of a low-cost party card for €20. Although this method was negatively assessed by socialist militants, the PS membership increased quickly from 120,000 to 220,000. This is quite a singular case of instant membership encouraged by the party itself; and it should be taken seriously, as the latecomers, curbing the influence of the older ideological members, strongly contributed to the success of the outsider Ségolène Royal.

As already reported, the 2011 primaries were no longer restricted to members, but rather opened to all citizens. In addition, the selectorate was made up of those minors who would have been 18 at the time of the presidential election, or who alternatively were enrolled either in the main PS or in the party's youth organisation. Foreigners enrolled in the party were also allowed to vote. Pre-registration was not requested, but all voters were required to subscribe to the Charter of Values of the left coalition and to pay a €1 fee.

Candidacy

In the 2005 Italian primary entry was regulated in a straightforward manner: aspirants had to collect at least 10,000 signatures from ordinary people, and it was also required that they had not previously worked for a right-wing party (see Table 7.1). Such a low threshold allowed seven candidates to enter. The frontrunner, Romano Prodi, former Prime Minister and former President of the European Commission, was an independent lacking a partisan brand, but he was openly supported by the two main left-wing parties – Democrats of the Left (DS) and The Daisy (DL) – and some other small parties. Four other candidates were leaders of minor parties, while two less well-known, underdog independent candidates simply sought to use the campaign to force their agenda on particular topics, such as gender policy, or to propagate anti-capitalist criticisms.

In the run-up to the 2012 primaries, a completely transformed left coalition was led by the pivotal Democratic Party. According to the PD statute, only the incumbent leader, Pier Luigi Bersani – a 61-year-old selected in 2009 through an open party primary – was allowed to participate in a coalition primary to select the prime ministerial candidate. Hence most of the pre-primary period was dedicated to the contestation of this rule, particularly by Matteo Renzi, who was demanding renewal for the sitting party leadership. Finally, Bersani agreed to suspend the statute in order to allow additional candidates. Thus both Renzi and Laura Puppato – a PD regional councillor and the only female candidate to run – could challenge their own party leader. Besides the three PD candidates, Nichi Vendola from the post-Communist Left Ecology Freedom and Bruno Tabacci from the small, new Democratic Centre (CD) also ran after gathering the signatures of 20,000 ordinary people.

In 1993 Henri Emmanuelli had been selected leader of the Socialist Party by a large majority of the congress of delegates. During the lead-up to the 1995 presidential election, several candidatures were announced in a row, pushing the National Council to abdicate and to entrust the members as 'justice of the peace'.

Given the time restraints and the absence of precedents, it was simply stated that aspirants had to submit their candidature to the National Council (see Table 7.1). On the basis of this rudimentary rule, Jospin first presented his self-nomination for the primaries on 4 January 1995. To combat him, Emmanuelli immediately launched his own nomination. He was endorsed by some Socialist leaders who hoped to replicate in the primaries the favourable result obtained in the 1993 congress. However, their hopes were soon dashed.

In 2006 Ségolène Royal appeared to be the only electable Socialist candidate against the rampant popularity of Nicolas Sarkozy. Indeed, an alternative candidature was initially introduced by the Socialist establishment, but it definitively vanished when the party leader – and Royal's husband – François Hollande gave up. According to the rules of primaries adopted by the National Council, prospective candidates were required to be endorsed by at least 30 of the 200 Council members; as such, no more than six entries were feasible. Because of this rule, prominent Socialist politicians such as Jack Lang and Arnaud Montebourg were not able to enter, and only three candidates could compete: Ségolène Royal, former minister and MP, and current regional governor (endorsed by 59 members of the National Council); Laurent Fabius, former prime minister, minister, president of the Lower House and incumbent MP (endorsed by 58); and Dominique Strauss-Kahn, MP and former minister (endorsed by 40).

Five years later the would-be candidates for the 2011 open presidential primary needed to meet at least one of several alternative requirements. The aspirants had to be endorsed by:

- 5 per cent of the parliamentary group (17 endorsements);
- 5 per cent of the members of the National Council (16 endorsements);
- 5 per cent of the incumbent regional councillors (100 endorsements) coming from at least 10 different *départements* and four regions; or
- 5 per cent of socialist mayors of cities with more than 10,000 inhabitants (16 endorsements) from at least four different regions.

As a result, six candidates ran for the 2011 primary: Martine Aubry, PS leader and mayor of Lille; Jean-Michel Baylet, president of the Radical Party of the Left (PRG); François Hollande, MP and former Socialist Party leader; Arnaud Montebourg, MP and PS member responsible for renewal; Ségolène Royal, former presidential candidate; Manuel Valls, MP and mayor of Evry.

Voting System and Results

In the 2005 Italian primary the result was largely anticipated, and the definition of the basic rules was not contested. Only one contender recriminated about the territorial distribution of the 11,000 polling stations, a minor question raised to gain some popularity. More importantly, all parties and candidates agreed on the plurality electoral system. Unsurprisingly, the seven contenders played fair;

the primary was not competitive at all; and Romano Prodi obtained a landslide victory, gaining 74 per cent of the total votes and surpassing the runner-up, Fausto Bertinotti, by 60 percentage points (see Table 7.2; also Venturino, 2007).

As stated above, in 2012 the pre-primary period was completely different due to the presence of an aggressive challenger, Matteo Renzi. Therefore, the entourage of the frontrunner, Pier Luigi Bersani, managed to modify the electoral rules in order to disadvantage Renzi. The plurality system successfully experimented with in 2005 – and also predominantly used in local primaries – was deserted in favour of a two-round system, with a runoff if no candidate secured more than 50 per cent of the votes. This disingenuous rule innovation predisposed what followed (Valbruzzi, 2013). In the first round, turnout fell to close to 3 million, in part because of the new obstacles to participation (Emanuele et al., 2013). Bersani and Renzi took part in the runoff, the former holding a lead of 10 percentage points (45 vs 35 per cent). The people who wanted to vote in the second round without having participated in the first round were not allowed to enter the competition, thus a resurgence for Renzi was not viable in practice. In any case, the strategic attitudes of the first-round losers boosted Bersani's final results. Vendola's supporters in the first round amounted to 15 per cent of the total vote, and in the runoff most of them voted for Bersani, who was considered to be a Democrat candidate friendly to the left (Bernardi and Rombi, 2013). In the runoff the turnout fell again by 350,000 in comparison with the first round. In the end, Bersani won the nomination, beating Renzi by 60 to 40 per cent.

In the French case, the two-round system used for both presidential and parliamentary elections was also adopted for all the primaries. In two cases the runoff was unnecessary because the winner reached 50 per cent in the first round (see Table 7.2). In 1995, 82,000 out of 112,000 Socialist members turned out, and Lionel Jospin won with 65.8 per cent. In 2006, 180,000 out of 220,000 voters selected Ségolène Royal with 60.6 per cent, compared to 21 per cent for Dominique Strauss-Kahn and 19 per cent for Laurent Fabius. However, in the 2011 open primary no candidate reached 50 per cent. François Hollande and Martine Aubry entered the second round, and the former gained the nomination by attaining 56.6 per cent.

Turnout levels are completely different in the closed and open primaries. In the former, voters represent tens of thousands, while in the latter they amount to millions. While this is an obvious consequence of the rules on the inclusiveness of the selectorate, it is intriguing to consider what happened in the two rounds of the 2011 primary. In that case 2,661,231 voters turned out in the first round, while in the second their number grew to 2,860,157. This serves as indirect evidence of the media and public interest raised by the open primary elections. And in comparison with Italy, where new voters were denied a voice in the runoff, it highlights the importance of the rules of the game for the final result.

Table 7.2 Main features of primary election competitions in Italy and France

Country	Party	Year	Turnout	Number of candidates	Incumbent running	Incumbent winner	Winner's votes (%)	Runner-up's votes (%)	Women running	Women winning	Winner's age	National seniority
Italy	Centre-left coalition	2005	4,294,487	7	No	n.a.	74.1	14.7	Yes	No	66	No
Italy	Centre-left coalition	2012	3,110,210[a]	5	No	n.a.	44.9[c]	35.5	Yes	No	61	Yes
France	Socialist Party	1995	82,649	2	No	n.a.	65.8	34.2	No	n.a.	57	Yes
France	Socialist Party	2006	180,557	3	No	n.a.	60.6	20.7	Yes	Yes	53	Yes
France	Socialist Party, Radical Party of the Left	2011	2,661,231[b]	6	No	n.a.	39.2[c]	30.4	Yes	No	57	Yes

Notes: [a] First round (second round 2,802,382);
[b] first round (second round 2,860,157);
[c] first round.

Political Consequences for Parties

The assessment of the possible penalties brought about by primary elections is a widely debated problem in American research (Hacker, 1965; Wichowsky and Niebler, 2010). To shed light on this, we deal first with the electoral performances of the parties after the use of primaries. For sake of comparison, we focus on the parliamentary elections both in Italy and in France, although in the latter presidential elections are more directly linked with primaries. Secondly, a minor strand of American research addresses the consequences of primary elections for party organisations (Miller et al., 1988). The differences between American and European parties are substantial. In any case, here we replicate that approach by considering whether and how primaries affect party membership.

Several factors concur to make the relationships between primaries, electoral results and participation in government highly problematic. In Italy, the left-wing coalition has, in the last decade, repeatedly changed denomination and composition; in 2005 the rightist parliamentary majority implemented contested electoral reform; and the 2013 election featured the highest volatility in the whole array of Western European elections since 1945, due to the success of the populist Five Star Movement which gained 25 per cent of the vote in its first campaign. In France the party system is more stable, but primaries have been used in closed and open form, making any evaluation extremely difficult.

While taking into account these external conditions, one can observe in Table 7.3 that in Italy, between the 2001 to the 2006 parliamentary election, in correspondence with the 2005 primaries, the left coalition led by Romano Prodi gained about 3 million votes, and progressed from opposition to government after a narrow victory over Berlusconi's alliance. The Prodi government lasted only two years, and then the left-wing coalition was ruinously defeated in the 2008 early election. In this case, the two-party coalition did not select the candidate Prime Minister through primaries, preferring instead to appoint the leader of the Democratic Party, Walter Veltroni. The result was disastrous. But it should also be noted that Veltroni had been selected as party leader the previous year through an open primary, and that in 2008 the PD received a noteworthy 33 per cent of the vote (about 12 million).

Immediately after the 2012 primary, opinion polls showed a large advantage for the nominee, Pier Luigi Bersani, over the usual right-wing competitor Silvio Berlusconi. But a weak campaign by Bersani dissipated the lead; both the coalition and the Democratic Party suffered a huge loss of votes; and in the newly elected parliament each of the three major forces – left, right and M5S – were unable to attain a majority. Moreover, the left-wing coalition lost over 3.5 million votes in comparison with the previous election. After lengthy negotiation a government was formed, led by the deputy leader of the PD, Enrico Letta, and supported by a grand coalition including Berlusconi's party. This choice provoked a split in the left-wing coalition, as Left Ecology Freedom refused to enter a government

Table 7.3 Effects of primary elections on political parties in Italy and France

Country	Party	Year	Members		Change (N)	Electoral performance (Votes)		Change (Votes after primaries - votes before primaries)
			Year before primaries (N)	Year after primaries (N)		Before primaries (N)	After primaries (N)	
Italy	Centre-left coalition	2005	555,481[e]	561,193[e]	+5,712	16,019,388[a]	19,002,598[b]	+2,983,210
Italy	Centre-left coalition	2012	804,217[f]	577,169[f]	-227,048	13,689,330[c]	10,047,808[d]	-3,641,522
France	Socialist Party	1995	102,991	111,536	+8,545	4,415,495	5,961,612	+1,546,117
France	Socialist Party	2006	127,374	201,397	+74,023	6,086,599	6,436,136	+349,537
France	Socialist Party	2011	145,361	173,000	+27,639	6,436,136	7,618,326	+1,182,190

Notes: [a] Ulivo (coalition), 2001 parliamentary election;
[b] The Union, 2006 parliamentary election;
[c] Democratic Party and Italy of Values, 2008 parliamentary election;
[d] Democratic Party, Left Ecology Freedom, Democratic Centre and South Tyrolean People's Party;
[e] only Democrats of the Left (data concerning The Daisy not available);
[f] Democratic Party and Left Ecology Freedom.

including right-wing parties. In this case, the initial success of the primaries was followed by disaster involving the left, and indeed all of Italian politics.

In spite of the growing importance of primaries in France, few researches have so far focused on their presumable consequences (De Luca, 2014). To obviate such a limitation, Table 7.3 shows the relationships between the primaries and the Socialist Party's results in parliamentary elections. In 1995, after the first ever primary, Lionel Jospin was defeated as presidential candidate in an open seat race; but in the 1997 early parliamentary election, called by the incumbent President, Jacques Chirac, the PS and its allies won a majority in the lower chamber. At that time, Socialists gained over 1.5 million votes more than in the previous parliamentary election. Thus a left-wing government formed in a situation of cohabitation, and as the leader of the PS selected in 1995 Lionel Jospin was appointed Prime Minister. In this case the primaries played only an indirect role: Jospin progressed to the party leadership as winner of the primaries, and then quite fortuitously to the premiership.

As stated above, the Socialists performed very poorly in the 2002 presidential election. To recover after this failure the primaries were revived for the 2007 presidential election. In that case, Ségolène Royal was defeated by Nicolas Sarkozy, but in the parliamentary election which immediately followed the Socialist Party was at least able to block the feared landslide victory by the Gaullists, realising an increase in their electoral support of around 300,000 votes if compared to 2002. In this case the primaries were ostensibly unable to completely reverse a critical state of affairs, but they do seem to have contributed to saving the Socialists from a major breakdown.

After two closed primaries, in 2011 the PS opened up the selection of the presidential candidate to all voters. The outcome was a great success for the party: the nominee, François Hollande, won the 2012 race against the incumbent Nicolas Sarkozy, and the subsequent parliamentary election guaranteed the Socialists a large majority and the formation of a left-wing government. The PS obtained over 1 million votes more than in the earlier electoral performance. The Hollande presidency may have been helped by Sarkozy's low popularity rating, but the margin of the result points to open primaries being a valuable tool to improve party prospects.

With regard to membership, let us now consider the effects of primary elections on the recruitment of party members. This relationship must be assessed differently depending on the rules of the game. When parties make use of closed primaries, usually membership rises immediately before the primaries, and those instant members frequently leave the party just afterwards, or they may remain as passive, low-quality participants (Cross and Rahat, 2012). The situation is different in the case of open primaries. If the strategies deployed by the politicians to gain nominations are by and large similar, interested citizens are not spurred to acquire a party card, as they may vote for a preferred candidate without becoming a party member. Therefore, no growth should happen before the primaries, and in any case an increase in membership should not be considered in any way deceitful. Moreover, if the primaries play any role, the number of partisans is expected to rise after the primaries as a consequence of improved party image. A decrease, or an erratic rise and fall, instead shows the irrelevance of the primaries for party membership.

These cases may be controlled in reference with Table 7.3, which also describes the variations in membership of the left-wing parties in the two countries. In the Italian case, once more, things are blurred by the party politics of the last 20 years. One should at least bear in mind that Democrats of the Left and The Daisy have been the main parties of the left-wing coalition for the first half of the 2000s; that they merged in 2007 to form the Democratic Party; and finally that the post-Communist Left Ecology Freedom was the main PD partner in the 2012 coalition primary and in the subsequent 2013 parliamentary election. That said, after the first case of primary elections in 2005, the main left-wing party, the Democrats of the Left, slightly enhanced its membership in 2006. For the 2012 primary election, PD and SEL memberships experienced a combined fall of 227,000 members. Here the ups and downs of the membership appear to be unconnected with the primaries, and rather linked to the transformation of the left-wing parties.

In the French case, the membership variation registered a positive trend after all primary elections. After the 1995 primary the membership increased by 8,500 compared to data before the primary. In this case, membership figures have declined steadily from the early 1990s, to increase immediately after the primaries – in full disagreement with the point of view of the (closed) primaries as a pathology. The pattern has been partially different in the case of the 2006 primaries, when there was an abrupt rise in membership in comparison with the previous year. The main reason is that, as stated above, the Socialist Party then promoted a membership recruitment drive immediately before the primary by selling low-cost party cards. Finally the Socialist membership increased by 27,600 after the 2011 primaries, confirming the positive trend of the precedent years. It is important to recall again that in this case the open primaries lacked any incentive for instant membership, and the rise is to be credited to the improvement of the party image.

Conclusion

Drawing a general 'conclusion' from the analysis of the five cases that we have analysed in this chapter is extremely risky. Hence we simply advance a few considerations about possible trends of party democratisation.

Starting with the rationales for the primaries, first of all the French cases show a tendency to evolve from closed to open primaries by emulating the Italian experiences. As other parties throughout Europe strive to increase the inclusiveness of their selectorates,[3] a case of cross-national contagion may be suspected which upholds primaries open to all citizens. Moreover, the set of rules used to regulate

---

3 See Chapter 4 on Spain and Portugal in this volume.

the electoral processes has grown in complexity both in Italy and in France, and in a couple of cases the rules have been shaped disingenuously to benefit a candidate. These examples support the idea of a fraudulent use of primaries by the party elites to surmount internal opponents, as feared by the cartel party theorists. In these cases, the manipulation concerns the rules rather than the party members, so it may also affect open primaries – as happened in Italy in 2012 – in addition to the closed primary as originally supposed by Katz and Mair (1995).

Let us now briefly assess the possible consequences of using primary elections. Considering first electoral results, we note that all three open primaries analysed here have been followed by successes for the changing Italian left-wing coalitions and the French Socialist Party. By 'success' we mean that the parties and coalitions involved gained a substantial number of votes, and were able to form a government. However, the case of the Italian left after the 2013 parliamentary election remains controversial. The coalition collected the greatest number of votes, but it was not able to achieve a parliamentary majority. The events that followed – the breakdown of the coalition, the Democratic Party entering an unexpectedly oversized government, and the resignation of its secretary – can hardly be depicted as a 'success'. In any case, one can at least reject the thesis of the unavoidable penalty due to the use of primaries which is borne out by mainstream American research.

Examining party membership, we have found some support for the pessimistic thesis according to which closed primaries mobilise instant members scarcely involved in politics, who are predestined to quickly leave the party or to become inactive grassroots. In any case, it may be expected that the success of the nominee in the subsequent general election might balance this tendency. Unfortunately, because both the closed primaries under examination here resulted in the defeat of the Socialist presidential candidate, this is only an interesting research question. In contrast with full member vote, open primaries seemingly do not bring such inconveniences. They do not entail incentives to membership, and can improve party image without undesirable collateral effects.

As with all political events, electoral results and levels of party membership are affected by a range of factors. Therefore readers should be aware that the relationships discussed above could be spurious – namely, they could involve variables not considered here. For instance, in considering the consequences of the 2012 primaries in Italy, it seems likely that party choices after the primaries, vocally opposed by the grassroots, may have influenced the plummeting of membership more than any other event. In the case of the ebb and flow of the Socialist membership in France it would be necessary also to fully assess the selection of the party leader. S/he is chosen through a traditional congress of delegates, where the role of the members is still crucial and an incentive to join exists. Not so for the Italian Democratic Party, whose leader is once more selected through open primaries lacking incentives to sign up. As usual, only further comparative researches will shed light on these shadowy areas.

Chapter 8
Democratising Candidate Selection in Romania and Slovakia

Sergiu Gherghina and Peter Spáč

Introduction

In more than two decades of post-communist party politics, the use of inclusive selection methods in Central and Eastern European (CEE) has been episodic. The control of the party in central office and the limited recruitment and involvement of party members appeared to be the rules of the game (Lewis, 1996; van Biezen, 2003; Millard, 2004; Deegan-Krause, 2006). In this environment only a handful of parties formally specify primary elections – open to their members – as a means of selecting their candidates (Gherghina, 2013). Two important political parties from Romania and Slovakia had a similar approach towards primaries: they both formally adopted primaries, but failed to use them on a systematic basis. The Romanian Social Democratic Party (PSD) used primaries for the selection of its legislative candidates in 2004, made them optional immediately afterwards and never used them again. The Slovak Democratic and Christian Union-Democratic Party (SDKÚ-DS) adopted primaries in 2000 but used them only in 2002 and 2010.

The comparison between these two parties is more relevant if we account for the dimensions proposed by Gallagher and Marsh (1988). According to these dimensions, the parties have developed in different political environments and played different roles in the domestic political arena. The PSD is the largest Romanian party, being the successor of the communist party (Pop-Eleches, 1999) from which it inherited the organisation. Between 1992, the year of its formation, and 2012 the PSD won five out of six legislative elections and formed four coalition governments. It has formed coalition governments with a variety of political parties, ranging from the Conservative Party (PC) – with which it also competed in alliances on several occasions – to liberals or democrat liberals, the latter sharing origins with the PSD. These achievements indicate that the PSD is the largest and relatively most stable political party of the left, both features being remarkable in the context of relatively high electoral volatility at party system level. In Slovakia, the SDKÚ-DS was formed from the debris of a wider movement which played a crucial role in securing the democratic system in the country at the end of the 1990s. Since its emergence, the party has become the leading actor of the centre-right, with ambitions to dominate this side of the political spectrum. Although the party has never lived up to such expectations, it joined two coalition governments from the position of *formateur*, holding the position of prime minister. These governments, formed after elections in 2002 and 2010, were rather ideologically homogeneous as they included liberals, conservatives and parties representing the Hungarian minority. However, in recent years the SDKÚ-DS watched its own decline and in the 2012 election it barely gained access to Parliament.

Having these features as points of departure, this chapter analyses the use of primaries in Romania and Slovakia with a focus on the PSD in 2004 and the SDKÚ-DS in 2010.[1] Our goal is to identify similarities in the formal rules, organisation and potential effects of primaries.[2] The first section presents the contextual determinants and rationales behind the adoption of primaries. Next, we briefly describe the election process, with an emphasis on formal rules, electoral campaign, competitiveness and degree of participation. The third section analyses the political consequences of primaries on the PSD and the SDKÚ-DS. The empirical evidence reveals no impact of the inclusive candidate selection methods on electoral performance or membership organisation for either party. The conclusions summarise the key findings and elaborate on the broader implications of the analysis and further avenues for research.

Contexts and Rationales for Adopting Primary Elections

As mentioned earlier, the PSD is the largest Romanian party, with an average electoral support higher than 30 per cent. It won five out of the six legislative elections held since its creation, and participated in four coalition governments (three times as the leading party). It emerged after a split in the National Salvation Front (FSN), the communist successor party, early in the transition (1992). The split followed a divergence of opinions among the leaders of the Front. Ion Iliescu's ideological group lost the internal elections and formed a new party – the Democratic National Salvation Front (FDSN). In 1993, it changed its name to Party of Social Democracy in Romania (PDSR), and from 2001 the PSD. The PSD retained most of the party elites and local branches of the Front, and thus ended up with a relevant organisational heritage similar to that of the other successor parties in the region (Ishiyama, 1999). The party has a tradition of centre-dominated candidate selection. While both local and central organisations can propose candidates, the final decision belongs to the central office. The latter is quite strong in the everyday life of the party, being backed by long-standing leaders of

---

1 The 2002 primaries were partly spoiled by the internal turmoil that relativised their results. At the same time, no data on those primaries is available.

2 One political party in Romania – the Democratic Alliance of Hungarians in Romania (UDMR) – has always selected its candidates on the basis of primaries for all legislative elections. This case cannot be included in the analysis due to data availability and a relatively different type of organisation, in that it is not a party *per se* but a conglomerate of associations and foundations.

territorial organisations. This increased support of territorial leaders for the central organisation is one reason why factionalism is quite limited within the PSD. In this context, the party leader has often had the task of ensuring the organisation's cohesiveness and diminishing potential dissent.

The PSD proactively used its heritage and worked to develop its organisation, being oriented towards the enlargement of its membership base. The result was a dramatic increase in membership between 1992 and 1996 – from 60,000 to 309,000 (Gherghina, 2014a). In general, the PSD maintained this high level until 2008, the average number of members being around 330,000 or approximately 1.6 per cent of the electorate. In spite of this solid membership base, inclusiveness of candidate selection was limited between 1992 and 2004. Selection was exclusively an elite affair that involved negotiation between the central and local layers. The representatives of local organisations proposed candidates for the legislative elections and the executive committee approved these proposals. At the same time, after 1999 the central layer could make its own proposals after discussion with the local organisations. In 2004, the PSD decided to change this selection method and introduce primaries open to all its members. This decision was triggered by four major determinants:

1. the stability or augmentation of membership
2. stronger ties with the electorate
3. a better image
4. high-quality candidates.

First, although the PSD had an important membership organisation, one of the largest in Central and Eastern Europe, its claim to represent the masses required a stable or even higher number of members. This concern was also relevant in the context of a small decrease in terms of membership between 1996 and 2000, when the party lost approximately 5,000 members. Second, the electoral support registered fluctuations in the elections organised in the first post-communist decade. Its victory in the 1992 elections with almost 28 per cent of the vote was followed by a decrease to a little more than 21 per cent in the subsequent 1996 elections – its lowest electoral performance – that threw the party into opposition. Then in 2000, the PSD's electoral support witnessed a boost. This absence of electoral stability indicated the need for stronger connections with the voters, and the adoption of primaries could have acted as a catalyst.

Third, among the Romanian political parties the PSD was considered greatly indebted to its local notabilities, and accused of clientelistic practices. In general, the local leaders and Members of Parliament (MPs) play important roles in voter mobilisation at constituency level in Romania. This is partly why the emergence of strong local leaders and MPs is encouraged by parties. However, in the case of the PSD, more than in other parties, local leaders and MPs follow their own interests and agendas, playing the nepotism card and thus receiving extensive public criticism in the media. For example, corruption allegations following the

1992–96 term in government and during the 1996 electoral campaign negatively affected the party and contributed to its failure to win the elections. Thus, a better image of the party was necessary and the primaries could help achieve this goal. The PSD wanted to illustrate that its internal decisions are governed by democratic principles. Along the same lines, the adoption of candidate-centred primaries converged with the movement for electoral reform at national level. Following the 2000 parliamentary elections, the closed-list proportional representation (PR) system was seen as the key driver for popular discontent in Parliament, the quality of MPs and the general performance of this institution (Gherghina and Jiglau, 2012). The aim was to replace the electoral lists controlled by the party with candidates running in single-member districts. While this reform was implemented nationally in 2008, the PSD – in government when the discussions on electoral reform emerged – conveyed a clear message to the masses. It was willing to adopt first the required electoral change in its internal procedures.

Fourth, the primaries aimed to improve the quality of candidates. The PSD is one of the CEE political parties with most MPs present in almost all legislatures during the post-communist period. These MPs are usually the leaders of county organisations or politicians with strong electoral support in the territory. The adoption of primaries could have ensured a higher percentage of reliable candidates on which the party could count for renomination.[3] Furthermore, primaries could provide useful tools to 'clean' the party and present new faces to the voters. The same idea was emphasised in a report issued by the PSD's research institute, Ovidiu Sincai, in July 2004. According to this report, primary elections could allow the reform of the political class. This was particularly important due to the strong competition faced by the PSD in the 2004 legislative elections. The country's second and third parties – the National Liberal Party and the Democrat Party (later Democrat Liberal Party) – joined forces in an alliance to defeat the social democrats. Before the 2004 legislative elections the new alliance (Truth and Justice) had high levels of support in public opinion polls.

Let us now focus on the Slovak case to assess similarities and differences between the two experiences. The PSD and the SDKÚ-DS had similar formations and shared some reasons to adopt primaries. The SDKÚ-DS is a classic case of a top-down created party which emerged after internal disputes within the Slovak Democratic Coalition (SDK). The latter was the main opposition group that contributed to the defeat of the semi-democratic regime of Prime Minister Vladimír Mečiar in the 1998 elections. After these elections the parties involved in the SDK's formation advocated a return to its original coalition form.[4] The newly appointed Prime Minister Mikuláš Dzurinda rejected this idea, and asked

---

3   For a detailed explanation regarding the concept of candidate renomination and one way to calculate it for parliamentary parties see Gherghina (2014b).

4   The SDK was originally founded as a coalition of five parties. Due to Mečiar's electoral reform, which intentionally disadvantaged this type of cooperation, the SDK was finally forced to transform into a single party (Rybář, 2005, pp. 136–7).

the original parties that created SDK to merge into a single unit.⁵ When mutual agreement proved impossible, Dzurinda, together with several other SDK leaders, released a declaration in January 2000 announcing the emergence of the SDKÚ-DS (Haughton and Rybář, 2004, pp. 124–7).

The way in which the SDKÚ-DS was created strongly influenced its internal mechanisms. The original idea was to create a political entity including several ideological platforms, ranging from liberal to conservative – but this idea faded quite quickly (Kopeček, 2007). Alongside their weakening, the position of the leader and his inner circle improved strongly and until the party's first general election in 2002 it was near to dominant. Unlike the proclaimed idea, the party was built as a centralised structure with decision making controlled by the leadership – with only few possibilities for permanent internal factions.

Shortly after its emergence the SDKÚ-DS introduced a mechanism for selecting its candidates through primaries; this made it the first and so far the only party in Slovakia to do so. There are two main reasons behind this decision which may be identified. First, the SDKÚ-DS tried to present itself as the main successor to the SDK and its democratic legacy. The 1998 election was not only a competition about programmatic issues; it was also about the basic principles of the political system. Being the strongest opposition party/alliance, the SDK strongly supported the ideas of liberal democracy and presented itself as the main guarantee of Slovakia's entry into the European Union (EU) and NATO. This had a strong symbolic connotation as the country was disqualified from accession under Mečiar's rule (Haughton, 2003). After its emergence, the SDKÚ-DS tried to follow the line of the SDK, and this was obvious even from its name. It tried to commit to liberal democracy by mentioning it in its manifesto and by applying it to internal processes. Accordingly, it adopted primaries and stressed their inclusive character as proof of the party's devotion to democratic values.

Second, similar to the PSD, the SDKÚ-DS also acquired an instrument to distinguish it from the other competitors who selected their candidates behind closed doors. The idea of opening candidate selection to all members conveyed a message of commitment to democratic values within the party. In this sense, primaries were thought to differentiate the other political competitors and make membership of the SDKÚ-DS more attractive. This was necessary in order to recruit a larger membership base, an important part of its vision for integration.⁶ In Slovakia the willingness of citizens to become party members remained rather low after 1989. The biggest membership from all was acquired by party of Mečiar

---

5   However, it is questionable whether a stable subject could be created from all the parties that established the SDK. These parties included Christian Democrats, Liberals, Social Democrats and Greens, a mixture which was able to cooperate only because of a common enemy – the Mečiar regime.

6   Although the previous discussions about merging the parties which established the SDK ended without success, the SDKÚ-DS continued to stress the need to integrate the various ideological currents (Kopeček, 2007, pp. 382–3).

in the 1990s, reaching 70,000 (Kopeček, 2007, p. 163) – a figure that dramatically exceeded that of any other party until the present. Thus, the SDKÚ-DS adopted an instrument to boost its membership, but this was situated in an environment working under rather different rules – and the later development of the number of party members confirmed this (see below). However, from the standpoint of party elites, the introduction of primaries was seen as a pragmatic step towards backing up the party's public proclamations and general aims.

The Primary Election Process

This section focuses on the main features of primary election processes in Romania and Slovakia. It presents and analyses in a comparative way the selectorate, decentralisation, the electoral system and candidates of the two political parties under scrutiny. Consistent with the decision to organise its primaries at constituency (that is county) level, the PSD delegated the responsibility for candidate nominations to the county organisations. As shown in Table 8.1, the procedure was similar for candidates running for a seat on the list for the Chamber of Deputies (the lower chamber) and for the Senate (the upper chamber). Each constituency compiled ballot papers including the names of all the candidates fulfilling the eligibility criteria. The latter were a combination of fuzzy and concrete issues. Any member could become a candidate as longs as (s)he gathered 1,000 signatures from supporters; was known as an 'honest person', with professional recognition; had no prior criminal convictions; was not under judicial investigation; and had never been suspended or dismissed from a leadership position. Also, no party member who held an official elected position at local and county level could run in primaries. As an extra criterion, foreign language skills were an asset. Finally, in deciding who could run in primaries, two quotas were enforced: 25 per cent women candidates and 30 per cent young candidates (that is under 35 years old). The candidates also required formal approval from the party leadership at county level.

The 2010 primaries for legislative elections in the SDKÚ-DS followed a different logic, with complicated nomination procedures and inclusive eligibility criteria. In terms of nominations, they distinguished between two separate elections: for leader of the candidate list; and for the composition of the list of candidates. For the first type of election, the party chairman is expected to run, although he can choose not to. Candidates for this position can be nominated by the central office (Presidium), regional party leaders or groups of at least 300 members. If no such nominations are made, the chairman becomes the candidate list leader by default. For the second type of election, the candidates are formally divided into two groups: 15 candidates nominated by the central office for national-level lists; and candidates nominated for the regional constituencies. The executive committee has a monopoly on the nominations and order of candidates for the first group. The candidates for the regions are nominated by the remaining party bodies, two associated party organisations (women and youth) or at least 100

Table 8.1 Main features of primary elections processes in Romania and Slovakia

Country	Party	Year	Selectorate	Decentralisation	Candidacy	Voting system	Timing	Deselection
Romania	PSD	2004	Only party members	Subnational/regional level	1,000 signatures Honest, with professional recognition No convictions or under investigation	Electronic voting Individual candidates Multiple votes (N=district magnitude)	Less than three months before legislative elections	Not regulated
Slovakia	SDKÚ-DS	2010	Only party members	National level	300 signatures for leader of the list 100 signatures for list candidates	Paper voting Open lists Multiple votes (N=20: 5 for central office, 15 for regions)	Four months before legislative elections	Regulated

members. The order of these candidates is determined by the regional leaderships (each region deciding the order of its candidates) and associated organisations. To be nominated, a person has to fulfil the requirements stated by law to run for the office. The SDKÚ-DS also formally allows non-members to run in primaries, which is valid both for the candidates on the list and for the leader.

The electoral system used by the two parties reflected the above-mentioned differences in nominations. The PSD opted for an electronic voting system that allows the members to choose between individual candidates – that is, completely different from the closed-list PR system in legislative elections. As a result of elections being organised at constituency level, each member had a number of votes equal to the constituency magnitude. Winners were declared the candidates with the highest share of the vote, and the order on the list was supposed to reflect their popularity. However, this did not happen in practice. Although having no formally specified role, the executive committee altered the results of the primaries and either replaced some candidates with some of its own or changed the order on the list for the legislative elections.

The electoral procedures followed by the SDKÚ-DS resembled the system used in parliamentary elections, and voting took part on open lists. Each party member could cast 20 votes: five for the candidates proposed by the central office and 15 for regional candidates.[7] With respect to the latter, every voter had to cast at least one vote for a candidate from every region and every associated organisation. After votes were counted, the candidates were ranked according to share of votes, but both groups of candidates were placed in predetermined positions. The candidates nominated by the centre occupied positions 2–6 and all the even positions up to number 26. The candidates nominated by the regions got all the remaining positions, but there is an obligatory rotation of all regions and associated organisations at the top. The first 10 seats reserved for the candidates nominated by the regions were occupied by one candidate per region each plus two candidates of the associated organisations. A region's second candidate can thus occupy at best the 11th position among this group of candidates, which is the 27th position on the list. This mechanism ensured territorial and social representation in the composition of the list. According to the regulations, the final word belonged to the executive committee, which holds the power to alter the order of the selected candidates.

As for the campaign, the formal regulations of the two parties showed similar concern for the duration and means used to convey messages. The electoral campaign for the PSD primary elections was 18 days and started after all candidates were validated; it ended one day before the elections. Candidates could only use meetings with members – no campaigning in the media, over the phone or through public advertisement. The SDKÚ-DS candidates could start campaigning after they were officially nominated, which in practice means that the campaign lasts for

---

7   The SDKÚ-DS statutes stipulate that only members who have been in the party for at least 12 months may vote in primaries.

about one month. They could present themselves at meetings of party members or via the party's webpage. As in the Romanian case, the campaign lasted until the day before the primaries. The SDKÚ-DS has a special provision according to which any form of negative campaign against party competitors was strictly forbidden. If candidates break this rule they risk sanctions up to the loss of functions held in the party organisation (Primary Election Rules of SDKÚ-DS, 2009).

Participation and Competitiveness

The two primary elections appear to be quite attractive to members. The turnout percentages in Table 8.2 reflect a similar popularity, with four out of five members casting a vote. This similarity gains relevance in the context of contrasting approaches to the membership organisations. The PSD inherited and developed one of the largest membership organisations in Central and Eastern Europe, while the SDKÚ-DS relies on a minimal number of members. This high level of participation can provide legitimacy to the primaries. However, this figure is not reliable in the case of the PSD as it is an estimate provided by the party president, Adrian Năstase (Radulescu, 2004). There are three reasons why his statements are likely to be biased;

1. Năstase was the initiator of the primaries, and a large turnout would have supported his idea.
2. When referring to the turnout he mentioned that almost 500,000 members voted, equivalent to 82 per cent; this means that the total number of party members was over 600,000. However, the PSD's official number of members around the legislative elections in 2004 was less than 400,000 (Gherghina, 2014a).
3. The aggregate number of votes was not recorded at country level, since the primaries took place at constituency level. Turnout was reported only in some constituencies, and thus aggregate calculations are not possible.

Even the reported turnout in constituencies is not reliable due to several problems. In the Suceava constituency the PSD secretary polled 18,022 votes while the turnout was 15,710 members. In the Vrancea constituency a PSD minister polled 13,539 votes but only 13,155 members voted. A similar case was in the Mehedinti constituency, where a central party figure received 10,200 votes from the 9,918 who went to the polls (Georgescu, 2012).

Contrary to these fuzzy percentages, the figures for the SDKÚ-DS are accurate and indicate no real difference in levels of participation between the three competitions. The explanation for this is relatively simple: the party as a whole held its elections on one day. Thus the selectors were motivated to participate in primaries in all constituencies. Equally important in explaining the similar levels of participation is that the candidates for the national lists and for the regional constituencies were listed on the same ballot.

Table 8.2 Main features of primary election competitions in Romania and Slovakia

Country	Party	Year	Turnout (%)	Number of candidates	Number of incumbents	Incumbents nominated (%)	Nominations to be allocated	Realistic seats	Number of women	Women nominated (%)	VCI
Romania	PSD	2004	82.0	722 deputies	98	13	314	110	n.a.	n.a.	n.a.
				287 senators	31	11	136	55	n.a.	n.a.	n.a.
Slovakia	SDKÚ-DS	2010	List leader: 80.3	2	2	100	2	2	1	50	0.62
			Candidate for national lists: 80.0	14	10	71	14	14	3	21.4	0.52
			Candidates for regional lists: 80.0	150	11	7	134	14	22	14.6	0.51

A key aspect of primaries is their degree of competitiveness. In reporting the situation for the PSD we distinguish between the candidates for the Chamber of Deputies and the Senate. The lower chamber of the Romanian Parliament has more seats, and in the 2004 legislative election the political parties competed for 314. Its size varies across elections, and this number does not include the seats reserved to the ethnic minorities. The Senate, with fairly similar functions and electoral procedures, consisted of 136 seats in the 2004 legislative elections; due to these similarities the Romanian parties gain similar percentages of seats in elections for both chambers. The number of candidates in the primaries mirrored the size of the chambers, but the ratio was comparable. For the Chamber of Deputies there were 2.3 candidates for one seat and 5.6 candidates for one realistic seat, while for the Senate there were 2.1 candidates for one seat and 5.2 candidates for one realistic seat. In the primary elections 98 incumbent deputies have run (out of 170 elected in the 2000–04 legislature) and 31 senators (out of 69 elected in the 2000–04 legislature).[8] In the absence of data regarding gender distribution we can hardly know the exact number of women candidates. While there is no doubt that the quota mentioned in the regulations to organise primaries has been respected, the relatively poor history of female representation in the Romanian Parliament raises doubts about a high number of women as candidates in the primaries.

The SDKÚ-DS has significant differences across the competitions. Above all, there was almost no competition for the list leadership or between the candidates proposed by the central office. In essence, all the candidates could be sure of getting into the final ballot.[9] Moreover, all the allocated positions – according to the rules (see above) – were realistic and gave them good chances of being elected in the legislative elections.[10] Consequently, even if they wanted to, party members were not able to throw these candidates completely off the list in the framework of the primaries, but only determine their order. On the other hand, the regional candidates experienced a highly competitive process because the number of nominees was 10 times higher than the number of realistic seats. Although in this case, too, a majority of the candidates were assured of a place in the ballot, only a small number of them were able to place sufficiently high on the list.

---

8   In 2004 there was a decrease in realistic seats compared to 2000 for two reasons: the number of MPs was reduced and the PSD faced competition from a strong alliance formed by the democrats and liberals.

9   This guarantee also affects the loser of the contest for leader. As only elite party officials enter this competition, the loser gets second position on the list. This happened in both cases when primaries were used. Based on this, only 14 candidates from the centre are nominated, and the best of these gets the third position on the list.

10   The number of realistic seats a party is expected to win was determined as the average of the party's previous results in 2002 and 2006. In them the SDKÚ-DS won 28 and 31 seats, which yields and average of 30 seats (rounded). For each of the competitions it was determined how many of the realistic seats belonged to it, and these numbers were used independently in the calculations.

A look at the incumbents also provides important information. Out of the 31 party MPs from the previous term in office, 23 have run in the primaries. Their distribution across competitions is also illustrative: incumbents were the only ones competing for the list leadership and made up the majority of the centre-based list of candidates. The competition within the SDKÚ-DS was mostly closed, with little room for newcomers; the latter were given more chances for the regional nominations.

As for the representation of women, we have data only for the SDKÚ-DS.[11] The results of the 2010 primaries indicate the existence of 23 women on the final list, six of whom occupied realistic positions – including Iveta Radičová as the leader. In the group of candidates for the centre, three women won realistic positions and one of them was in third place on the list. Among the candidates from the regions, two women were successful, but both placed below the first 20 positions (23 and 27). This shows that women can expect better placement in the more centralised and exclusive nominating processes. In the case of the SDKÚ-DS, the executive committee proposes the candidates for the centre, by which its rules in effect place them in the foremost positions on the list. When compared to other Slovak parties, the SDKÚ-DS stands fairly well with regard to women's representation.

The way in which primaries were implemented in Romania and Slovakia allows for three general conclusions. First, the two examined parties used different formal rules to conduct closed primaries for candidate selection. For example, the Romanian PSD placed emphasis on quotas for women and young members or used a different electoral system than in legislative elections (for example electronic voting and candidates as opposed to closed lists), issues that were completely ignored by the Slovak SDKÚ-DS. Instead, it formally separated the candidates and thus created different competitions within the party. Second, primaries were appealing to party members: in spite of large differences in the size of membership organisations, participation was very high in both cases – that is, four out of five members cast their votes. Third, the involvement and control of the central office existed in both parties but took different forms. The PSD elite partially altered the results of the vote after primaries, while in the case of the SDKÚ-DS the party leadership reserved the highest positions on the final list for its nominees.

Political Consequences for Parties

At a glance, the adoption of primaries appears to have a beneficial influence on the PSD's membership organisation. Between 2000 and 2004, the number of members showed a significant increase (Table 8.3). In subsequent legislative elections, when primaries were no longer used, the number of members decreased. However, this positive relationship between primaries and party membership is likely to be

---

11 The quota mechanism for women in the SDKÚ-DS guarantees only that a woman will be nominated in at least one unpaired slot from 7th to 25th place.

spurious. The history of PSD membership from the first post-communist decade illustrates that the party gained members when it was in government. This was also the case for the 2000–04 legislative term, while between 2004 and 2008 the party was in opposition. In addition, the increase must be considered in light of unfair competition and electoral fraud during primaries. Therefore, it is more likely that the high number of members in 2004 was the result of candidates' desire to win primaries by any means rather than an increased attractiveness of the party for citizens. For example, in their attempt to create unfair advantages during the primary elections, some local leaders enrolled new members overnight. In the Iasi constituency, party membership increased by more than 3,000 (from 14,000 to 17,500) in less than two months. Media reports, based on accusations by opponents of the local leaders, claim that most of these new members were offered financial benefits in the form of social assistance (Onofrei, 2004). Illustrative of this argument is the increase in membership during primaries and the decrease until 2008 (after primaries). The members recruited to enhance electoral support during primaries had only short-term commitments and left the party immediately after.

The data on SDKÚ-DS membership tell a similar story where the primaries appear to have no impact on attracting new members. The party is situated on a descending slope starting in 2006 irrespective of the use of primaries. The explanations for these changes lie in the party's longitudinal political development and performance. The number of members changed from year to year, reflecting the party's position in the system of power. After losing the 2006 elections the party went into opposition, and membership declined rapidly. A turnaround came midway through the electoral term, with membership growth culminating at the end of 2010, when the party again found itself in government. In the following years membership fell sharply again, along with the breakup of the Radičová government and the outbreak of the 'Gorilla' scandal.[12]

Regarding electoral performance, the PSD appears to have a stable electorate in the three most recent legislative elections (2000, 2004 and 2008). In 2004, the party managed to secure a fairly similar share of the vote as in 2000 (almost 37 per cent). This electoral stability does not appear to be necessarily linked to the adoption of primaries, as in 2008 the party registered a similar electoral result. Instead of primaries, one possible explanation for the stable electoral performance is the structure of competition. In the last decade, once the number of parliamentary parties was reduced to five, the alternatives were simpler for voters. Two parties – the radical right and the ethnic party – have clear target audiences. Practically, the rest of the electorate (approximately 80 per cent) has three options: the PSD, the Democrats or the Liberals. Moreover, the PSD's decision to merge with many centre-left parties allowed the party to encapsulate the preferences of the voters on the left.

---

12 A document was circulated ahead of the 2012 election, alleging large-scale corruption during the period of Dzurinda's second government. This led to a sharp drop in the SDKÚ-DS's electoral performance (Spáč, 2010, p. 101).

Table 8.3 Effects of primary elections on political parties in Romania and Slovakia

Country	Party	Year	Members		Change (N)	Electoral performance (Votes)		Change (Votes after primaries % - votes before primaries %)
			Year before primaries (N)	Year after primaries (N)		Before primaries (%)	After primaries (%)	
Romania	PSD	2004	304,713[a]	385,481[a]	80768	36.9	37.0	0.2
Slovakia	SDKÚ-DS	2010	6,275	6,842	567	18.4	15.4	-2.9

Notes: [a] M/E ratios – PSD before primaries 1.72; PSD after primaries 2.09.
Sources: IDEA, Central Electoral Bureau in Romania, Statistical Office of the Slovak Republic, Gherghina 2014a.

As for the consequences of primaries for the SDKÚ-DS, the most important aspect is the party's results in the general elections. Four parliamentary elections have been held since the party's inception, but primaries have been held only twice. The party did not hold primaries ahead of the 2006 and 2012 elections, officially citing time constraints as both elections were called early. The data in Table 8.3 show that, with the exception of the most recent elections, the SDKÚ-DS's results were fairly balanced. Given the importance of the relative values, both the best and worst results (18.4 and 6.1 per cent respectively) were achieved in elections which were not preceded by primaries. On the contrary, when primaries were held they did not have a substantial effect on the party's results, which were rather average.

One possible explanation would be insufficient public awareness of the primaries. Although the SDKÚ-DS gained some media coverage because of the primaries, in 2010 this was overwhelmingly devoted to the competition for the position of the list leader between Radičová and Ivan Mikloš. Conversely, filling the remaining positions on the list was solely an internal party matter, with little publicity. The SDKÚ-DS also plays into this effect by not releasing the results of its primaries to the public. Objectively speaking, the primary elections are barely registered by society, which limits the influence of this process on the party's election results. As practice shows, the party's election results were dependent on other, more pronounced factors.[13]

The public debate about primaries was fairly limited in both countries. While the media reported on their novelty for domestic politics and drew parallels with the American examples, none of the other political parties engaged with the topic in a constructive manner. In Romania, following the PSD's bad experience, some marginal discourses about the use of primaries as political strategy emerged among the political competitors. However, not even this approach was solid and the subject died out quite fast. The lack of interest in primaries from both the public and the political parties is an important reason why no political actor has used primaries to select its candidates or leaders since 2004. A similar situation occurred in Slovakia, where the topic of primaries received some attention after this method was adopted by the SDKÚ-DS but never led to any broader public or political discussions. With no visible profit for the SDKÚ-DS, motivation for other actors to follow this party was low. As a result, the remaining Slovak parties only rarely opened debates about primaries and never made any notable effort to make their candidate selection more inclusive.

---

13 These phenomena include tactical voting of SDKÚ-DS's electorate in 2010 leading a section of the party voters to support other, smaller centre-right parties. The aim was to prevent a possible slump of this segment of the party spectrum. The party's devastating result in 2012 was mainly caused by the so-called Gorilla scandal.

Conclusions

This chapter analysed the use of primaries in two CEE political parties. Each of these had its own rationale behind the implementation of inclusive candidate selection. The Romanian PSD adopted primaries more than a decade after its creation and understood them mainly as an experiment. The major goals were to maintain a stronger link with the electorate, improve the party's image and raise the quality of its candidates. The Slovak SDKÚ-DS launched primaries immediately after its formation, as this step helped the party emphasise its uniqueness. In light of these different drivers, the organisation of primaries varied greatly. The comparison reveals that the PSD uses various criteria to restrict candidacies to members, whereas the SDKÚ-DS allows all Slovak citizens to enter the competition. The differences also affect the use of quotas, which are extensively implemented by the PSD but in a minimalist way by the SDKÚ-DS.

With respect to the most important formal aspects, the PSD's primary elections were rather decentralised, but with a strong final say from the executive committee which could alter the will of participating members. In the SDKÚ-DS this type of control was only formally stated, but without real implementation. The main reason may be that the party elites held in any case a very strong position due to a majority of realistic seats reserved for their candidates. The executive committee of the SDKÚ-DS had no need to alter the results of primaries as it controls the main part of the whole process from the beginning. Both parties also differed in some practical aspects – such as electronic or paper ballots and the electoral system itself – mainly caused by the system used for legislative elections. What is important is the fact that in both parties the primaries were very attractive for members and participation rates were high.

Apart from these differences, the use of primaries shares a few features. One of them is their closed character, being available to members only. One further similarity is the character of the campaigns: short and limited with respect to the way candidates can promote themselves. As for the consequences, none of the primaries had a significant effect on party membership size and electoral performance; their development and changes have different determinants.

The latter can be one explanation for the absence of the systematic use of primaries in the PSD and the SDKÚ-DS. Another explanation lies in the attitudes of the party elites. Our description of the primaries indicated that elites continue to understand the selection of candidates as a process in which they must hold a strong say and rarely allow regular members to get the upper hand. Both elements are likely to perpetuate the poor tradition of inclusive intra-party decision-making processes in the region.

Chapter 9
Democratising Candidate Selection in Iceland

Indridi H. Indriðason and Gunnar Helgi Kristinsson

Introduction

When the Icelandic parties began opening up their candidate selection processes during the 1970s they probably had no idea that what they were doing was rather unusual in a European context. Primaries were adopted, without much consideration of the consequences they might have, in response to immediate pressures and were adapted along the way in response to unforeseen circumstances and events. Prior to the development of formal mass membership organisations there had been occasional experiments with primaries in Iceland, but the consolidation of party organisations during the 1930s saw greater party control of the selection processes. The long history, since the 1970s, of party primaries in Iceland in the context of proportional representation (PR) and multiparty politics provides an opportunity for exploring the origins of primaries and evaluating their impact in a well-established European democracy.

According to Bengtsson et al. (2013, p. 32), Icelandic party politics is relatively polarised by comparison with the other Nordic countries, and more divisive in terms of voters' evaluations of the parties. The political culture is characterised by a relatively strong sense of nationalism, which played a crucial role in Icelandic state building during the late nineteenth and the early twentieth century. Nationalism is a strong force both on the political right and left, and has functioned as both a unifying and divisive factor in Icelandic politics.[1]

Iceland is a parliamentary democracy with a popularly elected president who can initiate referenda (a right which he has exercised three times) but otherwise plays a marginal political role. The country is normally governed by majority coalition governments of two or three parties, and minority governments are rare. Patterns of coalition formation are fairly fluid although, given its size, the Progressive Party (PP) has participated in a disproportionately large number of government coalitions, due to its willingness to form coalitions with both the left

---

1   Although confidence in the system was badly shaken in the financial meltdown of 2008, Iceland ranks highly even after the crash among the states of the world on such indexes as the Human Development Index (14 in 2013), Freedom House press freedom measure (6–9 in 2014) and Transparency International's Corruption Perception Index (12 in 2013).

and the right. Government coalitions are, however, typically not long-lived, with a few exceptions: between 1971 and 2014, Iceland experienced 19 government coalitions. As in most parliamentary systems the government is the main initiator of policy and legislation, but Iceland's parliament, the Alþingi (Althingi), nonetheless plays a more active legislative role than its counterparts in the other Nordic countries (Kristinsson, 2013). Unlike the other Nordic countries, Iceland has a tradition of patronage and constituency service where individual politicians play a linkage role between clientele groups and the state (Indriðason, 2005; Kristinsson, 1996).

D'Hondt's formula for proportional representation is used in parliamentary elections, with special arrangements aimed at maintaining overrepresentation for the rural areas while minimising disproportionalities between the parties. There are six constituencies (Northwest, Northeast, South, Southwest, Reykjavík North and Reykjavík South), with district magnitude ranging from eight to 13 (2013) and electorates from 21,000 to 63,000. Although the electoral system is a semi-open list, allowing voters to strike candidates off the list and alter the order of the candidates, in effect the system functions as a closed-list system due to the number of votes required to alter the party list. The composition of the Alþingi has not been affected in recent elections even though voters have made greater use of the option to change the party lists. There have been increasing demands in recent years for strengthening the preferential element in the election system and the individual accountability of parliamentarians. The low level of individual accountability in parliamentary elections may be a contributing factor to the popularity of party primaries. A radical system of preferential voting would most likely eliminate the primaries, which would become rather pointless if the lists they produced could be easily changed in the ensuing election.

In the almost total absence of ethnic, linguistic or religious divisions the party system which developed during the twentieth century was shaped primarily by the industrial revolution. On the right the urban middle classes and conservative farmers were joined in the Independence Party (IP), which was the largest in electoral terms. Its main competitor for the farm vote was the Progressive Party, which was the main party of government during the inter-war period, benefiting from a highly skewed system of representation. Two parties competed for the working-class vote: the Social Democrats (SDP) and the People's Alliance (PA), an alliance of communists and left socialists. The People's Alliance was usually the larger of the two from 1942 until a reshuffle on the left in 1999 created two new parties, the Social Democratic Alliance (SDA) and the Left-Green Movement (LGM), where the balance was reversed.

The occasional fifth party challenged the four-party system, and five or six parties have usually been represented since the 1970s. The class basis of the system, however, appears to have been significantly eroded as early as the 1950s, and in recent elections class voting in the traditional sense (Alford, 1962) has disappeared altogether. Left–right issues dominate the political agenda and voter choice. Foreign policy issues, however, have often played a major role in Icelandic politics (including a defence agreement with the US, membership of NATO, foreign economic policy and European integration) and the rural–urban divide remains a significant influence on electoral behaviour. Environmental issues have also become increasingly prominent in recent years.

Contexts and Rationales for Adopting Primary Elections

Although all four of the main parties in Iceland had adopted formal membership organisations outside the Alþingi by the 1930s, the parliamentary groups remained at the centre of party work and decision making. This applies in particular to the two parties which were created internally, that is actually founded as parliamentary parties – the Progressive Party and the Independence Party. The Social Democrats (formed in 1916) were originally the political wing of the trade union movement, but pressure from communists and trade union conservatives gradually undermined this connection and it was abolished in 1942. The Social Democrats took on the organisational form of a mass party, but they were from that time the least organised of the four main parties. The left-socialists gained a strong foothold in the trade union movement and among left-wing and nationalistic intellectuals who were critical of Icelandic participation in Western security cooperation.

The central role of the parliamentary groups was accentuated by the relatively active policy and legislative functions of the Alþingi, compared to other legislatures in parliamentary systems (Arter, 1999). Private members' bills constituted a uniquely large proportion of bills passed by the Alþingi, and its highly active standing committees regularly made substantial changes to government bills. In many cases individual members of parliament (MPs) were active in promoting the cause of special interest groups and constituency interests in the legislative and budgetary process and through the executive as well when their party was in government.

Cross and Blais (2012b, p. 2) note that in many democracies there is a struggle between different parts of the party organisations – that is party on the ground, in central office and in elected office – for control over leadership selection. There is, they maintain, 'clear evidence of an ongoing shift in authority away from the parliamentary party towards grassroots members'. The Icelandic party leaders, as a rule, receive their mandate from the party conference. The 'internally created' parties of the centre and right (IP and PP) were slower to accept this principle than the working-class parties, but the IP introduced the principle of direct election of the party leader by party conference in 1961 and the PP in 1986. The new parties in 2013 (Bright Future and the Pirate Party) have similar principles. The only party with the option of holding a general membership election for party leader according to party statutes is the Social Democratic Alliance. This rule has been invoked twice, in 2005 and 2013. In 2005 former Reykjavík Mayor Gísladóttir challenged Skarphéðinsson for the position of party leader and won by a convincing 2/3 of the vote. According to press reports, party membership rose by close to 50 per cent during the campaign, largely due to the efforts of the contenders (Fréttablaðið, 25 April 2005). In January 2013, upon Jóhanna Sigurðardóttir's retirement, two candidates competed for the leadership in an open election among registered party members. Árni Páll Árnason won by 62 per cent to Hannesson's 38 per cent. Turnout was 30.6 per cent, and most votes (93 per cent) were cast electronically. No large-scale increase in membership was reported in connection with the election.

Even if direct election of the party leader by the mass membership is an exception in Icelandic party politics, nominations in parliamentary elections are in some cases used as indicators of how strong party leaders stand with the voters. The decision of Progressive Party leader Gunnlaugsson to move his candidature from the Reykjavík area to the Northeast constituency before the 2013 election and challenge a former contender for the leadership position was taken as a sign of strength after he was convincingly elected in the double district council. Similarly, after a contender for the SDA leadership, Árnason, won a convincing victory over one of his main rivals in the Southwest constituency, this strengthened his bid for the leadership considerably. By the same token, Independence Party leader Benediktsson's relatively poor performance in the IP primary election in the Southwest in November 2012, where he polled only 54 per cent for first place, fired speculation concerning his position as party leader and weakened his campaign to the extent that he threatened to resign only days before the parliamentary election in order to get his party into line. Similar considerations have played a role in earlier elections (see for example Eyjan, 2009).

Little research exists on the degree of factionalism in Icelandic political parties. Factions have existed at times in all of the major parties, often centred on individuals or single issues, and in some cases these have led to actual party splits (for example PP in 1974, SDP in 1983 and IP in 1987). Long-standing factions, however, combining a broader collection of individuals and policy orientations, are rare. The main long-term factor which may cause a certain amount of friction within parties is the competition of geographical interests for representation and political attention. This affects, among other things, the nomination process, the selection of ministers, lawmaking and budgeting (for example Kristinsson, 1999).

Two factors contributed, above all, to the introduction of relatively inclusive primaries in the Icelandic parties around 1970. In the first place there was a certain amount of dissatisfaction with the established party organisations that were thought to constitute a closed system of power and political privilege dominated by middle-aged or elderly men. Traditionally underrepresented groups, such as young voters and women, were making themselves increasingly felt in political life and saw the primaries as a way of gaining better access to representation. On behalf of these groups the primaries were presented as a challenge to established power structures. The parties themselves, however, saw the primaries as a way of resolving conflicting claims for representation not only of different social groups but also of different localities. Following the introduction of proportional representation in multimember constituencies in 1959 the parties made far-reaching changes in their organisational structures which in many cases led to intensified competition for representation of local interests within the newly formed district organisations. Given a relatively decentralised structure of nominations, the parties found it difficult to deal with such conflict. The old practice of resolving nomination disputes through primaries, which never quite disappeared, gained sudden appeal. Early discussions of primaries may be found in local and national newspapers in the period around 1900 when the first political groups were taking shape.[2] In the early twentieth century primaries were used above all where party organisation was weak or nonexistent as a method of agreeing upon candidates. Without organising such primaries, the political groups faced the risk of too many candidates from within their ranks contesting elections in the single- or double-member districts used at the time. This consideration became more important with the introduction of parliamentary government in 1904. The early primaries had no binding effect and the parties had very weak control over their own candidatures until the 1920s or 1930s.

With the establishment of a permanent party structure the national and local party organisations took over the task of looking for suitable candidates and adjusting their number to the number of seats on offer. Nonetheless, primaries were never fully abolished and could be useful – especially in cases of disagreements concerning eligible candidates. The central committee of the Progressive Party, for example, accepted statutes on primaries in 1945 when it wanted to replace its former party leader with an alternative candidate in a strong PP constituency (Progressive Party, 14 December 1945). Nominations have developed in different directions in the parties since 1970, with the IP and the Social Democrats tending towards more inclusive forms and the PP and left socialists towards less inclusive ones. Some form of primary election was used for candidate selection for about 46 per cent of party lists in the four main parties between 1971 and 2009 (Indriðason and Kristinsson, 2013). Newly established parties, on the other hand, often face difficulties in holding full-scale primaries, which is a costly project, and tend to adopt less inclusive forms of nomination, if only for practical reasons.

The Primary Election Process

Primary elections in Iceland have been a strange mixture of uniformity and similarity. For the most part, the parties have used a unique voting system, *rank ordered plurality*, while other aspects (openness, candidate requirements, gender quotas) have varied across party, district and time. There are some noticeable trends. The popularity of the open primary has waned in recent years: around the 1980s about 30 per cent of candidate nominations were conducted using open primaries, while

---

2   See for example Pétursson et al. (1851, p. 172) for the earliest mention of primary elections in Iceland we are aware of; Guðmundsson (1886) for a call for a primary election from a candidate for Alþingi; Ísafold (1890) about primaries for and elections to Alþingi; and Ísafold (1900) about town council elections.

Table 9.1 Features of primary election processes in Iceland, 2012–2013

Party	Year	District	Selectorate[a]	Decentralisation	Candidacy	Voting system	Timing[b]	Deselection
PP	2012	NA=NE	Limited-wide	Local	Member and requirement	Runoff	5	Not regulated
PP	-	NV=NW	Limited-narrow	Local	Member and requirement	Nomination committee	-	Not regulated
PP	-	R	Limited-narrow	Local	Member and requirement	Nomination committee	-	Not regulated
PP	2013	S	Limited-wide	Local	Member and requirement	Runoff	3.5	Not regulated
PP	2012	SV=SW	Limited-wide	Local	Member and requirement	Runoff	4.5	Not regulated
IP	2013	NA	Registered members	Local	Member and requirement	Rank ordered plurality	3	Not regulated
IP	2012	NV	Limited-wide	Local	Member and requirement	Runoff	5	Not regulated
IP	2013	R	Registered members	Local	Member and requirement	Rank ordered plurality	5	Not regulated
IP	2012	S	Registered members	Local	Member and requirement	Rank ordered plurality	3	Not regulated
IP	2012	SV	Registered members	Local	Member and requirement	Rank ordered plurality	5.5	Not regulated
SDA	2012	NA	Support declaration	Local	Member and requirement	Rank ordered plurality	5.5	Not regulated
SDA	2012	NV	Registered members	Local	Member and requirement	Rank ordered plurality	5	Not regulated
SDA	2012	R	Registered members	Local	Member and requirement	Rank ordered plurality	5	Not regulated
SDA	2012	S	Support declaration	Local	Member and requirement	Rank ordered plurality	5	Not regulated
SDA	2013	SV	Support declaration	Local	Member and requirement	Rank ordered plurality	5.5	Not regulated
LGM	2012	NA	Registered members	Local	Member and requirement	Rank ordered plurality	4.5	Not regulated
LGM	2013	NV	Registered members	Local	Member and requirement	Rank ordered plurality	3	Not regulated
LGM	2012	R	Registered members	Local	Member and requirement	Rank ordered plurality	5	Not regulated
LGM	-	S	Limited-narrow	Local	Member and requirement	Nomination committee	-	Not regulated
LGM	2012	SV	Registered members	Local	Member and requirement	Rank ordered plurality	5	Not regulated

Note: [a] 'Limited-narrow' refers to nomination committees that are typically composed of fewer than 10 party members; 'limited-wide' refers to arrangements such as the double district councils as described in the text. [b] Months before the general elections.

the corresponding number is less than 5 per cent after 2000. Gender quotas, on the other hand, have become increasingly common. Explanations about what factors explain local party decisions are limited and primarily anecdotal. Decisions about the openness of participation appear at times to have been influenced by weak incumbents with strong ties to the local organisations. The adoption of gender quotas has likely been driven by increased emphasis on gender equality in society as well as by the improved representation of women in politics.[3]

In recent years the central party organisations have sought to apply common standards for primary elections while affording the local parties a considerable degree of choice. The Left-Green Movement adopted certain minimal requirements; the Progressive Party offered its constituency organisations five options for selecting candidates[4]; and the Social Democratic Alliance offered four options.[5] A two-thirds majority in the Independence Party's constituency councils can opt to adopt the process of 'ranking', a nomination committee or a more inclusive primary instead of a closed primary. Table 9.1 shows the main features of the candidate selection process.

The Independence Party, the Progressive Party, the Social Democratic Alliance and the Left-Green Movement all used a primary in at least one district, but the primaries varied in terms of the electoral system employed as well the size of the selectorate. Openness has been a notable feature of primary elections in Iceland – 16 per cent of the party lists put forth between 1971 and 2009 were the product of open primaries. None of the primaries held ahead of the 2013 parliamentary election were open. That said, the obstacles to participating in a primary were often far from insurmountable. Some of the primaries were in effect open – that is, they simply required the voter to sign a declaration of support for the party or join the party as late as on primary day.[6]

The candidate selection methods used for the 2013 election appear less open than in the past. The inclusiveness of the primaries varied greatly, as Table 9.1 shows. At one end of the spectrum were the PP (NE, S, SW) and the IP (NW). The PP's 'double district councils' and the IP's 'ranking' method restricted voting rights to some combination of local party chairs, members and supplemental members of the district council, members of the central party's board living in the district and local party representatives.

---

3   The causal effect is often assumed to be in the opposite direction – that is, gender quotas increase female representation.

4   Postal voting, closed primary, double district council, committee and open primary (*Póstkosning, lokað prófkjör, tvöfalt kjördæmisþing, uppstilling, opið prófkjör*).

5   The Social Democratic Alliance debated removing open primaries from among those options, but the proposal failed. The most permissive option requires non-members to sign a declaration of support seven days before the primary.

6   For the Independence Party, voters can join the party up to the end of the primary date, while the Progressive Party requires voters to join the party 30 days before the primary and the Left-Green Movement requires 10 days.

At the other end of the spectrum the most common requirement for participation was party membership, which was required in 10 out of 13 primaries. Three of the five SDA primaries also allowed voters to participate after signing a statement of support. Most of the parties allow voters to join the party as late as on the primary day. The requirement of party membership sounds more restrictive than it really is. The parties generally do not charge membership fees – becoming a party member is as easy as putting one's name on a piece of paper. The exception is the Left-Green Movement, which has the additional requirement of primary voters having paid a minimum annual fee (*lágmarksviðmiðunarárgjald*) – about €3.[7]

As one would expect, primary candidates are required to be party members. In addition, the parties typically require a candidate to be recommended by 10–30 party members.[8] The SDA and the PP allow the district organisation to charge candidates a fee. All of the SDA's district councils charged fees, which were in the range of €125–310.[9]

In some instances the parties also impose stronger limitations on campaign spending than those imposed by law. The LGM does not allow candidates to buy advertisements and the SDA requires candidates to limit their spending to 20 per cent of the legal limit. The PP and IP do not regulate campaign spending.

The electoral system reflects the inclusiveness of the primary. In the less inclusive primaries, the 'double district council' and 'ranking' employ a similar electoral system. The councils fill the seats sequentially, starting with the first seat. After the first seat has been filled, losing candidates may announce their candidacy for the second seat. This process continues until all the seats have been filled. There is, however, a slight difference between the rules of the PP and the IP. The PP employs a majority runoff election for each seat, with the top two vote winners facing one another, while the IP simply uses plurality rule.[10]

The *rank ordered plurality* system typically used in the more inclusive primary elections is, as far as we can tell, an Icelandic invention. Presented with a list of candidates, the voters are asked to rank or to cast one vote for each seat on the party list to be filled. The first seat is allocated to the candidate who received the most votes for the first seat. The second seat is then allocated to the candidate who received the most first and second place votes among the remaining candidates. This process is continued, filling each seat with the candidate who received the most votes for that seat or a seat higher on the list. Table 9.2 shows the results

---

7 The district parties generally charge higher membership fees, but paying the minimum annual fee is sufficient to vote in the primaries.

8 The Left-Green Movement has no requirement about recommendations for a candidate.

9 The Social Democratic Alliance sets the maximum fee for students at 125 Euros.

10 Plurality rule may be more likely to result in the rejection of a candidate who is majority-preferred to the winner. Haraldur Benediktsson for example won the second seat with 90 out of 228 votes, but we do not know whether he would have beaten the second runner-up (with 73 votes) in a runoff.

of the SDA's primary in the Southwest constituency. Árnason, a contender for the party leader position, received the most votes for the first seat, and is thus allocated the first seat. Júlíusdóttir received 910 votes for the first seat and 454 for the second, for a total of 1,364 votes. We can thus see that Árnason was not necessarily the majority-preferred candidate for the first seat on the party list – although Júlíusdóttir would have needed to be the preferred candidate of nearly all of those who ranked some other candidate first. Schram won the third seat with a total of 1,250 votes for seats 1–3.

Table 9.2   Example of rank ordered plurality voting

Candidate	Seat request	Votes for seats					
		1	1–2	1–3	1–4	1–5	1–6
Árni Páll Árnason	1	1,041	1,250	1,385	1,503	1,590	1,685
Katrín Júlíusdóttir	1	910	1,364	1,567	1,701	1,764	1,829
Magnús Orri Schram	2–3	57	632	1,250	1,548	1,747	1,841
Lúðvík Geirsson	2	60	576	812	1,105	1,350	1,520
Margrét Gauja Magnúsdóttir	3–4	3	43	306	611	889	1,158
Margrét Júlía Rafnsdóttir	3–4	11	71	279	575	877	1,185

Note: SDA primary, Southwest constituency (partial results).

The fact that plurality rule is used to allocate each seat implies that the electoral system has certain characteristics. First, it does not satisfy independence of irrelevant alternatives: that is, a candidate's ability to win a particular seat depends not only on their relative standing vis-à-vis their main competitor but also on who else is in the race. This has some interesting implications in primaries that employ gender quotas, as discussed below. Second, the system is highly majoritarian and is not guaranteed to produce a 'proportional' outcome where ideological differences or factions exist. A coordinated majority faction is guaranteed all the seats on the party list if it ranks the candidates in the same way.

When announcing their candidacy, the great majority of contenders announce which seat(s) they are seeking, even though they are generally not required to do so.[11] It is not obvious why the candidates choose to adopt such a strategy, but electoral alliances are a possible motivation. That is, an informal alliance between candidates competing for different seats on the party list allows the candidates to

---

11   The Progressive Party does require candidates to declare which seats they wish to be considered for. The rules of the other parties do not require candidates to do so, but it is possible that the constituency parties may have required candidates to do so – although we have found no such instances.

encourage their supporters to vote for the other candidate. Announcing a candidacy for particular seats might shield the candidate from negative campaigning – in particular for candidates not aiming for seats high on the list that are usually contested by incumbents or other high-ranking party members.

The candidates' announcements do not bind the hands of voters – they can rank the candidates in any manner they see fit.[12] But, as the primary results in Table 9.2 show, voters seem to heed the candidates' announcements.[13] For example, about 93 per cent of the votes for the first seat were given to the two candidates who had announced that they wanted to lead the list. However, a candidate's preference for a particular seat does not prevent voters from ranking the candidate lower. Júlíusdóttir, for example, sought the first seat, yet about half of her votes were for seats lower on the list.

The primaries were held, on average, about five months ahead of the election scheduled for 27 April 2013. The first primaries were held in early November 2012 and the last ones in late January 2013. The timing of the primaries varies as much within parties as across parties, with the exception of the SDA whose primaries all took place in mid-November.

Comprehensive data on participation is difficult to gather, but the available data shows that the number of registered voters ranged from 439 to 9,064; the number of votes cast from 139 to 7,546; and turnout ranged from 25 to 62 per cent.[14] Although the data is incomplete, a couple of comments are warranted. First, there is substantial variation in the size of the primaries, which is not surprising since the rules governing participation vary greatly. Second, turnout is surprisingly low. In only two of the nine primaries, where turnout data is available, does a majority of eligible voters cast a vote. This appears to be the case even where primary participation is restricted, as in the double district councils.

Gauging the competitiveness of the primaries is challenging for two reasons. First, the parties often only report partial results in the primaries. Second, even when complete results are available, it is not clear how to measure competitiveness because multiple seats are being filled and contenders declare their candidacy for particular seats. For example, there may be little competition for the first seat on the list, while competition for the second seat is very stiff – for instance where the party leader seeks the first seat. If we focus on competition for the first seat, sufficiently detailed results are available for 12 districts. Focusing on the first seat on the list, in eight of these the winner won more than twice as many votes as the runner-up for the seat. Focusing on the second seat, that was true for half the primaries.

---

12 We have found one exception to this where voters were restricted to placing a contender in a seat that she announced her candidacy for. This happened in a Social Democratic Party primary in Reykjavík for the 1991 parliamentary election.

13 Of course, it could be the case that the announcements simply reflect that the candidates have fairly reasonable expectations about how they will fare in the primaries.

14 The Independence Party was reported to have 20,000 registered voters in the Reykjavík district.

Table 9.3a Party leaders: features of primary election competitions in Iceland

Party	Year	Turnout	Number of candidates	Incumbent running	Incumbent winner	Winner's votes (%)	Runner-up's votes (%)	Women running	Woman winner	Winner's age	National seniority
SDA	2013	30.7	2	No	n.a.	62.2	37.8	No	n.a.	46	Yes
IP	2013		1	Yes	Yes	78.9	18.8	No	n.a.	43	Yes
LG	2013		1	No	n.a	98.4	-	Yes	Yes	37	Yes
PP	2013		1	Yes	Yes	97.6	-	-	-	38	Yes
Mean	-	30.7	1.3	50.0	50.0-	84.3	14.2	0.3	-	41	-

Table 9.3b Candidates: features of primary election competitions in Iceland

Party	Year	Turnout	Number of candidates	Number of incumbents	Incumbents nominated (%)	Winner's votes (%)	Nominations to be allocated	Realistic seats	Number of women	Women nominated (%)	VCI
IP	2012	18,978	65	13	43.3		30	16	19	23.1	74.1
LG	2012	14,260[a]	47	8	33.3		24	13	14	37.5	64.0
PP	2012	1,079	26	4	19.0		21	5	13	34.6	66.1
SDA	2012	7,729	47	17	73.9		23	20	13	56.5	60.3
Mean	-	7,303	46.3	10.5	42.4		24.5	13.5	14.8	-	-

Notes: The vote concentration index (VCI) is simply calculated as the average of the share of votes received by the winner of the primary across the districts in which the party held a primary or a nomination method other than nomination committee. Note that the VCI is not fully comparable as the voting method employed differs across parties and districts. The vote concentration in individual districts was the following: PP – NA 62.9%, S 88.6%, SV 46.9%; IP – NA 81.9%, NV 100% (uncontested); R 72.1%, S 62.6%, SV 53.8%; SDA – NA 73.0%, NV 76.0%, R 38.7%, S 65.1%, SV 48.9%; LGM – NA 76.2, NV 41.0%, R 85.1%, SV 53.6%. [a] Average turnout in the three districts where the rate is available was 30.9 per cent.

Political Consequences for Parties

Primary elections have been hypothesised to influence party politics in a variety of ways. Often these are seen as being primarily negative, for example by weakening parties by increasing intra-party competition or by increasing the importance of money in politics (Hazan and Rahat, 2010). However, much of the criticism of primaries derives from the US experience, and we argue elsewhere it is not clear that those lessons are directly applicable to, for example, parliamentary systems or elections that operate under rules of proportional representation (Indriðason and Kristinsson, 2013). Thus, it is possible that the overall effect of primary elections is a positive one, for example by increasing the representativeness of the parties and enhancing accountability. Here we examine a few of the outcomes of the candidate selection methods in Iceland.

Inclusive party primaries can pose a challenge to institutionalised political parties in the sense that they can open up avenues for external influence on candidate selection in the form of money and non-attached participants, which in turn may undermine fair representation and party cohesion. Worries of this kind are well known from the Icelandic debate and deserve looking into.

Since 2007 primary candidates have been required to disclose information regarding fundraising and campaign expenditures if they exceed 2,500 Euros. The great majority of candidates seeking a seat on the party lists in 2013 did not exceed that limit. Of the 189 candidates, only 30 exceeded the limit.[15] The average level of spending for those 30 candidates was 8,500 Euros. The Left-Green Movement's ban on paid advertising and the Progressive Party's choice of less participatory methods of candidate selection had a clear effect – no candidate for these parties exceeded the limit. Meanwhile, eight of the Social Democrat's 47 candidates exceeded the limit, spending on average 3,660 Euros. The Independence Party stood out, with half of its 44 candidates exceeding the limit and spending on average 10,270 Euros. While the Social Democrat's limit on campaign spending to 20 per cent of the legal maximum helps explain why average spending for those of its candidates exceeding the limit is lower than for the Independence Party candidates, it does not explain why a much smaller fraction of its candidates exceeds the reporting limit – that is, why a cap on spending should affect the average level of spending but not the number of candidates required to report.[16] Arguably, the amounts spent on campaigns are not large; but it must be kept in mind that the number of voters in the primaries tops out at several thousand – and the most expensive campaigns spend around 4 Euros per voter.

---

15 Candidates who do not exceed the limit are asked (but not required) to sign a statement to that effect: 28 candidates neither turned in a report nor signed a statement declaring that their spending had not exceeded the disclosure limit.

16 The legal maximum limit on spending varies by constituency and is lowest in the Northwest, where it was 29,425 Euros in 2012–13; 20 per cent of that amount is 5,885 Euros, which is higher than the disclosure limit.

In addition to the general concern about the influence of money, it has also been considered important for its potential for influencing the under-representation of women. Smaller political networks and fewer resources have been offered as explanation for the difficulty women have in achieving equal representation. One concern, then, is that more inclusive candidate selection methods demand more resources, which disadvantages women. Focusing on the candidates who exceeded the disclosure limit, the genders are almost evenly balanced – 16 men and 14 women. Men thus appear to have a slight edge, except that 62.5 per cent of the candidates were men; that is, we would have expected 19 men and 11 women to exceed the disclosure threshold if gender were not important. Of the candidates whose spending exceeds the threshold, male candidates outspend female candidates by about 1,500 Euros on average. Using regression analysis, there are also some indications that incumbents, candidates competing in the Reykjavík constituency, older candidates and candidates aiming for seats higher on the party list spend more. However, only the constituency and party have a statistically significant effect and, importantly, the effect of gender does not.[17]

It is interesting to briefly compare the level of campaign spending on primaries in preparation for the 2013 election with previous elections: 50 per cent more candidates exceeded the disclosure threshold in 2009 (the first for which disclosure was required) than ahead of the 2013 election, but the average among those was slightly lower at 7,440 Euros. The legislation on campaign finances had been adopted ahead of the 2007 election but did not apply to it. Nevertheless, several candidates did disclose their campaign spending, and the average for those who did so was 25,510 Euros. The averages are, of course, not comparable, but the highest levels of spending were far higher ahead of the 2007 election than the 2009 and 2013 elections. The economic crisis likely played some part, making it more difficult for the candidates to raise campaign funds; voters may also have become more suspicious of the ties between business interests and politicians in the wake of the crisis.

But does campaign spending matter in Icelandic primary elections? To examine that possibility we ran a logit regression where the dependent variable was whether or not a contender won the highest seat announced for their candidacy. If campaign spending has any effect, then by definition the probability of winning a seat depends on the candidate's own spending as well as on the spending of other candidates contesting the same seat. Thus, as a measure of campaign spending we use a relative measure that captures how much more or less one candidate spent than other candidate(s) seeking the same seat. We then controlled for gender, incumbency status, the highest seat sought and the total number of candidates in the primary. The results show some indications that campaign spending matters. While the effect of

---

17 We also considered a Heckman model to account for sample selection. As our sample is small the results are not very robust to model specification, but overall they tend to be in line with a simple regression model. In some specifications, female candidates are found to spend more on their campaigns than men.

campaign spending is always estimated as being positive, its magnitude depends on which seat on the party list the candidate is seeking. Spending an additional 500,000 ISK (3,125 Euros) on one's campaign increases the probability of winning the second seat about 4 percentage points, while the change in the probability of winning the fourth seat is estimated to be about seven percentage points.[18]

Thus, there is reason to think that money matters when it comes to candidate nomination, and that female candidates may be disadvantaged because they may be less well connected than their male counterparts. A simple way to examine this question is by comparing the shares of female candidates among those nominated and among those occupying seats with a realistic chance of winning a seat in parliament (which we simply define by the number of seats that were currently held by the party in the constituency), which is shown in Table 9.4.[19] Primaries perform fairly well compared with other candidate nomination methods: the share of female nominees is similar to the share nominated by party congresses and, when it comes to viable seats, far better than when the nominations are handled by committee. It is surprising that committees perform as badly as they do as one might have expected the party elite to be more attuned to concerns about gender representation. We caution that these results must be taken with a grain of salt as only three constituencies used nomination committees. In addition, the Progressive Party accounts for two of these; that is, it is difficult to say whether this finding is a function of the nomination method or the party.

Table 9.4   Women on party lists by nomination method

Nomination method	Percentage of nominations	Percentage of realistic positions
Committee	–	29
Congress	42	52
Primary	39	50

While women appear to do relatively poorly when it comes to the share of overall nominations, one must keep in mind that they only accounted for about 40 per cent of the primary candidates, which is very close to their share of nominations. Seen in this light, women actually appear to be favoured when it comes to viable seats. This is an interesting development as Indriðason and Sigurjónsdóttir (2008, 2014), in studying primary elections up to the 2009 election, found that while

---

18 The sample only includes the candidates for the Social Democratic Alliance and the Independence Party, as candidates from other parties did not exceed the disclosure limit. The full results are in the Appendix, below.

19 We do not count the share of female nominees when a committee is in charge as the committees propose a complete list whereas nominations by congresses and primaries normally limit the number of nominations to 4–8 candidates.

women were more successful in primary elections overall, that was not true when they competed for the top seats on the party lists.

Table 9.5   Effects of primary elections on political parties in Iceland, 2013

Party	Members		Change %	Electoral performance (Votes)		Change (Votes after primaries % - votes before primaries %)
	Year before primaries (N)	Year after primaries (N)		Before primaries (N)	After primaries (N)	
SDA	-	-	-	55,758	24,294	-16.9
IP	-	-	-	44,369	50,355	3.0
LGM	4,953	5,133	180	40,581	20,546	-11.2
PP	2,833	2,704	-129	27,699	46,173	9.6

Note: Membership numbers are only available for Reykjavík.

There is little doubt that inclusive nominations in the Icelandic parties have influenced the number of registered members substantially. This holds in particular for instances where applying for membership or joining the party is a prerequisite for voting in a primary. But there may also be effects from coming into contact with the party even when there are no such formal requirements. Table 9.5 shows that membership in the PP in Reykjavík, which used a nomination committee to select candidates, declined from the year before the election to the year after, while membership in the LGM, which used primaries in four out of five districts, increased slightly. Of course, one cannot infer much from such limited evidence, but those trends in membership run counter to the electoral success of the parties. The PP gained nearly 10 percentage points while the LGM lost about 11. There is, thus, also little support for the hypothesis that more inclusive methods of candidate nomination mobilise support for parties when the 2013 election is considered. Indriðason and Kristinsson (2012), however, found some limited indications that parties do better when they hold primaries, and that these effects are smaller or nonexistent when more of the other parties in the constituency also hold primaries.[20]

Table 9.6 supports the findings from previous research (Indriðason and Kristinsson, 2013) that there is a clear relationship between participation in primaries and the number of self-reported party members. Thus, membership figures are highest in the Independence Party, where participation in primaries is greatest, and also relatively high in the Social Democratic Alliance. Although the Progressive Party has an old and well-established membership organisation

---

20   The limited number of observations, along with the fact that they are not independent, makes it difficult to accurately estimate the effects of primary elections on electoral outcomes. Therefore, findings should be considered suggestive at best.

Table 9.6 Votes, participation in primaries and membership density in Iceland, 2013

Party voted for	Voted for party	Voted in party primary	Registered members	Membership density
Independence Party	26.7	15.2	16.4	61.4
Progressive Party	24.4	3.4	4.4	18.0
Social Democratic Alliance	12.9	6.8	6.5	50.4
Left-Green Movement	10.9	1.9	1.7	15.6
Others	25.1	1.0	1.5	5.6
Total	100.0	28.5	30.4	30.4

Notes: Values are percentages. Membership density is the percentage of members relative to voters.

Sources: Party voted for refers to election results, while the remaining columns are based on results of the 2013 Icelandic National Election Study (ICENES). Figures on primaries and members are adjusted in accordance with the total (thus discounting non-replies on party).

its membership figures are lower, and they are lowest in the Left-Greens. The ratio of members to voters is also of interest, although this is inevitably affected by the electoral fortunes of the parties in question (the Progressives did well, while the Social Democrats and Left-Greens lost heavily). Membership density is much higher in the parties with relatively inclusive nomination processes, the Independence Party and the Social Democrats, than in those with more exclusive arrangements. It is lowest in the new parties, which have hardly any membership organisation and non-inclusive nominations.

The findings are consistent with the idea that inclusive primaries work as a method of attracting new party members, and the total figure for party members in Iceland is among the highest found in any established democratic system (Whiteley, 2011).

The Icelandic experience of party primaries in the nomination process does not support the contention that they weaken party cohesion. The idea may seem plausible that individual parliamentarians are tempted to act independently when they owe their seats not to the party hierarchy but to a hybrid congregation of supporters (Carey and Shugart, 1995). Party leaders may not be able to punish non-conformity by getting rid of difficult members of the parliamentary group. It is important to note, however, that there are countervailing tendencies. One is the increasing independence of the party leaders from the parliamentary group. With a direct mandate from the party conference, or even the members at large, party leaders are in a position to play an assertive role vis-à-vis the parliamentary party. They have increasingly used this position in the Icelandic parties to direct the allocation of positions of responsibility among members of the parliamentary group. A member of parliament who wishes to be seen as a potential cabinet minister, chair of a parliamentary committee, chair of the parliamentary group or speaker of the house must cultivate their reputation as a team player and a reliable party member (Kam, 2009). Parliamentary government helps, in this respect, to maintain party cohesion given the strong desire by most MPs to be considered ministerial material. Another factor which contributes to cohesion in the Icelandic case is the electoral formula in place which, as already indicated, has strong majoritarian features. This makes the strategy of representing party factions rather than the mainstream party less rewarding than it might be under a more proportional formula.

Empirical evidence lends little support to the thesis that primaries undermine party cohesion in Iceland. Party cohesion is at a similar level as in the other Nordic states. The spread of more inclusive nomination methods over time has not led to a corresponding erosion of party cohesion. The parties which use the most inclusive methods of nomination are also the ones with the highest level of cohesion (IP and Social Democrats), while the party using the least inclusive methods has the lowest level (Kristinsson, 2011).

Conclusion

The Icelandic experience of primaries is unique with regard to frequency, openness, participation and the length of time they have been employed. It is possible that some other unique features of the case affect the outcome, for example the small size of the political system, but to our knowledge there is no theory which explicitly links the effects of nominations with country size. Thus there is no *prima facie* reason to assume that size affects our findings in a crucial manner.

Party primaries clearly have the potential of recruiting larger groups of voters for the party registers than more conventional forms of nomination. Moreover, the Icelandic primaries developed in response to criticism of the established parties and their lack of responsiveness to the claims of disadvantaged groups for representation. At a time when parties all over seem to be experiencing crises of membership recruitment this is a highly relevant finding (van Biezen et al., 2012). The important question is whether primary elections have side effects which may adversely affect the parties or their role in the political system. Any organisational feature as broadly defined as 'inclusiveness of nominations' may have both beneficial and negative effects. To study their effects we have to know more about their inner dynamics and the environment in which they operate.

The experience of the Icelandic parties suggests a learning process in which they have managed to minimise the potential dysfunctions of primaries by adapting them to party needs. The use of partially open rather than open primaries tends to boost party membership and establish links between parties and voters. There has been a clear move away from open primaries to more restricted forms. To the extent that the under-representation of certain groups of voters may be feared, this may be offset by combining primaries and zipper lists or quotas. Although this has created some irritation at times, it has not been considered a major problem. The tradition of indicating which seat a candidate is seeking and a majoritarian electoral formula add structure to the competition and reduce the risk of factionalism. Several features of the party environment have also proven helpful in making the primaries function without undermining the parties and their roles. In particular, parliamentary government and more assertive party leaders have contributed to a high level of party cohesion, despite the potentially disruptive effects of primaries. The Icelandic experience, so far, also suggests that the dangers of excessive campaign spending can be held in check through proper regulation and supervision. Spending, nonetheless, does affect performance in primaries, and the greatest reservation to be held in connection with their introduction concerns the ability of the parties and national government to prevent the development of corruption in relation to campaign spending.

Appendix

Here we examine the effect of campaign spending on primary candidates' success in obtaining the highest seat on the party list they sought. That is, a candidate may declare their wish to be considered for the second, third or fourth seat on the list. For this candidate the dependent variable would be coded 1 if the candidate ends up winning the second (or first) seat, but zero otherwise. Substantively similar results obtain if success is coded as obtaining any seat the candidate declares candidacy for.

The key independent variable is *relative spending*, which captures how much the candidate spent relative to other candidates in the same constituency. It is measured as the difference between the candidate's own spending and the total spending of other candidates in the constituency. The variable *high seat* is the highest seat on the party list that the candidate declared candidacy for. The variable interacts with *relative spending* as the importance of campaign spending is likely to depend on whether the candidate is competing for one of the top spots on the list or a seat fairly low on the list. We also include indicator variables for female candidates, incumbents and the total number of candidates competing in the primary. We estimate a logit model with standard errors clustered by primary; that is, observations within a primary will be correlated as the success of one candidate, which usually means that some other candidate was not successful.

Table 9.7 Effects of campaign spending on primary success in Iceland

	Model 1	Model 2
High seat	-0.45 (0.15)	-0.42 (0.12)
Relative spending	0.52 (0.35)	-0.43 (0.55)
High seat*relative spending		0.51 (0.00014)
Female	0.29 (0.58)	0.33 (0.51)
Incumbent	0.087 (0.77)	0.26 (0.28)
Number of candidates	-0.047 (0.26)	-0.069 (0.084)
Constant	0.099 (0.87)	0.12 (0.84)
Observations	109	109
Log Likelihood	-47.41	-46.35
Chi^2	58.93	58.65

Note: p-values in parentheses.

Chapter 10
Conclusion

Giulia Sandri, Antonella Seddone and Fulvio Venturino

The Case Studies: An Overview

This volume aims to provide a general overview of the processes of democratic innovation within political parties. In practice, this has led to an in-depth examination of the introduction of primary elections. The need for a comparative analysis on this topic is a result of the recent spread of inclusive procedures for recruiting political personnel in parties outside the United States. Over the last two decades, a growing number of parties have introduced primary elections for selecting candidates and leaders, including Belgium, Italy, France, Romania, Slovakia and Iceland. Beyond Europe, intra-party democracy also has improved in Israel, Canada, Japan, Taiwan and South Korea, not to mention in various Latin American countries. Many parties in these countries promote participative opportunities involving their members, or even the entire electorate, to choose candidates for public office and party leadership. Nevertheless, despite recent trends towards involving activists and voters in parties' decision-making, analysis of the implementation of primary elections outside the US is not equally developed. There is also a lack of analysis on the impact of these intra-party reforms at electoral and organisational level. If anything, the few studies on primaries outside the US have underlined the differences from the American case taken as a reference, providing a framework of analysis which now needs to be supported by empirical research.

This book investigates primary elections from a wider perspective. Specifically, the point at issue is not to understand whether and to what extent the intra-party democracy practised in other countries diverges from the American ideal. Rather, here we aim to clarify *why* and *how* political parties in different countries choose to reform their methods of selecting candidates and leaders in an inclusive direction, and *what* the effects brought about by that choice are. Hence, the main contribution is to describe the causes and consequences of primary elections (open and closed) outside the US, offering an analysis of the procedural features and their outcomes in terms of participation, representation and competitiveness.

The comparative approach has contributed to an understanding of the actual functioning of primary elections within different political and party systems. By focusing on such a large set of heterogeneous case studies it has been possible to collect information on a wide range of inclusive selections in order to understand how causes, procedures, outcomes and consequences are mutually interrelated. We have considered countries from different geopolitical areas, ranging from Western (Belgium, France, Iceland Italy Portugal and Spain) and Eastern (Romania and Slovakia) Europe to Israel and Asia (specifically Japan and Taiwan). This comparative approach has considered differences concerning types of democracies (established and new) as well as political systems (parliamentary and semi-presidential).

A further distinction concerns the offices to be selected. This volume addresses both candidate and leader selection; and, besides the case analysed, it deals with the issue of the differences between the two types of selection thoroughly from a theoretical point of view. Other differences concern the experience of resorting to such elections: the length of the period of time during which primaries have been used, the regular and reiterated use of the instrument, etc. These variables could vary significantly from one case to the other: from Iceland, with its long tradition of primary elections; to Slovakia and Romania, where party internal democratisation is at its very beginnings. In this regard, the Italian and French cases provide several insights for understanding the ongoing process of introducing primaries within a party system.

Each empirical chapter analysed candidate or leader selection in two countries, with the exception of Iceland which, due to its specificities, required a chapter to itself. This paired comparison was justified by similarities in political institutions of the two countries. Analogies and specificities of each case were pointed out, providing a detailed analysis on:

- political background, investigated from both a political and a historical point of view;
- rationales, including potential factors pushing political parties to change their selection methods;
- procedural features and rules adopted by political parties to regulate primaries;
- outcomes of primaries from the point of view of participation, competitiveness and representation;
- consequences at systemic and organisational level.

These analytical dimensions were evaluated in the light of their mutual interaction in order to better understand the functioning of such inclusive procedures.

Differences between American and Non-American Primaries

A well-known difference between the American and non-American experience of primary elections concerns their public regulation. While in the US they have been extensively regulated by state laws since the beginning of the twentieth century, in all the countries analysed here public regulation is so far lacking. An important consequence stems from this disparity. While in the US the timing of compulsory primaries is strictly regulated – also due to the presidential system of government – where primaries are not mandatory their occurrence is unsystematic. This is especially important for leader selection, as parties are often considered private actors not subject to state regulation in their internal affairs. However, the candidate selection for both parliamentary and executive offices is also unpredictable.[1]

The lack of regulation is related to another relevant aspect. The manipulation of primaries by party elites is hypothesised by scholars adopting the cartel party perspective, who argue that party leaders give members power in internal decision-making to overcome opposition from the mid-level leadership. By so doing they assume that the members may be easily manipulated, although evidence supporting this is quite limited. In any case, we have explored some cases of elite manipulation supporting the cartel party theory. However, rather than engage in a costly strategy for influencing presumably unaware party members, the leaders prefer to craft the rules for primaries in such a way as to foster preferred results. This somewhat deceitful choice is costless because, in the absence of public regulation, the leaders are necessarily entitled to make the rules concerning candidacy, selectorate, electoral system and so on. Moreover, manipulation of the rules, if compared to manipulation of the members, has the advantage of applying to open primaries involving non-members, an increasingly common practice in European party politics.

The lack of regulation is linked to the absence of public financial support. At first glance, this might seem an obstruction to the spread of primary elections. However, primaries entail very low organisational and logistical costs, and activities that can be easily covered by the voluntary work of activists and party members. And in the case of open primaries, where turnout peaks to millions of voters, a small fee from each voter gives the parties substantial, self-financed support. Finally, the lack of public funding might enhance sympathy for party democracy among ordinary people, most of whom are also taxpayers. There are no comparative data concerning the general electorate that explore their views on primaries, but on the basis of a few exploratory case studies it seems that most citizens have favourable opinions on primaries in Western Europe, even when they are not particularly interested in politics.

Besides the type of regulation for primaries, another important difference between the US and other countries is related to substantive variations in the organisational structures of parties. Due to the well-known 'exceptionalism', American parties do not have formally enrolled members. Thus, the organisational consequences brought about by the use of primaries are usually assessed in terms of lower mobilisation of dissatisfied activists and potential electoral 'penalties'. Compared to US political organisations, European parties still count on a

---

1 The current situation is rapidly evolving because public funding of parties and electoral politics has given national governments the necessary tools for promoting intra-party democracy. In some – admittedly rare – cases the inflow of money from the state to the parties is subject to the requirement of adopting primary elections.

substantial number of formally enrolled members, even though the membership size has radically decreased in the last decades. Thus, our empirical chapters have explored the electoral effects of primaries, and have also examined variations in party membership related to the use of internal elections.

Scholars advocating the cartel party theory argue that party leaders deliberately demobilise members in order to wield power without restraint – perhaps because the public financing of politics makes activists less relevant. Additionally, by so doing they favour a steady decline in party membership figures, together with several other ecological factors such as post-materialism and the end of ideologies. What we have discovered through the analyses developed here is that the use of primary elections improves party image, and in turn it may at least partially reverse this downward trend. An open and democratic party may still be attractive, electorally speaking, to many citizens.

The final difference between American and non-American party politics that we consider here concerns the party systems. The US is the archetypal example of a two-party system, in this case dominated by Democrats and Republicans. Outside the US multiparty systems clearly prevail; indeed, all the cases analysed in this book feature a high number of parties. Several research projects have assessed the consequences of party fragmentation for government stability, voter choice or effectiveness of public policies. From the point of view of intra-party democracy, a multiparty system allows for organising coalition primaries. It should be added that in principle they are not relevant for selecting a party leader, and potentially useful in the case of selecting parliamentary candidates when a plurality electoral system is in use.[2] However, so far this has never, to the best of our knowledge, been put into practice. Above all, they are becoming relevant in the selection of a single candidate for a single elected office. In practice, this means that parties resort to coalition primaries when faced with selecting an electable chief executive candidate. As shown by the French case in 2002, this may easily happen after an unexpected and momentous defeat.

Candidate vs Leader Selection: Differences and Similarities

As clarified by Alan Ware in his chapter, in the American political system the distinction between candidate and leader selection is somewhat nonsensical. Once elected, a candidate simply becomes the party leader. The distinction is more relevant in non-American contexts, and in principle it is unproblematic. Primaries for selecting a candidate represent the first step towards the decision to compete in

---

2 Coalition primaries for selecting candidates for parliamentary elections could also be used when a runoff system is adopted for electing the members of the lower (or upper) house. However, in this case, parties could find it more practical to use the first round of the parliamentary election to filter out several candidates and to choose their best/most electable candidates.

a general election to take up a public office. Primary elections for selecting a party leader are designed to choose the head of a political organisation, and in this case the electoral process does not require a second step. If the conceptual distinction is clear, the actual working of party politics needs some clarification.

Let us deal first with candidate selection. In Europe the first examples of primaries have exclusively involved the selection of candidates for parliament. Here, the case in point is Iceland – perhaps a minor country in the field of geopolitics, but a crucial case when intra-party democracy is at stake. As Indriðason and Kristinsson clearly demonstrate in their chapter, parliamentary primaries were introduced in Iceland some decades ago, and later other countries such as Israel and Italy have intermittently imitated that ground-breaking experience. At first this (moderate) increase in the use of primaries induced academics to equate primaries for *parliamentary* candidates with primaries for all candidate types.[3] However, in recent years this systematisation has been challenged by political reality. Today in some countries, parties and coalitions also make use of primaries to choose their (single) candidate to the office of chief executive. The chapter by De Luca and Venturino explores a few cases of this type of primary in Italy and France.

We have stated above that the distinction between candidate and leader selection is *conceptually* evident. This is the case for those countries where a party leader is, above all, the head of the organisation, and is less involved in electoral politics. As shown by Wauters, Rahat and Kenig, Belgium is a good case in point. However, in most cases the actual politics has evolved in such a way as to blur the distinction and make the consequences of selecting leaders through primaries more complicated. This happens because *de facto* a growing number of parties use primaries – often in the one member one vote (OMOV) form – to select a leader who automatically becomes their candidate chief executive. This practice is not directly linked to primaries. Indeed it is well entrenched in several English-speaking, majoritarian democracies, where the parliamentary group is entitled to select the party leader, and party democratisation did not take place until recently. Neither is it established in those constitutions and laws dedicated to the regulation of party life, usually lacking or not enforced in most countries. Nevertheless it is today a compelling rule even in those countries where the overlap between the office of party leader and prime minister was forbidden by parties' internal statutes.

The consequences of this state of affairs should be clear. When choosing their party leader, members, activists and citizens – according to the inclusiveness of the selectorate – are fully aware that they are voting for the party leader *and* for the man – rarely the woman – who will represent them (and the party) in the next electoral campaign. This is also the person who is expected to become the prime minister if the party wins the election. The consequences of this awareness

---

3 It should be noted that all the primaries to select parliamentary candidates analysed in this book – in Romania, Slovakia and Iceland – have been held when a proportional representation (PR) system was used to elect the parliament. This marks another important difference with the American case.

are made more pressing by the climate of permanent campaigning affecting all established democracies. In fact the (quite rare) research projects on primary elections based on survey data clearly show that electability is a motivation for choosing the candidate, and is as important as viability. In other words, when choosing the leader of their party, the selectors single out the preferred candidate, but they vote for him/her only if he/she is expected to win the forthcoming parliamentary election. If not, they prefer to vote strategically for another primary candidate considered to be more competitive in a general election.

The path from primaries to party leadership to head of government is becoming the expected career for the most important and ambitious politicians. However, the processes just described take place only in parliamentary systems. Here, a prime minister sustained by a parliamentary majority fills a partisan role which is clearly separate from the head of the state, either republican or monarchical. The institutional design of semi-presidential systems is completely different and, as a consequence, the selection of political personnel and the role of primaries also function according to completely different logics. A president chosen through primaries and successively directly elected by the voters –as in the case of François Hollande in France –is contemporaneously head of the executive and president of all citizens. In summary, he or she is prevented from having a partisan profile. Hence in a parliamentary system the party leader – chosen or not through primaries – is often the only admitted prime ministerial candidate. Instead, in a semi-presidential system, a party leader is allowed to eventually vie for the presidency, by running first in a primary election. But they are not the only admitted candidate from the party and, if elected president, they must necessarily leave the office of party leader.

Contexts and Rationales for Adopting Primary Elections

The crucial question which this book tries to address is why political parties are introducing inclusive methods into their decision-making despite the risk of weakening their control over access to the ballot, and therefore to political offices. What is the trade-off? What are the rationales encouraging leaders to renounce their prerogative and accept the risk of losing control over their own organisation?

According to the literature, changes in candidate and leader selection methods, especially towards more open and inclusive procedures, arise from a combination of factors usually related to three main levels: political system level, party system level and intra-party level (Barnea and Rahat, 2007). In addition, Cross and Blais (2012a) underlined how a sort of contagion effect at party system level could be a further incentive for the adoption of inclusive methods.

As underlined in Chapter 3, the personalisation of politics and the need to react to disaffection with politics are the most relevant factors that, at the *political system level*, are pressing political parties to adopt inclusive methods. Therefore, as shown by the Israeli parties, primaries play out as events that catalyse media attention and public opinion, providing a new source of legitimacy for party leaders and candidates. In this regard, the example of Romania and Slovakia is also of interest. In these countries, primaries are intended as an antidote to anti-party feelings in order to promote a new public image of the party based on transparency and democracy. In these Eastern European democracies, parties use primaries as an instrument to distinguish them from the other competitors who select their candidates behind closed doors. Opening up the candidate selection procedures conveys a message of commitment to democratic values within the party. Indeed, such an evocative label of democracy and transparency could be a powerful mobilising message to the electorate.

At *party system level*, our analyses show that a crisis determined by an electoral defeat is likely to trigger huge reforms within a political party. Primaries launch a process of renewal which would bedifficult to achieve by other means. Icelandic primaries seem to be the result of this kind of dynamic. In Iceland, reforms towards inclusiveness are based on the need to react to disaffection with the established party organisation and electoral de-alignment. Thus, through primaries it would be possible to appoint a new party elite, directly involving activists and giving them an active role in the process of party renewal. This is true also for Israeli, Belgian, Italian or French primaries as well as for those in Romania and Slovakia.

At party system level another factor that might influence parties in promoting inclusive procedures is related to the so-called *contagion effect*. This implies that if some parties adopt internal democracy then other parties will be forced to resort to such inclusive selection. This kind of dynamic has been extensively illustrated in the analysis of the Japanese and Taiwanese cases where, following the same logic, there is a trend for new parties to adopt primaries in order to differentiate themselves from other challengers. Or, as in the Romanian case, primary elections are used as a brand of democracy which characterises the party as one that is truly committed to democratic values, in contrast withother contenders.

Finally, our cases confirm how at *intra-party level* several factors contribute to enhancing the inclusive procedure. In this regard, we can identify two main dimensions. The first concerns the relationship between factions and party elites. According to cartel party theorists, motivations for the democratisation of selection methods could be interpreted as manipulation by the party elite to limit the power of middle-level elites in the party. Our analysis points out how elites could also aim to control internal conflict between factions by creating a wider consensus for a weak leader, as happened in Portugal. Nevertheless, the Japanese and Taiwanese experiences offer suggestions for the use of inclusiveness as an instrument adopted by less powerful leaders to challenge the established party elites in order to reduce the latter's influence.

The second dimension relates to the so-called party on the ground,which refers to the role played by party members within the organisation. In Spain, primaries have been used as a reaction to activists'dissatisfaction. From this angle, primaries could be considered as a new participative tool for involving activists in party life. In the case of the Portuguese Social Democratic Party (PSD), the adoption of inclusive selection was aimed at promoting internal mobilisation ,and above all improving the accountability of leaders.

Overall, it seems that at intra-party level primaries could serve different aims. On the one hand, they represent a tool used by the elite to tackle internal challenges from factions and for strengthening leader consensus within the party. On the other hand, they are presented to activists as an opportunity for participation in order to show that they are valued within the organisation. Therefore, they serve as a strategy for reactivating relationships with activists and enrolling new members.

Two main findings have emerged from our analyses. First, seldom is there a prevailing incentive; rather, reforms of candidate or leader selection methods are often the result of a combination of factors and political contingencies. Second, each of these factors can facilitate, but not determine, resort to the use of primaries. What emerges with clarity from the comparative analyses is that primaries are commonly recognised as effective strategies of reaction for parties which are facing crisis both at electoral and organisational level. The main added value of using primaries can be found in their capacity to promote a new public image of the party responding to anti-party feelings and disaffection with politics.

In sum, in most cases the rationale for the introduction of primaries has been twofold. On the one hand, this change followed electoral defeats, with the aim of demonstrating party renewal in order to appeal to voters and recruit new members. On the other hand, democratising reforms have been used to contest internal power. Opposition leaders have often defended the deepening of intra-party democracy to challenge incumbents, whereas weak leaders have tried to strengthen their position through the use of membership ballots.

However, in most democracies the adoption of primaries has shown a low level of institutionalisation, and this method of leadership and candidate selection is still a controversial issue in several parties. Also, the absence of accurate regulation in most party statutes (with exceptions, such as the Italian Democratic Party) and the fact that in some cases few contests have taken place since the adoption of the instrument show the strategic use that party elites often make of primaries. Party elites are the driving force in introducing primaries in most cases.

The Primary Election Process

The process of primary elections is marked by a clear final step. It is the nomination of the winner(s), and this is also when the campaign for the general election begins. It is less clear when the primaries themselves begin. Scholars allude to this situation by speaking about a period of 'pre-primaries'. This is the time from the first rumours about the decision to use primaries to the start of the primary campaign. In this interlude, the type of electoral system and the basic rules about the inclusiveness of candidacy and selectorate are decided upon. Then some would-be candidates are excluded, and the likely candidates are endorsed by politicians, entrepreneurs and celebrities from the worlds of sport or showbusiness. Once the electoral supply is defined, the primary electoral process actually starts. Three dimensions are considered relevant: participation, representation and competition.

When assessing citizens' participation in primary elections the distinction between the candidate and leader selection processes is less relevant. Social background, voting motivations and political reasoning are similar among the selectors in both cases. Rather, the fundamental distinction is between closed and open primaries. By and large, the latter involves a greater, and sometimes far greater, number of people than the former. From this evidence stems important differences. A significant level of citizens involvement brings media attention, hence the primary may easily gain attention at national level. This is more obvious in case of a candidate selection, because the nominee, upon winning the next general election, will represent the whole nation, as stated in the political rhetoric of many constitutions. However, an open primary may activate public attention also in case of a leader selection, in principle an affair involving only a party, its members and possibly its sympathisers. By contrast, a closed primary may gain a high level of interest only exceptionally. This depends upon the importance of the promoting party, the national political culture and the kind of media system operating in the country. The cases of the Romanian and Slovakian parties analysed by Gherghina and Spáč definitively show that closed primaries may, at best, involve a small number of professional politicians and party members.

'Representation' is a multidimensional concept. A political institution – parliament or government – is said to be representative from a sociological point of view when there is a correspondence between citizens and elected representatives in terms of socio-demographic profile. This dimension is thus measured by the degree of representativeness in socio-demographic terms of the selected officials. This question could be dealt with from several points of view; however, the most usual approach entails an assessment of the presence of women in politics. When the gender gap issue is analysed in reference to primary elections, two questions are relevant: how many women are candidates; and how many of these women candidates win the primaries and obtain the nomination?

Outside the US, primaries are a tool for innovating parties; thus one could suppose that they equally promote the presence of men and women inside the elected institutions. De Luca and Venturino analyse an important case – perhaps *the* case – where a woman gained the nomination for one of the most important roles in Western European democracies. We allude to Ségolène Royal, winner of the 2006 closed primaries promoted by the French Socialist Party who was then defeated by Nicolas Sarkozy in the 2007 presidential election. However, it should be noted that the general picture is not so favourable in terms of boosting the presence of women in politics. On the whole, the number of female candidates in primary elections is extremely low, and therefore the number of female nominees is also strikingly low. As the percentage of women leading a party is less than the percentage of women sitting in parliament, we may also assume that the gender gap is particularly persistent in primaries for leader selection.

'Competition' covers the dimensions dealing with the degree of competitiveness of the primary election process. This is a concept often associated with the concept of a 'negative electoral campaign'. Both competitive elections and negative campaigns relate to the struggle to win elected offices, but the two cases are rather different. A campaign is negative when candidates aggressively attack their competitors rather than promoting their own policies, whereas an election is competitive when the number of votes gained by the winner is not much larger than the number gained by the challengers. While the investigation of negativity addresses an important but different strand of research, assessment of competitiveness once more requires that the difference between candidate and leader selection is taken into account.

All things considered, the competitiveness of a primary election for selecting a candidate – either closed or open – may be measured by the same indicators utilised for the study of general elections.[4] This is because outside the US, where the level of competition is lamentably decreasing, primaries still feature the same characteristics as a general election: several candidates, an effective campaign and a disputed result. The case of primaries for selecting a party leader is often completely different. In most circumstances (sometimes reaching 90 per cent of cases) the selection goes uncontested – that is, there is just a single candidate. Often a race with more than one candidate is dominated by the incumbent. In any case, the number of votes gained by the frontrunner averages well above 60–70 per cent.

This situation discourages the use of those sophisticated measures for selecting candidates established for general elections and adapted for primaries. Rather, some raw indicators used for the highly uncompetitive American direct primaries could be more useful. There, the most important difference concerns the (infrequent) presence of more than one candidate, which may be measured by the simple distinction between contested and uncontested primaries. Alternatively, the competitiveness of party leader selections could be gauged through undemanding indicators such as the presence of incumbents and the percentage of votes gained by the winner.

Consequences of Using Primary Elections

According to our analyses, the adoption of primaries could be interpreted as a party's reaction to a crisis. On the one hand, an electoral failure and a climate of negative, dissatisfied public opinion could act as incentives for organisational renewal of the party. And often this renovation starts from reforms of internal procedures which lead to a new party elite and then to a new public image for the

---

4 Electoral researchers have made available several measures of competitiveness, the most common being closeness, the Rae index and the effective number of parties. All of them may be indifferently applied to party lists and individual candidates. Kenig (2008) has proposed an amended version of Laakso and Taagepera's effective number of parties.

party. On the other hand, the weakened links with activists and the challenges of maintaining high levels of internal mobilisation demand that the party provide new opportunities for participation. Primaries seem to be an appropriate strategy for answering such challenges. Hence, understanding whether and to what extent primary elections could affect political parties requires taking into account two main dimensions. The first could be defined as external, and is related to the impact of primary elections on the electoral performances achieved by those political parties resorting to these methods. The second is instead referred to as an internal dimension, namely the reaction at membership level to the introduction of inclusive procedures.

Let us begin by summarising the main findings of our analyses addressing the effects produced by primary elections on the external dimension. In this regard, considering candidate or leadership selection cases, the effects of primaries on electoral performance do not seem to be particularly relevant. It is difficult to distinguish the actual and direct impact of the selection method on the election result obtained by the party promoting it. In particular, in cases of a leadership selection, it would be very difficult to assess the influence of primaries on the electoral dimension. If a process of candidate selection is clearly aimed at selecting nominations for an electoral competition, it is not necessarily also true for the selection of a party leader. In several cases, the two offices do not overlap, as happens in Belgium (and in Italy until the 1990s). Or, as shown by the Israeli case, the selection of a party leader may not immediately follow a parliamentary election. Hence, even considering the strong personalisation of politics which could characterise a political system, it is not easy to identify the specific impact of inclusive selection procedures on party performance. Furthermore, the influence of political culture has to be considered. In the Belgian case, due to consociational politics, the offices of prime minister and party leader often do not coincide. As a consequence, the role of the leader and, therefore, the methods by which he or she is selected may have no influence on boosting electoral support.

According to the analyses in this volume, however, an improvement in the public image of a party does not correspond to an equal increase in its electoral consensus. Rather, electoral success depends on several interrelated factors. The mere method for selecting a candidate, or a party leader, is not sufficient to stimulate electoral support. A good example of this comes from Italy, where the inclusive selection of the prime ministerial candidate by the centre-left coalition produced a growing consensus registered by opinion polls which eventually was not followed by a similar electoral success. In that case, the political context played a role in the electoral setback. A climate of negative public opinion, combined with the emergence of new political actors, jeopardised the positive image created by the primaries just a few weeks before election day. In other cases, it seems that electoral performance depends on other intervening factors, such as the quality of the candidates or leaders selected and their personal appeal.

Moving to the analysis of consequences at internal party level, there are other ambiguities to be clarified. In this regard, among our cases, a temporary increase in enrolment is often observed, since just before primaries new members decide to join the party. However, such growth is often short-lived. The fluctuating rate of membership suggests instead that the rising number of enrolments is, in many cases, limited to the primary contingency. The requirement for registration or enrolment to participate in primary elections indeed produces an artificial increase in activists. Nonetheless, this increase is often the result of manipulation by the party elite aimed at controlling the results of selections – that is, when it is not outright fraudulent, as in the case of Romania.

Further points of interest on this issue are evident from the Belgian case. The authors suggest that the lack of a real impact on party membership is because of the low level of competitiveness of the leadership selections. In other words, if the selection is not perceived as truly competitive, political parties and their elites are not incentivised to launch massive recruitment campaigns. Neither are potential party members, even if they are interested in political activities, given any incentive to formally enrol. On closer inspection, we observe that the impact of primaries on membership size could not be fully understood by solely focusing on quantitative data. Indeed, membership rates are not sufficient to assess the impact of primaries. On the contrary, they may actually be misleading if the increases are due to manipulation by the party elites.

In sum, primaries have a positive effect on public opinion and therefore on the citizens' perceptions of the party. For this reason the contagion effect at the party system level represents an effective incentive for the adoption of inclusive tools. However, this does not directly correspond to a positive impact at electoral or organisational level. Primaries are not likely to affect electoral results or the capacity to attract new members. On the contrary, if on the electoral side it is very difficult to identify a direct impact from primaries, on the organisational side the increase in the number of activists could instead result in a temporary rise in membership, followed by a steep fall (a phenomenon usually called 'instant membership'); or, at worst, it could be the result of manipulation by the elite.

Our evidence suggests that the differences in political context between the American and European (or Asian) cases play a crucial role in explaining the long-term impact of primaries on party organisational features. The lack of state regulation of candidate and leadership selection in European, Asian and Middle Eastern parties diminishes the disruptive effect that primaries had on party organisations in the US. In Europe, Asia and Israel, party leaders seem to have been able to retain ultimate control over candidate and leadership selection, while at the same time increasing internal participation. The democratisation of the processes have been more formal than real.

A New Research Agenda

Are primaries capable of bringing real change for political parties? Do they really have an impact on parties? Our findings seem, so far, to be discouraging for those hoping for momentous impacts to come from the introduction of primaries to select candidates and leaders. Indeed, if political parties are currently continuing to choose inclusion as an answer to the anti-party feeling, blame and delegitimisation they experience within the political scene, they barely perceive the outcomes in terms of electoral consensus and membership mobilisation. Furthermore, despite the myth of a possible democratisation of internal party life, these inclusive selection methods seem to be firmly in the hands of party elites which, due the absence of a clear and formal institutionalisation of primaries, can easily use them to control the organisation as well as manage internal conflict and challenges by emerging factions. Hence the conservation of primaries can be explained in most cases by the creation of a new power equilibrium that combines the benefits of improved party image via stronger internal (direct) democracy (which serves lower party strata and voters) with a weakening of the mid-level elites (which serves the party leadership). Furthermore, the lack of state regulation for candidate and leadership selection in non-US parties diminishes the disruptive effect that primaries have on party organisations in the US.

All things considered, these are not disappointing results. The difficulties in illustrating a clear and direct impact of primaries on political parties suggest the need to expand the research on this issue by enlarging the focus. In particular, the consequences of primaries concerning both candidates and leader selection may be further addressed by adopting two main dimensions of analysis: internal and external. The former relates to the intra-party dynamics which could be affected by the resort to primary elections and could give information about the functioning and consequences of such processes. The latter dimension refers to electoral dynamics and explores the impact of primaries on parliamentary cohesion and inter-party competition at a systemic level.

In Table 10.1, by combining these two analytical levels and the four theoretical dimensions proposed by Hazan and Rahat (2010) – namely competition, participation, representation and responsiveness – we attempt to summarise the main strands of research which could be adopted in future studies on this issue.

According to our initial research results, primaries could be considered as strategic tools in the hands of party elites. Due to the lack of formal rules, party elites areable to define primary regulations and, therefore, the inclusiveness of selectorate and candidacy rules, with an impact on the selection process in terms of participation and competition. However, as shown, their impact could also be measured at the membership level, in the sense of increased ability to promote (or not) massive recruitment campaigns.

For this reason, understanding the selection processes means dealing with the internal party organisation. To be more precise, the internal distribution of power among factions represents, from this angle, a starting point for the evaluation of primaries'consequences as well as the role played by the leader within the party organisation. The selection of leaders and candidates through an inclusive

Table 10.1 Dimensions of analysis of the effects of primary elections

	Candidate selection		Party leader selection	
	Internal	External	Internal	External
Competition	Degree of factionalism	Electoral performance	Leadership autonomy	Degree of personalisation of electoral campaigns
		Degree of personalisation and candidate-centred competition	Degree of presidentialisation of party structures	Negative primary electoral campaign
Participation	Membership features (size, recruitment, activism, attitudes)	Turnout	Membership features (size, recruitment, activism, attitudes)	Turnout
Representation	Degree of candidates' ideological consistency	Candidate profiles (socio-demographics, ideological features	Internal patronage	Leadership profiles (socio-demographics, ideological features)
Responsiveness	Legislative behaviour and degree of cohesion (PPG)	Candidates' accountability	Leadership structure (dominant coalition)	Leader-centred electoral campaigns and communication
		Legislative behaviour (parliament)		

selectorate constitutes a new competitive arena for internal party factions or new leaders challenging the incumbent. Especially in the case of open primaries, the exogenous legitimation of the selected candidates or leader and the participation of voters and supporters could provide an opportunity for minority factions and for individual ambitions to defy the party leadership and its dominant coalition. Thus, in order to understand the functioning of the main dimensions of primary politics from the point of view of *competition*, we need to focus on party organisation, looking at the degree of centralisation or decentralisation of its decision-making bodies and, especially regarding leadership selection, the level of leader autonomy.

From an empirical point of view, this means focusing firstly on analysis of the party organisation, namely the statutes and internal rules concerning the role of the leader; the level of internal democracy given to the opposition; the possibility for the removal of the leader; and the internal allocation of power among the party internal bodies, as well as the role played by local branches. For example, as illustrated by US literature, the analysis of endorsements of primary candidates could provide meaningful information about the functioning of primaries from an internal point of view, pointing out the kind of relationship that exists among candidates and the party's factions within the primary contest.

Conversely, assessing the impact of primary elections from an external point of view regarding the competition involves focusing on the primary election campaign by looking at two main dimensions: personalisation of the contest and the negative campaign advertising adopted by candidates in their communication strategy. As is well known, a primary contest could emphasise the personalisation of political competition and give greater political relevance to candidates and leaders rather than parties and their ideological platforms. In this kind of competition, often the role of the party is in the background. By investigating in more depth the primary electoral campaign dynamics it is possible to evaluate to what extent the primary debate is focused on parties or on personal rhetoric, understanding to what extent the contest has been personalised by candidates. Personalisation, it should be clear, could affect party organisation in the post-primary election phase as regards cohesion and responsiveness.

Concerning negative advertising within a primary election campaign, there is an extensive body of literature. Indeed, according to US scholars, a negative campaign could have a strong impact on voters' attitudes, harming candidates in general elections. This evidence suggests the need to better investigate this dimension also within the non-US experience. From an empirical point of view, dealing with the personalisation of primary election campaigns as well as negative campaigns requires adopting either quantitative or qualitative methodologies aimed at evaluating public debate about primaries, analysis of candidates' public image and media coverage of the various candidates; and, with regard to the contents of the campaigns, we should resort to discourse analysis in terms of frame and tone.

The second dimension of analysis, *participation*, relates to the evolution of the relationship between members and the party at the internal level, and between supporters and the party at the external level. So far, we adopted this approach from a quantitative and aggregate point of view. Rather, this issue should be addressed also at the individual level by looking at members' attitudes towards their role within the party and towards this participatory procedure. In the case of open primaries, this dimension could also be investigated at the external level, focusing in particular on the differences between selectors (non-members) and activists (members) from a socio-political point of view.

Primary elections, both open and closed, might represent a modern transposition of (or a viable alternative to) the old participatory procedures of mass parties, where members and activists played a crucial role within the party organisation. The (at least apparent) devolution of decision-making powers to the wider membership and party supporters (in the case of open primaries) involved in this kind of internal election could strengthen activists' and ordinary members' propensity to get involved in intra-party activities. Hence, besides the quantitative evaluation of the participatory dimension of primary politics, it might be useful also to address the evolutions in the quality of intra-party involvement that are argued to be linked to the use of primary elections. In terms of empirical methodology, this can be measured only at an individual level, by collecting data on the intensity, quality and type of intra-party mobilisation through tailored quantitative surveys of party members, and possibly panel surveys repeated over time.

Such data would contribute to an evaluation of whether primaries and the wave of political mobilisation they usually entail could have consequences in the long term, especially open primaries and particularly in terms of both campaign activities and turnout. These data could also contribute to assessing whether, conversely, primary elections represent a tailored participatory event exclusively related to the issue of candidate or leader selection, without any impact on members' (or supporters') propensity to mobilise within the party beyond participating in internal elections.

The bottom line is that further research should be aimed at assessing to what extent a primary election, meaning the entire process as well as its result, could affect party organisation. With regard to the dimension of *representation*, so far research has focused on the sociological profile of candidates selected for office or party leadership, devoting a great deal of attention to gender representation. In this regard, several scholars argue that primary elections do not produce a higher level of representation in terms of gender balance if compared to other candidate or leadership selection methods. Notwithstanding this, the result of a primary election, in terms of representation, may produce a relevant impact on party organisation at internal as well as external levels. One must simply consider how often primaries are associated with the idea of a potential party renewal.

The candidate or leader profile is the first evidence which could be considered in order to assess to what extent the result of a primary election could bring about significant reform of the party organisation. In this regard, there are many dimensions to be taken into account: firstly, the gender, but also the age (that is, the political generation) and the political seniority of the selected candidate or leader – namely their experience in politics (previous experience in public and elected office) – and their ideological orientation. This last dimension is one of the most important when looking at representation. As suggested by US scholars, often primary voters are more likely to select candidates who do not correspond to the preferences of the general electorate and who are extreme in their ideological positions.

In other words, the candidate appointed by inclusive elections may not be suitable for the electoral competition, as they are unable to gain support among a wide electorate. Hence, there is the need to develop a thorough investigation of representation focused on the ideological consistency of the candidates or leaders appointed with respect to party members, the party line and their electorate. Once again, empirical research must resort to a quantitative methodological approach focused on individual data on candidates and selectors, and members or sympathisers.

Leader and candidate selection procedures entailing a highly inclusive, participatory electoral contest often characterised by high political personalisation might affect in a crucial way overall party *responsiveness*. Especially in the case of open primaries, the legitimacy of the nominee comes from an external body, and this could generate a shift in the dynamics of internal accountability by marginalising the role of control played by central party bodies. Primaries obviously have a role in providing legitimacy for candidates and leaders. Indeed, the designation through primaries is strongly connected to the personality of the candidate and gives the nominee a significant amount of personal power. The primary vote in some way ignores the party; it is focused on the candidate. This also affects the dynamics of responsiveness between candidates, the party and primary voters.

Responsiveness concerns the obligation of leaders and candidates selected through primaries to answer for their political decisions and the control that their principals (voters and party bodies) can exert on their actions. The adoption of open primaries can transform the features of their principals, which change from mid-level party elites, central bodies or members (according to the previous method of selection) to primary voters. A direct link with the selectorate is created, and this is also true in the case of closed primary elections, which shift the focus of accountability from party elites (usually the parliamentary party group) or central bodies to the wider membership, either active or inactive.

In order to measure responsiveness for candidates appointed by inclusive procedures, we must consider the legislative behaviour of these candidates, with a particular focus on their parliamentary activities and their relationship within the parliamentary group. It has to be assessed in terms of their level of loyalty to the party line or their focus on personal initiatives, which could also challenge their own party. Considered at an organisational level, responsiveness requires taking into account the role played by the leader appointed through primaries within his or her own party. This means consideration must be given to possible changes in party statutes concerning the organisation or rules. Moreover, in this regard, the most effective research strategy consists of considering the communication strategies adopted by the leader, which should aim at verifying to what extent the leader adopts a personal style of communication and which kind of relationship he or she maintains with the party.

We have outlined here a framework for a new long-term research agenda. The increase in the use of primary elections suggests that we need to define a comparative research design to study their impact and consequences. So far, primary elections have been considered as an innovation within non-US political and party systems; but now this phenomenon is becoming increasingly relevant and requires a specific and tailored framework for analysis, focused not just on the process but also on its consequences both at systemic and organisational level.

Bibliography

Abramowitz, A.I., Rapaport, R.B. and McGlennon, J., eds, 1986. *The Life of the Parties: Activists in Presidential Politics.* Lexington: Kentucky University Press.

Adams, J. and Merrill, S., 2008. Candidate and party strategies in two-stage election beginning with a primary. *American Journal of Political Science*, 52(2), pp.344–59.

Alcántara, M. and Freidenberg, F., 2001. *Partidos políticos de América Latina.* Salamanca: Universidad de Salamanca.

Aldrich, J.H., 1980. A dynamic model of presidential nomination campaigns. *American Political Science Review*, 74(3), pp.651–69.

Alford, R.R., 1962. A suggested index of the association of social class and voting. *Public Opinion Quarterly*, 26(3), pp.417–25.

Ansolabehere, S., Hansen, J.M., Hirano, S. and Snyder, J.M., 2006. The decline of competition in US primary elections, 1908–2004. In: M. McDonald and J. Samples, eds. *The Marketplace of Democracy: Electoral Competition and American Politics.* Washington: Brookings Institution Press. pp.74–101.

APSA, 1950. Toward a more responsible two-party system: a report of the committee on political parties. *American Political Science Review*, 44(3), Part 2, Supplement.

Argelaguet, J., 2009. *The Power of Grass-Roots Members in a Political Party: The Case of Esquerra Republicana de Catalunya.* Paper delivered to the ECPR (European Consortium for Political Research) Joint Sessions of Workshops. Lisbon, 14–19 April.

Arter, D., 1999. *Scandinavian Politics Today.* Manchester: Manchester University Press.

Atmor, N. 2011. *The Relationship between Candidate Selection Methods and Electoral Systems.* PhD thesis, Hebrew University [in Hebrew].

Austin, R., 1976. *Participation in American Presidential Nominations.* Washington: American Enterprise Institute.

Aylott, N., Ikstens, J. and Lilliefeldt, E., 2012. *Ever More Inclusive? Candidate Selection in North European Democracies.* Paper delivered to the ECPR (European Consortium for Political Research) Joint Sessions of Workshops. Antwerp, 10–15 April.

Balmas, M., Rahat, G., Sheafer, T. and Shenhav, S., 2014. Two routes to personalized politics: centralized and decentralized personalization. *Party Politics*, 20(1), pp.37–51.

Barberà, O. and Rodríguez Teruel, J., 2012. *The Introduction of Party Primaries in Spain*. Paper delivered to the ECPR (European Consortium for Political Research) Joint Sessions of Workshops. Antwerp, 10–15 April.

Barberà, O., Rodríguez Teruel, J., Barrio, A. and Baras, M., 2014. The selection of party leaders in Spain. In: J.B. Pilet and W.P. Cross, eds. *The Selection of Political Party Leaders in Contemporary Parliamentary Democracies*. London: Routledge. pp. 108–23.

Barnea, S. and Rahat, G., 2007. Reforming candidate selection methods: a three-level approach. *Party Politics*, 13(3), pp.375–94.

Baum, J. and Robinson, J.A., 1999. Party primaries in Taiwan: trends, conditions, and projections in candidate selection. *Occasional Papers Reprints Series in Contemporary Asian Studies*, 6(155), pp.1–39.

Bengtsson, Å., Hansen, K., Harðarson, Ó.Þ., Narud, H.M. and Oscarsson, H., 2013. *The Nordic Voter: Myths of Exceptionalism*. Colchester: ECPR.

Bernardi, L. and Rombi, S., 2013. Nella testa dei selettori. Gli orientamenti di voto tra primo e secondo turno. In: B. Gelli, T. Mannarini and M. Talò, eds. *Perdere vincendo. Dal successo delle primarie 2012 all'impasse post-elettorale*. Milan: Angeli. pp.189–208.

Bille, L., 2001. Democratizing a democratic procedure: myth or reality? Candidate selection in Western European parties, 1960–1990. *Party Politics*, 7(3), pp.363–80.

Bolleyer, N., 2012. New party organization in Western Europe: of hierarchies, stratarchies and federations. *Party Politics*, 18(3), pp.315–36.

Bolleyer, N., 2009. Inside the cartel party: party organization in government and opposition. *Political Studies*, 57(3), pp.559–79.

Bordandini, P., Di Virgilio, A. and Raniolo, F., 2008. The birth of a party: the case of the Italian Partito Democratico. *South European Society and Politics*, 13(3), pp.303–24.

Bruhn, K., 2011. Electing extremists? Party primaries and legislative candidates in Mexico. Working Paper: University of California Santa Barbara.

Bruneau, T.C., Diamandouros, P.N., Gunther, R., Lijphart, A., Morlino, L. and Brooks, R.A., 2001. Democracy, Southern European style. In: P.N. Diamandouros and R. Gunther, eds. *Parties, Politics, and Democracy in the New Southern Europe*. Baltimore: Johns Hopkins University Press. pp.16–82.

Burden, B., 2004. Candidate positioning in US congressional elections. *British Journal of Political Science*, 34(2), pp.211–27.

Bynander, F. and 't Hart, P., 2007. The politics of party leader survival and succession: Australia in comparative perspective. *Australian Journal of Political Science*, 42(1), pp.47–72.

Cain, B.E., Dalton, R.J. and Scarrow S.E., eds, 2003. *Democracy Transformed? Expanding Political Opportunities in Advanced Industrial Democracies*. Oxford: Oxford University Press.

Canon, B.C., 1978. Factionalism in the South: a test of theory and a revisitation of V.O. Key. *American Journal of Political Science*, 22(4), pp.833–48.

Carey, J. and Polga-Hecimovich, J., 2006. Primary elections and candidate strength in Latin America. *Journal of Politics*, 68(3), pp.530–43.

Carey, J.M. and Shugart, M.S., 1995. Incentives to cultivate a personal vote: a rank ordering of electoral formulas. *Electoral Studies*, 14(4), pp.417–39.

Carty, R.K., 2004. Parties as franchise systems: the stratarchical organizational imperative. *Party Politics*, 10(1), pp.5–24.

Carty, R.K. and Blake, D.E., 1999. The adoption of membership votes for choosing party leaders: the experience of Canadian parties. *Party Politics*, 5(2), pp.211–24.

Carty, R.K. and Cross, W.P., 2006. Can stratarchically organized parties be democratic? The Canadian case. Journal of Elections, *Public Opinion and Parties*, 16(2), pp.93–114.

Central Electoral Bureau in Romania, 2004–12. Election reports and documents. [online] Available at: <http://www.bec2004.ro; http://www.becparlamentare2008.ro; http://www.becparlamentare2012.ro> [in Romanian].

CIA, 2014. *World Factbook*. [online] Available at: <https://www.cia.gov/library/publications/the-world-factbook/index.html> [accessed June 2014].

Coelho, M., 2014. *Os partidos políticos e o recrutamento do pessoal dirigente em Portugal*. Lisbon: Europress.

Cohen, M., Karol, D., Noel, H. and Zaller J., 2008. *The Party Decides: Presidential Nominations Before and After Reform*. Chicago: University of Chicago Press.

Corbetta, P. and Vignati, R., 2013. The primaries of the centre left: only a temporary success? *Contemporary Italian Politics*, 5(1), pp.82–96.

Costa Lobo, M., 2003. A elite partidária em Portugal, 1976–2002: dirigentes, deputados e membros do governo. In: A.C. Pinto and A. Freire, eds. *Elites, sociedade e mudança política*. Lisbon: Celta, pp.249–75.

Costa Lobo, M., 2006. Short-term voting determinants in a young democracy: leader effects in Portugal in the 2002 legislative elections. *Electoral Studies*, 25(2), pp.270–86.

Courtney, J.C., 1995. *Do Conventions Matter? Choosing National Party Leaders in Canada*. Montreal: McGill-Queen's University Press.

Cross, W.P. and Blais, A., 2012a. *Politics at the Centre: The Selection and Removal of Leaders in the Principal Anglophone Parliamentary Democracies*. Oxford: Oxford University Press.

Cross, W.P. and Blais, A., 2012b. Who selects the party leader? *Party Politics*, 18(2), pp.127–50.

Cross, W.P. and Katz, R.S., eds, 2013. *The Challenges of Intra-Party Democracy*. Oxford: Oxford University Press.

Cross, W.P. and Rahat, G., 2012. *The Pathologies of Party Primaries and their Possible Solutions*. Paper delivered to the ECPR (European Consortium for Political Research) Joint Sessions of Workshops. Antwerp, 10–15 April.

Dalton, R.J., 2002. *Citizen Politics: Public Opinion and Political Parties in Advanced Industrial Democracies*. Chatham: Chatham House.

Dalton, R.J, Farrell, D. and McAllister, I., 2011. *Political Parties and Democratic Linkage. How Parties Organize Democracy*. Oxford: Oxford University Press.

De Luca, M., 2014. Les électeurs socialistes dans les primaires présidentielles à Paris. *French Politics, Culture and Society*, 32(2), pp.123–42.

De Luca, M., Jones, M. and Tula, M., 2002. Back rooms or ballot boxes? Candidate nomination in Argentina. *Comparative Political Studies*, 35(4), pp.413–36.

De Winter, L., 2000. Liberal parties in Belgium: from freemasons to free citizens. In: L. De Winter, ed. *Liberalism and Liberal Parties in the European Union*. Barcelona: ICPS. pp.141–82.

Deegan-Krause, K., 2006. *Elected Affinities: Democracy and Party Competition in Slovakia and the Czech Republic*. Stanford: Stanford University Press.

Deschouwer, K., 2004. Political parties and their reactions to the erosion of voter loyalty in Belgium: caught in a trap. In: P. Mair, W. Müller and F. Plasser, eds. *Political Parties and Electoral Change*. London: Sage. pp.179–206.

Deschouwer, K., 2009. *The Politics of Belgium*. Basingstoke: Palgrave Macmillan.

Dolez, B. and Laurent, A., 2007. Une primaire à la française: la désignation de Ségolène Royal par le Parti Socialiste. *Revue Française de Science Politique*, 57(2), pp.133–61.

Dumont, P., Fiers, S. and Dandoy, R., 2009. Belgium: ups and downs of ministerial careers in a partitocratic federal state. In: K. Dowding and P. Dumont, eds. *The Selection and Deselection of Ministers in Europe*. New York: Routledge. pp.125–46.

Emanuele, V., Fruncillo, D. and Porcellato, N., 2013. La partecipazione al voto. In: B. Gelli, T. Mannarini and M. Talò, eds. *Perdere vincendo. Dal successo delle primarie 2012 all'impasse post-elettorale*. Milan: Angeli. pp.87–108.

Eyjan, 2009. *News Analysis: Primary Results May Determine Political Leadership over the Next Years*. [online] Available at: <http://eyjan.pressan.is/frettir/2009/03/14/frettaskyring-um-profkjorin-nidurstodur-geta-radid-urslitum-um-forystuhlutverk-i-stjornmalum-naestu-ara> [accessed 10 August 2014; in Icelandic].

Eyre, J.R. and Martin, C., 1967. *The Colorado Preprimary System*. Boulder: Bureau of Governmental Research.

Fell, D., 2010. Was 2005 a critical election in Taiwan? Locating the start of a new political era. *Asian Survey*, 50(5), pp.927–45.

Fell, D., 2012. *Government and Politics in Taiwan*. London and New York: Routledge.

Ferrand, O. and Montebourg, A., 2011. *Primaire. comment sauver la gauche*. Paris: Seuil.

Franklin, M., 2002. The dynamics of electoral participation. In: L. LeDuc, R.G. Niemi and P. Norris, eds. *Comparing Democracies 2: New Challenges in the Study of Elections and Voting*. London: Sage. pp.148–68.

Freire, A., 2005. Party system change in Portugal, 1974–2005: the role of social, political and ideological factors. *Portuguese Journal of Social Science*, 4(2), pp.21–40.

Fréttablaðið, 2005. *26 days*. [online] Available at: <www.visir.is/ExternalData/pdf/fbl/050425/pdf> [accessed 10 August 2014; in Icelandic].

Gallagher, M. and Marsh, M., eds, 1988. *Candidate Selection in Comparative Perspective: The Secret Garden of Politics*. London: Sage.

Gangas, P., 1995. *El desarrollo organizativo de los partidos políticos españoles de implantación estatal*. PhD thesis, Instituto Juan March de Estudios e Investigaciones.

García-Guereta, E.M., 2001. *Factores externos e internos en la transformación de los partidos politicos. El caso de AP-PP*. PhD thesis, Instituto Juan March de Estudios e Investigaciones.

Geer, J.G., 1989. *Nominating Presidents: An Evaluation of Voters and Primaries*. Westport: Greenwood.

Gelli, B., Mannarini, T. and Talò, M., eds, 2013. *Perdere vincendo. Dal successo delle primarie 2012 all'impasse post-elettorale*. Milan: Angeli.

Georgescu, R., 2012. USL asks voters to select its candidates. *Adevarul*, 9 January [in Romanian].

Gerber, E.R. and Morton, R.B., 1998. Primary election systems and representation. *Journal of Law, Economics, and Organization*, 14(2), pp.304–24.

Gherghina, S., 2013. One-shot party primaries: the case of the Romanian Social Democrats. *Politics*, 33(3), pp.185–95.

Gherghina, S., 2014a. *Party Organization and Electoral Volatility in Central and Eastern Europe: Enhancing Voter Loyalty*. London: Routledge.

Gherghina, S., 2014b. The MP renomination indicator: a measure of elite continuity and its importance for legislative research. *Parliamentary Affairs* [available online first, doi: 10.1093/pa/gst034].

Gherghina, S., and Jiglau, G., 2012. Where does the mechanism collapse? Understanding the 2008 Romanian electoral system. *Representation*, 48(4), pp.445–59.

Grunberg, G. and Haegel, F., 2007. *La France vers le bipartitisme? La présidentialisation du PS et de l'UMP*. Paris: Presses de Sciences Po.

Guðmundsson, J., 1886. On parliamentary candidacies 1886. *Ísafold*, 13(51) [in Icelandic].

Hacker, A., 1965. Does a 'divisive' primary harm a candidate's election chance? *American Political Science Review*, 59(1), pp.105–10.

Haines, A.A. and Rhine, S.L., 1998. Attack politics in presidential nomination campaigns: an examination of the frequency and determinants of intermediated negative messages against opponents. *Political Research Quarterly*, 51(3), pp.691–721.

Haughton, T., 2003. 'We'll finish what we've started': the 2002 Slovak parliamentary elections. *Journal of Communist Studies and Transition Politics*, 19(4), pp.65–90.

Haughton, T., and Rybář, M., 2004. All right now? Explaining the successes and failures of the Slovak centre-right. *Journal of Communist Studies and Transition Politics*, 20(3), pp.115–32.

Hazan, R.Y., 2000. Religion and politics in Israel: the rise and fall of the consociational model. In: R.Y. Hazan and M. Maor, eds, *Parties, Elections and Cleavages: Israel in Comparative and Theoretical Perspective*. London: Frank Cass. pp.109–37.

Hazan, R.Y., 2002. Candidate selection. In: L. LeDuc, R.G. Niemi and P. Norris, eds. *Comparing Democracies 2: New Challenges in the Study of Elections and Voting*. London: Sage. pp.108–26.

Hazan, R.Y. and Gerrit V., 2006. Electoral systems and candidate selection. *Acta Politica*, 41(2), pp.146–62.

Hazan, R.Y. and Rahat, G., 2010. *Democracy within Parties: Candidate Selection Methods and their Political Consequences*. Oxford: Oxford University Press.

Hazan, R.Y. and Voerman, G., 2006. Electoral systems and candidate selection. *Acta Politica*, 41(2), pp.146–62.

Heidar, K., 2006. Party membership and participation. In: R.S. Katz and W. Crotty, eds. *Handbook of Party Politics*. London: Sage. pp.301–16.

Heidar, K. and Saglie, J., 2003. A decline of linkage? Intra-party participation in Norway, 1991–2000. *European Journal of Political Research*, 42(6), pp.761–86.

Hopkin, J., 2001. Bringing the members back in? Democratizing candidate selection in Britain and Spain. *Party Politics*, 7(3), pp.343–61.

Hsieh, J.F., 2010. Is the Kuomintang invincible? In: Lee Wei-Chin, ed. *Taiwan's Politics in the 21st Century: Changes and Challenges*. Singapore: World Scientific Publishing. pp.25–40.

Hsu, Y. and Chen, H., 2007. Intra-party factional competition and the fate of the party election: a case study of the Democratic Progressive Party. *Taiwan Journal of Political Science*, 31(3), pp.129–74 [in Chinese].

ICENES (Icelandic National Election Study), 2012. [online] Available at: <http://www.fel.hi.is/en/icelandic_national_election_study_icenes> [accessed 23 February 2012].

Ichino, N. and Nathan, N.L., 2012. Do primaries improve electoral performance? Clientelism and intra-party conflict in Ghana. *American Journal of Political Science*, 57(2), pp.428–41.

IDEA (International Institute for Democracy and Electoral Assistance), 2014. [online] Available at: <www.idea.int> [accessed 18 July 2014].

IMF (International Monetary Fund), 2013. [online] Available at: <http://www.imf.org/> [accessed 31 October 2014].

Indriðason, I.H., 2005. A theory of coalitions and clientelism: coalition politics in Iceland, 1945–2000. *European Journal of Political Research*, 44(3), pp.439–64.

Indriðason, I.H. and Kristinsson, G.H., 2012. *Nominations through Party Primaries in Iceland*. Paper delivered to the ECPR (European Consortium for Political Research) Joint Sessions of Workshops. Antwerp, 10–15 April.

Indriðason, I.H. and Kristinsson, G.H., 2013. Primary consequences: the effects of candidate selection through party primaries in Iceland. *Party Politics* [available online first, doi: 1354068813487117].

Indriðason, I.H. and Sigurjónsdóttir, Á.J., 2008. Supply or demand? Women's success in the party primaries. *Icelandic Review of Politics and Administration*, 2(4), pp.205–29 [in Icelandic].

Indriðason, I.H. and Sigurjónsdóttir, Á.J., 2014. Primaries in a proportional representation system: girls vs boys. *Representation*, 50(1), pp.27–40.
Inoguchi, T., 2010. Fledgling two-party democracy in Japan: no strong partisans and a fragmented state bureaucracy. In: K. Lawson, ed. *Political Parties and Democracy*, vol. 3. New York: Greenwood. pp.173–90.
Ísafold, 1890. *Elections to Alþingi*. 51(202) [in Icelandic].
Ísafold, 1900. *City Council Elections*. 2(7) [in Icelandic].
Ishikawa, M., 1995. *Post-War Political History*. Tokyo: Iwanami shoten [in Japanese].
Ishiyama, J.T., 1999. The Communist successor parties and party organizational development in post-communist politics. *Political Research Quarterly*, 52(1), pp.87–112.
Ivaldi, G., 2007. Presidential strategies, models of leadership and the development of parties in a candidate-centred polity: the 2007 UMP and PS presidential nomination campaigns. *French Politics*, 5(3), pp.253–77.
Jalali, C., 2006. The woes of being in opposition: the PSD since 1995. *South European Society and Politics*, 11(3–4), pp.359–79.
Jalali, C., 2007. *Partidos e democracia em Portugal, 1974–2005*. Lisbon: Imprensa de Ciências Sociais.
Janda, K., 2009. *Laws against Party Switching, Defecting, or Floor-Crossing in National Parliaments: The Legal Regulation of Political Parties*. Working paper no. 2, August.
Jiji Press, 1981. *Party Cabinets of Postwar Japan: Analyses by Jiji Opinion Polls*. Tokyo: Jiji Press [in Japanese].
Jiji Press, 1992. *Japanese Parties and Cabinets, 1981–1991: Analyses by Jiji Opinion Polls*. Tokyo: Jiji Press [in Japanese].
Jiji Press, 1992–2013. *Jiji Opinion Poll Dispatches*. Tokyo: Jiji Press [in Japanese].
Kam, C., 2009. *Party Discipline and Parliamentary Government*. Cambridge: Cambridge University Press.
Katz, R.S., 2001. The problem of candidate selection and models of party democracy. *Party Politics*, 7(3), pp.277–96.
Katz, R.S. and Mair, P., 1995. Changing models of party organization and party democracy. The emergence of the cartel party. *Party Politics*, 1(1), pp.5–28.
Kaufmann, K.M., Gimpel, J.G. and Hoffman, A.H., 2003. A promise fulfilled? Open primaries and representation. *Journal of Politics*, 65(2), pp.457–76.
Kemahlioglu, O., Weitz-Shapiro, R. and Hirano, S. 2009. Why primaries in Latin American elections? *Journal of Politics*, 71(1), pp.339–52.
Kenig, O., 2009a. Democratization of party leadership selection: do wider selectorates produce more competitive contests? *Electoral Studies*, 28(2), pp.240–47.
Kenig, O., 2009b. Classifying party leaders' selection methods in parliamentary democracies. *Journal of Elections, Public Opinion and Parties*, 19(4), pp.433–47.

Kenig, O. and Barnea, S., 2009. The selection of ministers in Israel: is the prime minister a master of his domain?. *Israel Affairs*, 15(3), pp.261–78.

Kenig, O. and Rahat, G., 2011. *Leadership Selection and Candidate Selection: Similarities and Differences*. Paper presented at the workshop on 'The Selection of Party Leaders: Origins, Methods and Consequences'. ECPR Joint Sessions of Workshops, 12–17 April, University of St. Gallen, Switzerland.

Kenig, O. and Rahat, G., 2014. Selecting party leaders in Israel. In: J.B. Pilet and W.P. Cross, eds. *The Selection of Political Party Leaders in Contemporary Parliamentary Democracies*. London: Routledge. pp.206–21.

Kenig, O., Philippov, M. and Rahat, G., 2013. Party membership in Israel: an overview. *Israel Studies Review*, 28(1). pp.8–32.

Key, V.O., 1956. *American State Politics. An Introduction*. New York: Knopf.

Key, V.O., 1949. *Southern Politics*. New York: Knopf.

Kimmerling, B., 1999. Elections as a battleground over collective identity. In: A. Arian and M. Shamir, eds. *The Elections in Israel, 1996*. Albany: State University of New York Press. pp.27–44.

Kittilson, M.C. and Scarrow, S.E., 2003. Political parties and the rhetoric and realities of democratization. In: B.E. Cain, R.J. Dalton and S.E. Scarrow, eds. *Democracy Transformed? Expanding Political Opportunities in Advanced Industrial Democracies*. Oxford: Oxford University Press. pp.59–80.

Koole, R., 2012. *Party Primaries for Leadership Selection. The Dutch Case*. Paper delivered to the ECPR (European Consortium for Political Research) Joint Sessions of Workshops. Antwerp, 10–15 April.

Kopeček, L., 2007. *Political Parties in Slovakia, 1989–2006*. Brno: Centrum pro studium demokracie a kultury [in Slovakian].

Kristinsson, G.H., 1996. Parties, states and patronage. *West European Politics*, 19(3), pp.433–57.

Kristinsson, G.H., 1999. *Budgeting in Iceland*. Reykjavík: University of Iceland Press [in Icelandic].

Kristinsson, G.H., 2011. Party cohesion in the Icelandic Althingi. *Icelandic Review of Politics and Administration*, 7(2), pp.229–51 [in Icelandic].

Kristinsson, G.H., 2013. Realistic rationality or policy fumbling? *Icelandic Review of Politics and Administration*, 9(2), pp.257–77 [in Icelandic].

LeDuc, L., 2001. Democratizing party leadership selection. *Party Politics*, 7(3), pp.323–41.

Lefebvre, R., 2011. *Les primaires socialiste. La fin du parti militant*. Paris: Raison d'Agir.

Lewis, P.G., ed., 1996. *Party Structure and Organization in East Central Europe*. Cheltenham: Edward Elgar.

Lewis-Beck, M.S., ed., 2004. *The French Voter. Before and After the 2002 Elections*. Basingstoke: Palgrave Macmillan.

Lewis-Beck, M.S., Nadeau, R. and Bélanger, E., 2011. *French Presidential Elections*. Basingstoke: Palgrave Macmillan.

Lijphart, A., 2012. *Patterns of Democracy: Government Forms and Performance in Thirty-Six Countries*. 2nd edn. New Haven: Yale University Press.
Lipset, S.M. and Rokkan, S., 1967. Cleavage structures, party systems and voter alignments: an introduction. In: S.M. Lipset and S. Rokkan, eds. *Party Systems and Voter Alignments*. New York: Free Press. pp.1–64.
Lisi, M., 2009. *A arte de ser indispensável. Líder e organização no Partido Socialista Português*. Lisbon: Imprensa de Ciências Sociais.
Lisi, M., 2010. The democratization of the party leadership selection: the Portuguese experience. *Portuguese Journal of Social Sciences*, 9(2), pp.127–49.
Lisi, M., 2011. *Os partidos políticos em Portugal. Continuidade e transformação*. Coimbra: Almedina.
Lisi, M. and Freire, A. 2014. The selection of party leaders in Portugal. In: J.B. Pilet and W.P. Cross, eds. *The Selection of Political Party Leaders in Contemporary Parliamentary Democracies*. London: Routledge. pp.124–40.
Luther, K.R., 1999. A framework for the comparative analysis of political parties and party systems in consociational democracy. In: K.R. Luther and K. Deschouwer, eds. *Party Elites in Divided Societies: Political Parties in Consociational Democracy*. London: Routledge. pp.3–19.
Mair, P., 1994. Party organization: from civil society to the state. In: R.S. Katz and P. Mair, eds. *How Parties Organize*. London: Sage. pp.1–22.
Mair, P., 1997. *Party System Change: Approaches and Interpretations*. Oxford: Oxford University Press.
Mair, P. and van Biezen, I., 2001. Party membership in twenty European democracies, 1980–2000. *Party Politics*, 7(1), pp.5–21.
Makse, T. and Sokhey, A., 2010. Revisiting the divisive primary hypothesis: 2008 and the Clinton–Obama nomination battle. *American Politics Research*, 38(2), pp.233–65.
Maravall, J.M., 2008. The political consequences of internal party democracy. In: J.M. Maravall and I. Sánchez-Cuenca, eds, *Controlling Governments: Voters, Institutions, and Accountability*. New York: Cambridge University Press. pp.157–201.
Marsh, M., 1993. Introduction: selecting the party leader. *European Journal of Political Research*, 24(3), pp.229–31.
Matsumoto, M., 2010. The KMT's return to power: Ma Ying-jeou and his electoral strategies. In: M. Wakabayashi, ed. *Politics in Taiwan after Democratization: Eight Years of Chen Shui-bian Administration*. Chiba: Ide-Jetro. pp.95–121 [in Japanese].
Matsumoto, M., 2013. Presidential strength and party readership in Taiwan. In: Y. Kasuya, ed. *Presidents, Assemblies and Policy-Making in Asia*. Basingstoke: Palgrave Macmillan. pp.107–33.
May, J., 1973. Opinion structure of political parties: the special law of curvilinear disparity. *Political Studies*, 21(2), pp.135–51.

McElwain, K. and Umeda, M., 2011. Party leader election reform and party support. In: N. Hiwatari and J. Saito, eds. *Turmoil of Party Politics and Government Change*. Tokyo: Tokyodaigakushuppankai [in Japanese].
Meinke, S.R., Staton, J.K. and Wuhs, S.T., 2006. State delegate selection rules for presidential nominations, 1972–2000. *Journal of Politics*, 68(1), pp.180–93.
Méndez, M., 2000. *La estrategia organizativa del Partido Socialista Obrero Español, 1975–1996*. Madrid: Centro de Investigaciones Sociológicas.
Michels, R., 2009 [1911]. *Les partis politiques*. Brussels: Université de Bruxelles.
Mikulska, A. and Scarrow, S.E., 2010. Assessing the political impact of candidate selection rules: Britain in the 1990s. *Journal of Elections, Public Opinion and Parties*, 20(3), pp.311–33.
Millard, F., 2004. *Elections, Parties, and Representation in Post-Communist Europe*. Basingstoke: Palgrave Macmillan.
Miller, P.M., Jewell, M.E. and Sigelman, L., 1988. Divisive primaries and party activists: Kentucky, 1979 and 1983. *Journal of Politics*, 50(2), pp.459–70.
Mulé, R., 2007. *Dentro i Ds*. Bologna: Il Mulino.
Norrander, B., 1986. Selective participation: presidential primary voters as a subset of general election voters. *American Politics Quarterly*, 14(1–2), pp.35–53.
Norris, P., 2006. Recruitment. In: R.S. Katz and W. Crotty, eds. *Handbook of Party Politics*. London: Sage. pp.89–108.
Norris, P. and Lovenduski, J., 1995. *Political Recruitment: Gender, Race and Class in the British Parliament*. Cambridge: Cambridge University Press.
Öhman, M., 2004. *The Heart and Soul of the Party: Candidate Selection in Ghana and Africa*. PhD thesis, Uppsala Universitet.
Oñate, P., 2008. Los partidos políticos en la España democrática. In: M. Jiménez de Parga and F. Vallespín, eds. *La política*. Madrid: Fundación Sistema. pp.617–43.
Onofrei, C., 2004. PSD starts quarrelling. *Ziarul de Iasi*, 4 September [in Romanian].
Ostrogorski, M., 1902. *Democracy and the Organization of Political Parties*. London: Macmillan.
Palmer, N., 1997. *The New Hampshire Primary and the American Electoral Process*. Westport: Praeger.
Panebianco, A., 1988. *Political Parties: Organization and Power*. Cambridge: Cambridge University Press.
Party Politics, 2001. Special issue on democratization of candidate selection, 7(3).
Pasquino, G., ed., 2009. *Il Partito Democratico. Elezione del segretario, organizzazione e potere*. Bologna: Bononia University Press.
Pasquino, G. and Venturino, F., eds, 2009. *Le primarie comunali in Italia*. Bologna: Il Mulino.
Pasquino, G. and Venturino, F., eds, 2010. *Il Partito Democratico di Bersani. Persone, profilo e prospettive*, Bologna: Bononia University Press.
Pasquino, G. and Venturino, F., eds, 2014. *Il Partito Democratico secondo Matteo*. Bologna: Bononia University Press.

Peterson, D.A. and Djupe, P.A., 2005. When primary campaigns go negative: the determinants of campaign negativity. *Political Research Quarterly*, 58(1), pp.45–54.

Pétursson, P., Sigurðsson, J. and Magnússon, G., 1851. *Report on the Icelanders' National Assembly in 1851*. Reykjavík [in Icelandic].

Pilet, J.B. and Cross W.P., eds, 2014. *The Selection of Political Party Leaders in Contemporary Parliamentary Democracies*. London: Routledge.

Pilet, J.B. and Wauters, B., 2014. Party leadership selection in Belgium. In: J.B. Pilet and W.P. Cross, eds. *The Selection of Political Party Leaders in Contemporary Parliamentary Democracies*. London: Routledge. pp.30–46.

Píratar, 2013. *Constituency Councils and Primaries*. [online] Available at: <http://www.piratar.is/um-pirata/kjordaemisrad-og-profkjor> [accessed 6 October 2014; in Icelandic].

Poguntke, T. and Webb, P., eds, 2005. *The Presidentialization of Politics: A Comparative Study of Modern Societies*. Oxford: Oxford University Press.

Polsby, N., 1983. *The Consequences of Party Reform*. New York: Oxford University Press.

Pop-Eleches, G., 1999. Separated at birth or separated by birth? The communist successor parties in Romania and Hungary. *East European Politics and Societies*, 13(1), pp.117–47.

Progressive Party Central Office, 1945. *Records of the Central Committee*, vol. 12 (handwritten minutes).

Punnett, R.M., 1992. *Selecting the Party Leader: Britain in Comparative Perspective*. London: Harvester Wheatsheaf.

Quinn, T., 2012. *Electing and Ejecting Party Leaders in Britain*. New York: Palgrave Macmillan.

Radulescu, G., 2004. Adrian Nastase: the primary elections, a successful experiment. *Curierul National*, 7 (September) [in Romanian].

Rae, D.W., 1967. *The Political Consequences of Electoral Laws*. New Haven: Yale University Press.

Rahat, G., 2008. Entering through the back door: non-party actors in intra-party (s) electoral politics. In: D.M. Farrell and R. Schmitt-Beck, eds. *Non-Party Actors in Electoral Politics.:The Role of Interest Groups and Independent Citizens in Contemporary Election Campaigns*. Baden-Baden: Nomos. pp.25–44.

Rahat, G. and Hazan, R.Y., 2001. Candidate selection methods: an analytical framework. *Party Politics*, 7(3), pp.297–322.

Rahat, G. and Hazan, R.Y., 2006. Candidate selection methods: methods and consequences. In: R.S. Katz and W. Crotty, eds. *Handbook of Party Politics*. London: Sage. pp.109–21.

Rahat, G. and Hazan, R.Y., 2007. Political participation in party primaries: increase in quantity, decrease in quality? In: T. Zittel and D. Fuchs, eds. *Participatory Democracy and Political Participation*. London: Sage. pp.57–72.

Rahat, G. and Kenig, O., 2011. *Leadership Selection and Candidate Selection: Similarities and Differences*. Paper presented at the ECPR (European

Consortium for Political Research) Joint Sessions of Workshops, St. Gallen, Switzerland, April.

Rahat, G. and Sheafer, T., 2007. The personalization(s) of politics: Israel 1949–2003. *Political Communication*, 24(1), pp.65–80.

Rahat, G. and Sher-Hadar, N., 1999a. The 1996 party primaries and their political consequences. In: A. Arian and M. Shamir, eds. *The Elections in Israel 1996*. New York: State University of New York Press. pp. 241–68.

Rahat, G. and Sher-Hadar, N., 1999b. *Intra-Party Selection of Candidates for the Knesset List and for Prime-Ministerial Candidacy, 1995–1997*. Jerusalem: Israel Democracy Institute [in Hebrew].

Rahat, G., Hazan, R.Y. and Katz, R.S., 2008. Democracy and political parties: on the uneasy relationship between participation, competition and representation. *Party Politics*, 14(6), pp.663–83.

Ramiro, L., 2004. *Cambio y adaptación en la izquierda. La evolución del Partido Comunista de España y de Izquierda Unida, 1986–2000*. Madrid: Centro de Investigaciones Sociológicas.

Ramiro, L., 2013. Effects of party primaries on electoral performance: the Spanish socialist primaries in local elections. *Party Politics* [available online first, doi: 10.1177/1354068813514884].

Ranney, A., 1968. Representativeness of primary electorates. *Midwest Journal of Political Science*, 12(2), pp.224–38.

Ranney, A., 1972. Turnout and representation in presidential primary elections. *American Political Science Review*, 66(1), pp.21–37.

Ranney, A., 1981. Candidate selection. In: D. Butler, H.R. Penniman and A. Ranney, eds. *Democracy at the Polls*. Washington: American Enterprise Institute. pp.75–106.

Regenstreif, P., 1969. Note on the 'alternation' of French and English leaders in the liberal party of Canada. *Canadian Journal of Political Science*, 2(1), pp.118–22.

Reidy, T., 2011. Candidate selection. In: M. Gallagher and M. Marsh, eds. *How Ireland Voted 2011*. Basingstoke: Palgrave Macmillan. pp.47–67.

Reynolds, J.F., 2006. *The Demise of the American Convention System, 1880–1911*. Cambridge: Cambridge University Press.

Russell, M., 2005. *Building New Labour: The Politics of Party Organization*. New York: Palgrave Macmillan.

Rybář, M., 2005. Changes of party politics. In: S. Szomolanyi, ed. *Society and Politics in Slovakia: Paths to Stability, 1989–2004*. Bratislava: Comenius University. pp.132–53.

Sandri, G., 2011. *Leadership Selection Methods in Italy and their Consequences on Membership Mobilization*. Paper presented at the ECPR (European Consortium for Political Research) Joint Sessions of Workshops, St. Gallen, Switzerland, April.

Sandri, G. and Pauwels, T., 2011. Party membership role and party cartelization in Belgium and Italy: two faces of the same medal? *Politics and Policy*, 38(6), pp.1237–66.

Sartori, G., 1970. Concept misformation in comparative politics. *American Political Science Review*, 64(4), pp.1033–53.

Sartori, G., 1976. *Parties and Party Systems*. Cambridge: Cambridge University Press.

Scarrow, S., 1999. Parties and the expansion of direct participation opportunities: who benefits? *Party Politics*, 5(3), pp.341–62.

Scarrow, S., 2005. *Political Parties and Democracy in Theoretical and Practical Perspectives: Implementing Intra-Party Democracy*. Washington: National Democratic Institute for International Affairs.

Scarrow, S., 2015. *Beyond Party Members: Changing Approaches to Partisan Mobilization*. Oxford: Oxford University Press.

Scarrow, S.E. and Gezgor, B., 2010. Declining memberships, changing members? European political party members in a new era. *Party Politics*, 16(6), pp.823–43.

Scarrow, S.E., Webb, P. and Farrell, D.M., 2000. From social integration to electoral contestation: the changing distribution of power within political parties. In: R.J. Dalton and M.P. Wattenberg, eds. *Parties without Partisans: Political Change in Advanced Industrial Democracies*. Oxford: Oxford University Press. pp.129–51.

Seddone, A. and Venturino, F., 2013. Bringing voters back in leader selection: the open primaries of the Italian Democratic Party. *Modern Italy*, 18(3), pp.303–18.

Serra, G., 2007a. *Why Primaries? The Strategic Choice of a Candidate Selection Method*. Paper presented at the annual meeting of the American Political Science Association, Chicago, 30 August–2 September.

Serra, G., 2007b. *Primary Elections or Smoke-Filled Rooms: A Theory of Party Democratization in Latin America*. Paper delivered at the annual meeting of the Latin American Studies Association, Montreal, 5–8 September.

Serra, G., 2011. Why primaries? The party's tradeoff between policy and valence. *Journal of Theoretical Politics*, 23(1), pp.21–51.

Seyd, P. 1999. New parties/new politics? A case study of the British Labour Party. *Party Politics*, 5(3), pp.383–405.

Shefter, M., 1983. Regional receptivity to reform: the legacy of the progressives. *Political Science Quarterly*, 98(3), pp.459–83.

Shomer, Y., 2014. What affects candidate selection processes? A cross-national examination. *Party Politics*, 20(4), pp.533–46.

Social Democratic Party of Japan, 1986. *Documents of 40 Years History of the Social Democratic Party of Japan*. Tokyo: Nihon shakaito chuo honbu [in Japanese].

Social Democratic Party of Japan, 1996. *History of the Social Democratic Party of Japan*. Tokyo: Shakai minshuto zenkoku rengo [in Japanese].

Spáč, P., 2010. *Direct and Representative Democracy in Slovakia: Electoral Reforms and Referendum since 1989*. Brno: Centrum pro studium demokracie a kultury [in Slovakian].

Statistical Office of the Slovak Republic, 2013. [online] Available at: <www.statistics.sk> [accessed 30 July 2013].

Stone, W., 1986. The carryover effect in presidential elections. *American Political Science Review*, 80(2), pp.71–9.

Stone, W., Rapoport, R. and Schneider, M., 2004. Party members in a three-party election: major party and reform activism in the 1996 American presidential election. *Party Politics*, 10(4), pp.445–69.

Taebel, D.A., 1975. The effect of ballot position on electoral success. *American Journal of Political Science*, 19(3), pp.519–26.

Teixeira, M.C., 2009. *O povo semi-soberano. Partidos políticos e recrutamento parlamentar*. Coimbra: Almedina.

Tsurutani, T. 1980. The LDP in transition? Mass membership participation in party leadership selection. *Asian Survey*, 20(8), pp.844–59.

Uekami, T., 2008. Democratization of the party leader selection: comparative analysis of the LDP and the DPJ. *Annals of the Japanese Political Science Association*, 59(1), pp.220–40 [in Japanese].

Uekami, T., 2011a. Formation process, organization and policies of the DPJ. In: T. Uekami and H. Tsutsumi, eds. *Organization and Policies of the DPJ: From the Foundation to the Government Change*. Tokyo: Toyokeizaishinposha [in Japanese].

Uekami, T., 2011b. Electoral system reform and the conflict management in the party leader selection process of the DPJ: Structural problems facing new parties. In: T. Uekami and H. Tsutsumi, eds. *Organization and Policies of the DPJ: From the Foundation to the Government Change*. Tokyo: Toyokeizaishinposha [in Japanese].

United Nations, 2013. *Human Development Report*. [online] Available at: <http://hdr.undp.org/en/2013-report> [accessed 31 October 2014].

Valbruzzi, M., 2013. Vincere una battaglia e perdere la guerra. Il curioso caso delle primarie del 2012. In: B. Gelli, T. Mannarini and M. Talò, eds. *Perdere vincendo. Dal successo delle primarie 2012 all'impasse post-elettorale*. Milan: Angeli. pp.33–51.

van Biezen, I., 2003. *Political Parties in New Democracies: Party Organization in Party Organization in Southern and East-Central Europe*. Basingstoke: Palgrave Macmillan.

van Biezen, I. and Poguntke, T., 2014. The decline of membership-based politics. *Party Politics*, 20(2), pp.205–16.

van Biezen, I., Mair, P. and Poguntke, T., 2012. Going, going … gone? The decline of party membership in contemporary Europe. *European Journal of Political Research*, 52(1), pp.24–56.

van Haute, E., 2013. *Party Membership Figures for Belgium*. [online] MAPP working group data archive. Available at: <http://www.projectmapp.eu/> [accessed 18 October 2013].

van Holsteyn, J. and Koole, R., 2009. *Is It True What They Say? Dutch Party Members and their Opinion on Internal Party Democracy*. Paper delivered to the ECPR (European Consortium for Political Research) Joint Sessions of Workshops. Lisbon, 14–19 April.

Venturino, F., 2007, Le primarie nazionali dell'Unione: un'analisi della partecipazione con dati aggregati. *Rivista Italiana di Scienza Politica*, 37(3), pp.435–57.

Venturino, F., 2010. Italy: from partitocracy to personal parties. In: J. Blondel and J.L. Thiébault, eds. *Political Leadership, Parties, and Citizens: The Personalization of Politics*. London and New York, Routledge. pp.172–89.

Venturino, F., 2013. Le primarie comunali dal 2004 al 2012: un bilancio. In: A. Seddone and M. Valbruzzi, eds. *Le primarie viste da vicino*. Novi Ligure: Epoké, pp.17–35.

Verge, T., 2007. *Partidos y representación política: las dimensiones del cambio en los partidos políticos españoles, 1976–2006*. Madrid: Centro de Investigaciones Sociológicas.

Ware, A., 1984. *The Breakdown of Democratic Party Organization, 1940–1980*. Oxford: Oxford University Press.

Ware, A., 1979a. *The Logic of Party Democracy*. London: Macmillan.

Ware, A., 1979b. 'Divisive' primaries: the important questions. *British Journal of Political Science*, 9(3), pp.381–84.

Ware A., 2002. *The American Direct Primary: Party Institutionalization and Transformation in the North*. Cambridge: Cambridge University Press.

Wauters, B., 2009. *Intra-Party Democracy in Belgium: On Paper, in Practice and through the Eyes of the Members*. Paper delivered to the ECPR (European Consortium for Political Research) Joint Sessions of Workshops. Lisbon, 14–19 April.

Wauters, B., 2014. Democratising party leadership selection in Belgium: motivations and decision-makers. *Political Studies*, 62(S1), pp.61–80.

Wauters, B., 2015. Turnout rates in closed party leadership primaries: flash and fade out? *Government & Opposition*, 50(2), pp.218–39. [available online first, doi: 10.1017/gov.2013.45].

Wauters, B. and Pilet, J.B., 2015. Women as party leaders: does the selectorate matters? In: J.B. Pilet and W.P. Cross, eds. *The Selection of Political Party Leaders in Contemporary Parliamentary Democracies*. London: Routledge, pp.30–46.

Whiteley, P.F., 2011. Is the party over? The decline of party activism and membership across the democratic world. *Party Politics*, 17(1), pp.21–44.

Wichowsky, A. and Niebler, S.E., 2010. Narrow victories and hard games: revisiting the primary divisiveness hypothesis. *American Political Research*, 38(6), pp.1052–71.

Wintour, P., 2011. Labour considers plan to widen vote on party leadership. *The Guardian*, 3 February.

Wu, C., 2001. The transformation of the Kuomintang's candidate selection system. *Party Politics*, 7(1), pp.103–18.

Wu, Y., 2007. Semi-presidentialism. Easy to choose, difficult to operate: the case of Taiwan. In: R. Elgie and S. Moestrup, eds. *Semi-Presidentialism outside Europe: A Comparative Study*. London and New York: Routledge. pp.201–18.

Young, L., 2013. Party members and intra-party democracy. In: W.P. Cross and R.S. Katz, eds, *The Challenges of Intra-Party Democracy*. Oxford: Oxford University Press. pp.65–80.

Index

Notes: italics denote figures and tables; 'n' denotes footnotes.

actors, non-party 38, 50, 102
   see also media involvement
Africa 2, 3, 9
age *see* representation
America *see* Latin America; United States (US)
Argentina 1, 9, *10*
Arnar Bergmann Gunnlaugsson 164
Árni Páll Árnason 164, 169, *169*
Asia 2, 3, 9, 11, 12, 13, 15, 16, 182, 192, 193
   see also Japan; Taiwan; South Korea
Assis, Francisco 66
Aubry, Martine 133, 137
Australia 3, 9, *10*, *26*, 28, 29, *30*, 36, 36n, *37*
Austria *26*, *30*

backgrounds *see* representation
ballot paper position 49
ballots *see* general elections; primary elections
Bauzá, José Ramón 63–4
Baylet, Jean-Michel 137
Belgium, party leadership selection
   primaries 9, *10*, *23*, *26*, *30*, 85–7, 102–3
   rationale for adoption 87–90
   process of primaries 90–100, *92–3*, *95–8*
   political consequences for parties 100–102
Berlusconi, Silvio 131, 132
Bersani, Pier Luigi 131, 136, 138
Bertinotti, Fausto 138
Bolger, Jim 36, 36n
Bossi, Umberto 131, 132

Bright Future (Iceland) 163
Britain *see* United Kingdom (UK)
Brothers of Italy (FDI) (Italy) 132
Bryan, William Jennings 42–3

campaign expenditure (spending) 50, 168, 172–4, 172n, 173n, 178, *179*
campaign professionals (non-party actors) 38, 50, 102
Canada 3, 9, *10*, 24, *25–6*, 26–7, 29, *30*, 32, 33, 35, *35*, 36n, *37*
candidacy requirements 24, 188, 193
   Belgium and Israel 90–91, *92–3*, 94, *95–8*
   France and Italy *135*, 136–8, *139*
   Iceland 165, *166*, 167–8, 167n, *171*
   Japan and Taiwan 110–11, *112–13*, 115, *116–17*
   Portugal and Spain 67, *68*, 69n, *72–5*
   Romania and Slovakia 150–52, *151*, *154*
   United States 46–7
candidate-centred politics *see* personalised politics
candidate selection 1–19, *10*, 21–39, *23*, *28*, 184–6
   rationale for adoption 130–34, 146–50, 163–5, 186–8
   process of primaries 134–8, *135*, *139*, 150–56, *151*, *154*, 165–70 *166*, *169*, *171*, 188–90
   political consequences for parties 140–43, *141*, 156–9, *158*, 172–7, *174*, *175*, *176*, 190–97, *194*
   United States 41–5, 48–50
   see also party leadership selection
Carod-Rovira, Josep Lluís 63

cartel party theory 33, 38, 130, 144, 183–4, 187
Castro, Ribeiro e 65
caucuses 38, 42–3, 51, *124–6*
   see also elite, party
chancellors *see* chief executive selection
Chen Shui-bian 107
chief executive selection
   global use of primaries 9–11, *10*, 15, 24, 29, 39, 185
   vs. party leader selection 22–3, 185
   processes 27, 106–7, 130–34, 183–4
   responsiveness 38–9
   selectorates 24, 29, 32, 39, 46
   see also deselection; prime ministers
Chirac, Jacques 132–3, 142
Christian Democratic and Flemish Party (CD&V) (Belgium) *10*, *26*, *30*, 85, 89, *92*, *95*
Citizens' Party (Ciudadanos) (Spain) 61, 63
closed primaries 6–12, *10*, 16n, 19, 181, 189, 190, 195, 197
   Belgium *10*, 86
   France 130, 132, 133–4, 138, 142, 143–4
   Iceland 162, 167, 167n
   Italy 130, 131, 132
   Japan 111
   Portugal 59, 64–5, 66, 69–70, 71, 76–7, 82–3
   Romania and Slovakia 156, 160
   Spain 59, 63–4, 66, 71, 77
   Taiwan 108n–9n, 110
   United States 44–5, 45n
   see also open primaries
coalition primaries 184, 184n
Communist Party of Spain (PCE) (Spain) 60
competition (competitiveness) 35–6, 39, 190, 190n, 192, *194*, 194–5
   Belgium and Israel 99, 103
   Iceland 169–70
   Japan and Taiwan 114–15
   Romania and Slovakia 155–6
conflict, intra-party 7, 50–51, 56, 64, 76, 77, 83, 109n, 132, 165, 187, 193
   see also competition (competitiveness); factionalism

Conservative Party (PC) (Romania) 145
Conservatives (Canada) *10*, 24, *26*
Conservatives (UK) *10*, *32*, 35n, *37*, 90
contagion effect 5, 9, 15, 186, 187, 192
   across Europe 132, 143, 187
   in Japan and Taiwan 109–10, 187
   see also defeat, election, impact on parties
Costa, António 66–7, 69n
cross-filing primaries (US) 43

De Croo, Alexander 91
de Gaulle, Charles 129
decentralisation 26–7, *28*, 28–9, 35, 39, 44, 47, 51, 150, *151*, 166
defeat, election, impact on parties 5, 19, 33, 48, 65, 187, 188, 190–92
   Belgium and Israel 89, 102
   France 134, 184
   Japan and Taiwan 108–9, 110
   Spain 64, 76
Delors, Jacques 132
Democracy is Freedom - The Daisy (DL – La Margherita) (Italy) *135*, 136, 143
Democrat Liberal Party (Romania) 148
Democratic Alliance of Hungarians in Romania (UDMR) (Romania) *10*, 146n
Democratic Centre (CD) (Italy) *135*, 136
Democratic Movement for Change (DMC) (Israel) 87
Democratic National Salvation Front (FDSN) (Romania) 146
Democratic Party of Japan (DPJ) (Japan) *31*, 108, 109, 111, *113*, *116*, *120*, 122, *126–7*
Democratic Progressive Party (DPP) (Taiwan) *26*, *32*, 107, 108, 109, 110, 111, *113*, 114, 115, *117*, 118n, *121*
Democratic Social Centre – People's Party (CDS-PP) (Portugal) *10*, 61, 62, 65, *68*, 69, 70, 70n, *75*, *81*
Democrats of the Left (DS) (Italy) *10*, 131, 134, *135*, 136, 143
Democrats (US) 4, *10*, *25*, 41, 44, 47, 53, 56, 184

Denmark 9, *10*, 14, *30*, 37, *37*
deselection 27–9, *28*, 39
   candidates *135*, *151*, 166
   party leadership 68, 69, *92–3*, 94, *112–13*
Di Pietro, Antonio 132
Díez, Rosa 63, 76, 82
direct party primaries (US) 7, 12–13, 41–4, 47, 47n, 48, 50, 51, 54, 56, 190
Dzurinda, Mikuláš 148–9, 157n

Ecolo (Belgium) 10, 86
elections *see* general elections; primary elections
elite, party 24–5, *25*, *26*, 33–4, 38–9, 183, 187–8, 193
   Belgium and Israel 89–90
   France and Italy 144
   Iceland 164
   Japan and Taiwan 109–10, 111, *124–7*
   mobilisation of and against (US) 51–2
   Romania 152, 160
   United States 44, 48, 49–50, 51–2
   see also cartel party theory; manipulation concerns
Emmanuelli, Henri 132, 136–7
Energy (Meretz) (Israel) 86, *93*, *98*
equality *see* representation
Estarás, Rosa 63

Fabius, Laurent 133, 137, 138
factionalism 51, 54, 55–6, 56n, 63, 108, 147, 164, 178, *194*
fees
   candidates' 24, 91, 168
   party membership 168, 168n
   voting 67n, 111, 134, 136
females *see* women
Ferreira Leite, Manuela 37
Finland 9, *10*, 11, 12, 14, *25–6*, *31*, *37*
Five Star Movement (M5S) (Italy) *10*, 131
Flemish Greens (Groen) (Belgium) *10*, 86, 91
Flemish Interest (VB) (Belgium) *10*, 86, 88, 89
Flemish Liberals and Democrats (VLD) (Belgium) *10*, 88
Forward Italy (FI) (Italy) 131

Forward (Kadima) (Israel) *10*, *31*, 86, 88, 91, *93*, *98*
France, candidate selection primaries 22, *23*, *26*, *31*, 32, 33, 46n, 129–30, 143–4
   rationale for adoption 130–34
   process of primaries 134–8, *135*, *139*
   political consequences for parties 140–43, *141*
Francophone Democratic Federalists (FDF) (Belgium) *10*, 86
Free Party (Livre) (Portugal) 65n
funding 69, 183, 183n
fundraising activities 172, 172n

gender *see* women
general elections
   timing of primaries and *68*, 82, 91, *92–3*, 94, *112–13*, 118–22, *135*, *151*, *166*, 170
   United States, timing of primaries and 47–8, 182
   see also defeat, election
Germany 9, *10*, 12, 14, *25–6*, *31*, *37*
Gillard, Julia 36n, *37*
Greece 9, *10*, 11, *26*, *31*, 32
Greens (EELV) (France) *10*, 132, 133, 134
Grillo, Beppe 131
Guterres, António 64

Hannes Marino Hannesson 164
Haraldur Benediktsson 164, 168n
Harman, Harriet 53
Holland, François 133–4, 137, 142, 186
Humanist Democratic Centre (CDH) (Belgium) *10*, 85, 87, 91, *92*, *95–6*, 100

Iceland, candidate selection primaries *10*, *23*, *25–6*, *31*, 161–3, 177–8, 185, 187
   rationale for adoption 163–5
   process of primaries 165–70, *166*, *169*, *171*
   political consequences for parties 172–7, *174*, *175*, *176*
   effects of campaign spending on primary success 178, *179*

Ichiro Ozawa 110
Iliescu, Ion 146
Independence Party (IP) (Iceland) *31*, 162, 163, 164, 165, *166*, 167, 167n, 168, 170n, *171*, 172, 174n, 175, *175*, *176*, 177
Independent candidates 60n, 136
India 27n
Ingibjörg Sólrún Gísladóttir 163
Initiative for Catalonia Verds (ICV) (Spain) 62–3, 66, 67, *68*, 69, 70, 71, *72*, 77, *78*
Ireland 3, 9, *10*, 25–6, 29, *31*
Israel, party leadership selection primaries 3, 9, *23*, 25–6, *31*, 33, *35*, 37, *37*, 85–7, 102–3, 185, 186–7
  rationale for adoption 87–90
  process of primaries 90–100, *92–3*, *95–8*
  political consequences for parties 100–102
Issenberg, Sasha 1
Italian Democratic Party (PD) (Italy) *10*, *26*, *31*, 131, 134, 136, 143, 144, 188
Italy, candidate selection primaries 9, *10*, 22, 23, *26*, *31*, 32, 33, 129–30, 143–4, 185, 191
  rationale for adoption 130–34
  process of primaries 134–8, *135*, *139*
  political consequences for parties 140–43, *141*
Italy of Values (IDV) (Italy) 132, *135*

Japan, party leadership selection primaries 9, *10*, 22, *23*, 25–6, *31*, 105–6, 122, 187
  political and party systems 106–8
  rationale for adoption 108–10
  process of primaries 110–15, *112–13*, *116–17*
  political consequences for parties 118–22, *120–21*, *124–7*
Jewish Home, The (Israel) 86, *93*, *98*
Jóhanna Sigurtardóttir 164
Jospin, Lionel 132, 134, 137, 138, 142

Kadima (Forward) (Israel) *10*, *31*, 86, 88, 91, *93*, *98*
Katrín Júlíusdóttir 169, *169*, 170
Kuomintang (Nationalist Party) (KMT) (Taiwan) *10*, *32*, 107, 108–9, 108n–109n, 110–11, *113*, *117*, 118n, *121*, 122

Labor Party (Australia) *30*, 36, 36n, 37
Labour Party (Israeli Labour Party) (Israel) *10*, 25–6, *31*, 37, 86, 88–9, 91, *93*, 97–8, 101
Labour Party (UK) 1, *10*, 24, 32, 32, 53, 90
Lang, Jack 137
Latin America 3, 5, 7, 9, 12, 181
Le Pen, Jean-Marie 132
leadership selection *see* chief executive selection; party leadership selection
Left Bloc (BE) (Portugal) 61
Left Ecology Freedom (SEL) (Italy) *10*, 131, *135*, 136, 143
Left-Green Movement (LGM) (Iceland) *31*, 162, *166*, 167, 167n, 168, 168n, 170, *171*, *175*, 175–6, *176*
legislative candidate selection *see* candidate selection
Liberal Democratic Party (LDP) (Japan) *10*, *25*, *31*, 107–8, 109, 110, 111, *112*, 114, *116*, 118, 119, *120*, 122, *124–5*
Liberal Democrats (UK) *26*, 30n
Liberal Party (Canada) *10*, 24, 32, 36n
Lien Chan 107, 109
Likud (The Consolidation) (Israel) *10*, *26*, *31*, 86, 88–9, 91, *93*, *98*, 101
Livni, Tzipi 37
local level primaries 9–11, *10*, 16n, 26
  Europe 66, 69n, 70, 90, *92*, 132, 133, 134, 138, *166*
  Japan *113*
  United States 41–2, 41n, 43, 44, 47, 47n
  see also decentralisation

Ma Ying-jeou 109–10
Magnús Orri Schram 169, *169*

majoritarian system (voting system) 27, 29, 39, 61, 110, 129, 169, 177, 178, 185
  see also plurality systems; two-round majoritarian (run-off) systems; rank ordered plurality
manipulation concerns (fraudulent behaviour) 33, 35, 45, 82, 144, 157, 183, 187, 192
Matas, Jaume 63
Mečiar, Vladimir 148, 149–50, 149n
media involvement 7, 22, 38, 53–4, 186–7, 189, 195
  Belgium and Israel 89
  France and Italy 130, 131, 138
  Portugal and Spain 71, 71n, 76, 82, 83
  Romania and Slovakia 147, 152, 159
Members of Parliament (MPs) 24–5, 28, 35n, 66, 135, 163
  Japan, role in primaries 111, *112–13*, 114n, 115, 119
  Romania and Slovakia, development of role in 147–8, 155–6, 155n
members, party *see* closed primaries; membership, party; selectorates
membership, party 2, 5, 6, 8, 13, 18, 34, 184, 192–3, *194*
  Belgium and Israel 90, 91, *93*, 101–2, 103, 192
  France and Italy 136, *141*, 142–3, 144
  Iceland 163–4, 168, *175*, 175–6, *176*, 177
  Japan and Taiwan 111, 118, 118n, *120–21*, 122, *124–7*
  Portugal and Spain 67, 67n, 77, *78–81*, 82, 83, 84
  Romania and Slovakia 147, 149–50, 152, 152n, 156–7, *158*, 160
  United States 44–5, 46, 48, 53, 183–4
Mendes, Marques 65
Meretz (Energy) (Israel) 86, *93*, *98*
Middle East 3, 15, 192
  see also Israel
Mikloš, Ivan 159
Miliband, Ed 1
Milquet, Joëlle 37

Mitterrand, François 132
Montebourg, Arnaud 133, 137

Năstase, Adrian 153
National Front, The (FN) (France) 132, 134
National Party (New Zealand) 36, 36n, *37*
National Religious Party (NRP) (Israel) 86
National Salvation Front (FSN) (Romania) 146
Nationalist Party (Kuomintang) (KMT) (Taiwan) *10*, *32*, 107, 108–9, 108n–109n, 110–11, *113*, *117*, 118n, *121*, *122*
Netanyahu, Benjamin 101
Netherlands, The 9, *10*, 14, *26*, *31*
New Flemish Alliance (N-VA) (Belgium) *10*, *30*, 86, 89, 91, *93*, *97*
New Frontier Party (NFP) (Japan) 107–8, 109, 110, 111, *112*, *116*, *120*, *126–7*
New York Times (newspaper) 1n
New Zealand 3, *26*, 29, *31*, 36, 36n, *37*
non-partisan primaries 43
Northern League (LN) (Italy) *10*, 131, 132
Norway 14, *26*, *32*, *37*

one member, one vote (OMOV) (voting system) 11, 185
  Italy 131, 132
  Japan and Taiwan 107, 111
  Portugal and Spain 61–5, 69, 70, 70n, 77, 82, 83–4
  United Kingdom 1
Open Flemish Liberals and Democrats (OpenVLD) (Belgium) *10*, *26*, *30*, 86, 89, 90, 91, *92*, *96–7*, 100, 101
open primaries 6–12, *10*, 15, 18, 19, *32*, 181, 183, 189, 190, 194–7
  Belgium and Israel 90
  France 46n, 133–4, 133n, 136–8, 140, 142–4
  Iceland 165, 167, 167n, 176, 177
  Italy 130–32, 134, 136, 140, 142–4
  Japan 110, 111
  Portugal 65, 65n, 66–7, 69n, 83
  Spain 59, 66, *68*, 83

United States 45, 46
   see also semi-open primaries; closed primaries
Össur Skarphéðinsson 163

parliamentary party group (PPG) 25, *26*, 29, 30, *30–32*, 35, *35*, 36n, *37*, 38, 39, 185, 194, 197
parliamentary systems 13, 15, 22, 23, *23*, 33, 37, 48, 185, 186
   leadership deselection 28, *28*, 29
   see also Belgium; Iceland; Israel; Italy; Japan; Portugal; Slovakia; Spain
participation (voter turnout) 34–5, *35*, 39, 44–6, 44n, 49–50, *194*, 195–6
   Belgium and Israel 94–100, *95–8*
   Canada 35, *35*
   France and Italy 131, 134, 138, 139
   Iceland 170, *171*, 175
   Japan and Taiwan 114–15, *116–17*
   Portugal and Spain 70, 70n, *72–5*, 77, 82
   Romania and Slovakia 153, *154*
party elite *see* elite, party
party leadership selection 1–19, *10*, 21–39, *23*, *28*, *30–32*, 184–6
   rationale for adoption 61–5, 87–90, 108–10, 186–8
   process of primaries 66–76, *68*, *72–5*, 90–100, *92–3*, *95–8*, 110–17, *112–13*, *116–17*, 188–90
   political consequences for parties 76–83, *78–81*, 100–102, 118–22, *120–21*, *124–7*, 190–97, *194*
   see also candidate selection
party members *see* members, party
Party of Democratic Renewal (PRD) (Portugal) 61
Party of Social Democracy in Romania (PDSR) (Romania) 146
party primaries *see* primary elections; party leadership selection; candidate selection; open primaries; closed primaries
People of Freedom (PDL) (Italy) *26*, *31*, 132
People's Alliance (AP) (Spain) 60
People's Alliance (PA) (Iceland) 162

People's Party (PP) (Spain) *26*, *32*, 59, 62, 63, 66, *68*, 69, 71, *72*, 76, *78*
personalised politics (candidate-centred; personality politics) 42–3, 54–5, 71, 71n, 76, 101, 131, 186, 195
Pirate Party (Iceland) 163
plurality (voting system) 27, 184
   Belgium and Israel 91, *92–3*
   Iceland 168, 168n, 169
   Italy *135*, 137–8
   Japan and Taiwan 110, *113*, 114n
   Portugal and Spain 65, 67–9, *68*, 83
Podemos (We Can Party) (Spain) 61, 63
Portugal, party leadership selection
   primaries *10*, *23*, 24, *26*, *32*, 37, 59–61, 83–4, 187
   rationale for adoption 61–5
   process of primaries 66–76, *68*, *72–5*
   political consequences for parties 76–83, *78–81*
Portuguese Communist Party (PCP) (Portugal) 61
PPG *see* parliamentary party group (PPG)
pre-primaries 55, 188–9
presidential systems 12, 22, *23*
   see also semi-presidential systems
primary elections 1–13, *10*
   see also party leadership selection; candidate selection; open primaries; closed primaries
prime ministers 12, 15–18, 21–2, 32, 36n, 38, 185–6
   Belgium and Israel 87, 89, 103, 191
   France and Italy 130, 134, 136, 191
   Japan and Taiwan 106
   Portugal and Spain 59, 60, 62, 66, 67, 67n
   Romania and Slovakia 146
   women 36, 36n, 37, *37*
   see also chief executive selection
Prodi, Romano 131, 134, 136, 138
Progressive Party (PP) (Iceland) 161–2, 163, 164, 165, *166*, 167, 167n, 168, 169n, *171*, 172, 174, *175*, 175–6, *176*
proportional representation (PR) (voting system)
   Belgium and Israel 85, 86

France and Italy 129, 129n
Iceland 161, 162, 164–5, 172, 185n
Portugal 60
Romania and Slovakia 148, 152, 185n
publicity *see* media involvement

quotas 37, 150, 155–6, 156n, 160, 165, 167, 167n, 169, 178

Rabin, Yitzhak 101
Radical Party of the Left (PRG) (France) 137, *139*
Radičová, Iveta 156, 157
rank ordered plurality (voting system) 165–7, *166*, 168–9, *169*
Reformist Movement (MR) (Belgium) *30*, 86, *93*, *96*
regulation, state 41, 41n, 44, 45–6, 47, 183
Renzi, Matteo 134, 136, 138
representation 36–7, 36n, *37*, 39, 189, *194*, 196–7
　Belgium and Israel *95–8*, 100
　France and Italy *139*
　Iceland 164–5, 169, *171*
　Japan and Taiwan 115, *116–17*
　Portugal and Spain *72–5*, 76–7, 84
　Romania and Slovakia 150, 156
　see also women
Republican Left of Catalonia (ERC) (Spain) 63, 66, 67, *68*, 69, 71, *72*, *78*, 82
Republicans (US) *10*, *25*, 47, 53, 184
responsiveness, leaders' and candidates' 38–9, *194*, 197
Rocard, Michel 132
Romania, candidate selection primaries 9, *23*, *26*, *32*, 145–6, 160, 187, 189, 192
　rationale for adoption 146–50
　process of primaries 150–56, *151*, *154*
　political consequences for parties 156–9, *158*
Romanian Social Democratic Party (PSD) (Romania) *10*, *26*, *32*, 145–8, 149, 150, *151*, 152, 153, *154*, 155, 155n, 156, 157, *158*, 159, 160
Roosevelt, Theodore 43

Royal, Ségolène 133, 136, 137, 138, 142, 189
Rubalcaba, Alfredo Pérez 64
Rudd, Kevin 28, 36, 36n
run-off systems *see* two-round majoritarian systems

Salvini, Matteo 132
Sarkozy, Nicolas 133, 137, 142, 189
Seguro, António José 66–7, 69n
selectorates 24–5, *25*, *26*, *28*, 29–34, *30–32*, *35*, 36–7, *37*, 38–9, 185–6
　Belgium and Israel 90, *92–3*
　France and Italy 131, 134–6, *135*, 143
　Iceland 163, *166*, 167, 167n
　Japan and Taiwan *112–13*, *124–7*
　Portugal and Spain *68*
　Romania and Slovakia 150, *151*, 153, 160
　United States 44–6
semi-open primaries 32, 111, 162, 177
semi-presidential systems 15, 22, *23*, 106–7, 106n, 129, 130, 182, 186
　see also France; Romania; Taiwan
Shas (Israel) *26*, *31*
Shigeru Ishiba 111
Shinzō Abe 111
Slovak Democratic and Christian Union-Democratic Party (SDKU-DS) (Slovakia) *10*, 145–6, 148–50, 149n, *151*, 152–3, 152n, *154*, 155–7, 155n, 156n, 157n, *158*, 159, 159n, 160
Slovak Democratic Coalition (SDK) (Slovakia) 148–9, 149n
Slovakia, candidate selection primaries 9, *23*, 145–6, 160, 187, 189
　rationale for adoption 146–50
　process of primaries 150–56, *151*, *154*
　political consequences for parties 156–9, *158*
Social Democratic Alliance (SDA) (Iceland) *31*, 162, 163, 164, *166*, 167, 167n, 168–9, 168n, *169*, 170, *171*, 174n, 175, *175*, *176*
Social Democratic Party of Japan (SDPJ) (Japan) *10*, 107–8, 107n, 109, 111, *112*, 115, *116*, 120, *120*, *124–5*

Social Democratic Party (PSD) (Portugal) *10, 32,* 61, 65, 67, *68,* 69, 69n, 70, *75,* 76, 77, *80,* 82, 83, 187–8
Social Democrats (SDP) (Iceland) *26,* 162, 163, 164, 165, 170n, 172, 176, 177
Socialist Party – Differently (sp.a) (Belgium) *10,* 85, 89, 90, *92, 97,* 100, 101
Socialist Party (PS) (Belgium) *10,* 85, 89, 91, *92,* 97
Socialist Party (PS) (France) *10, 26, 31,* 130, 132–3, 134, *135,* 136–7, *139, 141,* 142, 143, 144, 189
Socialist Party (PS) (Portugal) *10, 26, 32,* 59, 61, 62, 64, 65, 67, *68,* 69–70, 69n, 71, *75,* 77, *80,* 82, 83
Socialists' Party of Catalonia (PSC) (Spain) 64, 67, *68,* 70, 72, 78
Sócrates, José 66
Soong Chu-yu, James 107
South Korea 9, 181
Spain, party leadership selection primaries 9, *10, 23, 26, 32,* 59–61, 83–4, 187
    rationale for adoption 61–5
    process of primaries 66–76, *68, 72–5*
    political consequences for parties 76–83, *78–81*
Spanish Socialist Workers' Party (PSOE) (Spain) *10, 26, 32,* 59, 60, 62, 64, 64n, 66, 67, *68,* 69, 70, 71, 71n, *72,* 76, *78*
Spirit Party (Belgium) *10,* 86
state regulation 41, 41n, 44, 45–6, 47, 183
Strauss-Kahn, Dominique 137, 138
Sweden 14, *26, 32*

Tabacci, Bruno 136
Taiwan, party leadership selection primaries 9, *23, 26, 32,* 105–6, 122, 187
    political and party systems 106–8
    rationale for adoption 108–10
    process of primaries 110–15, *112–13, 116–17*
    political consequences for parties 118–22, *120–21*
Takeo Miki 108, 109
Tavares, Rui 65n
Thatcher, Margaret 28, *37*

Thorning-Schmidt, Helle 37, *37*
Thyssen, Marianne 37
Touraine, Alain 133, 133n
Truth and Justice (Romania) 148
Tsai Ing-wen 115
turnout, voter *see* participation
two-round majoritarian (run-off) systems (voting system) 27, 43, 184n
    Belgium and Israel 91, *92–3,* 102
    France and Italy 129, 129n, *135,* 138, 142
    Iceland *166,* 168, 168n, 169
    Japan and Taiwan 110–11, *112–13*
    Portugal 65, *68,* 69

Union for a Popular Movement (UMP) (France) *10, 31,* 46n, 133, 134
Union of the Democratic Centre (UCD) (Spain) 60
Union, Progress and Democracy (UPyD) (Spain) *10,* 61, 63, 66, 67, 67n, *68,* 69, 71, *72–4,* 76, 77, *78–9,* 82, 82n, 84
United Kingdom (UK) 3, 9, *10,* 21–2, 24, *26,* 28, 29, *32,* 35, *35, 37,* 48
United Left (IU) (Spain) 60, 62
United States (US), primaries in 2, 3, 4, 5, *23, 25,* 41–4, 56–7, 130, 183–4, 196
    candidacy requirements 46
    candidate expenditure 50
    consequences of adoption 54–6
    participation 44–6
    parties' nominees 48–50
    rationale for adoption 50–54
    scheduling 47–8
    state regulation 47

Valls, Manuel 137
Vandenbroucke, Frank 101
Vázquez, Pachi 64
Vendola, Nichi 131, 136, 138
voter turnout *see* participation
voting systems *see* majoritarian; one member, one vote (OMOV); plurality; proportional representation (PR); rank ordered plurality; two-round majoritarian (run-off)

We Can Party (Podemos) (Spain) 61, 63
women 189
    candidate selections 133, *139*, 150, *154*, 155, 156, 156n
    party leadership selections 37, *72–5*, 76–7, *92–8*, 99–100, 115, *116–17*, 132
    as party leaders 36, 36n, 37, *37*
    Iceland 164, 165, 167, 167n, 169, *171*, 173–5, *174*, 174n

Yechimovich, Shelly 37
Yesh Atid (Israel) *25*